CW00662293

The Greatest Spy

The true story of the secret agent -
who inspired James Bond 007

John Harte

Cune

The Greatest Spy
by John Harte © 2022 John Harte
Cune Press, Seattle 2022 Second Edition
Hardback   ISBN 9781951082611

Library of Congress Cataloging-in-Publication Data

Names: Harte, John, 1925- author.
Title: The greatest spy : the true story of the secret agent that inspired
    James Bond 007 / John Harte.
Other titles: Dancing with death.
Description: Second edition. | Seattle : Cune Press, 2022. | Includes
    bibliographical references and index.
Identifiers: LCCN 2022030669 (print) | LCCN 2022030670 (ebook) | ISBN
    9781951082611 (hardcover) | ISBN 9781614574309 (epub)
Subjects: LCSH: Reilly, Sidney George, 1874-1925. | Spies--Great
    Britain--Biography. | Spies--Soviet Union--Biography. | Secret
    service--Great Britain--History--20th century. | Espionage,
    British--Soviet Union--History--20th century.
Classification: LCC DA574.R4 H37 2022 (print) | LCC DA574.R4 (ebook) |
    DDC 327.12092--dc23/eng/20220629
LC record available at https://lccn.loc.gov/2022030669
LC ebook record available at https://lccn.loc.gov/2022030670

 Aswat: Voices from a Small Planet (a series from Cune Press)

Looking Both Ways	Pauline Kaldas
Stage Warriors	Sarah Imes Borden
Stories My Father Told Me	Helen Zughaib & Elia Zughaib

Syria Crossroads (a series from Cune Press)

Leaving Syria	Bill Dienst & Madi Williamson
Visit the Old City of Aleppo	Khaldoun Fansa
The Plain of Dead Cities	Bruce McLaren
Steel & Silk	Sami Moubayed
Syria - A Decade of Lost Chances	Carsten Wieland
The Road from Damascus	Scott C. Davis
A Pen of Damascus Steel	Ali Ferzat
White Carnations	Musa Rahum Abbas

 Bridge Between the Cultures (a series from Cune Press)

Empower a Refugee	Patricia Martin Holt
Biblical Time Out of Mind	Tom Gage, James A. Freeman
Turning Fear Into Power	Linda Sartor
The Other Side of the Wall	Richard Hardigan
Equateur	Frederic Hunter
Curse of the Achille Lauro	Reem al-Nimer

Cune Cune Press: www.cunepress.com | www.cunepress.net

Contents

"Russia has always been a mystery for many westerners. The Americans, British and French have always misunderstood and underestimated the Russians and their allies. And because of that they have fallen for Russian deception and treachery for many times."
—*Latvian History* (online), September 19. 2012.

Among the fragments of Ancient Greek poetry attributed to Archilochus, is a mysterious line which says, "The fox knows many things, but the hedgehog knows one big thing."
—Archilochus (700 BC).

INTRODUCTION

"HISTORY REPEATS ITSELF," WROTE KARL MARX, "first as tragedy, second as farce." His claim was born out once again by Russia's unprovoked assault on Ukraine on February 24, 2022. Every day this conflict comes closer and closer to erupting into a Third World War, with threats from President Putin that this could be a nuclear conflict.

There was nothing farcical about the situation in Ukraine: the dead and dying women and children and old men, suffering from the constant artillery shelling and missile strike by the Russians. What is ludicrous is the stance of tyrannical leaders, such as the one in Moscow, who grasp at opportunities for self-aggrandizement at any cost to their own country and others.

The true story that follows describes how "it all happened before" when there was a Communist coup in Moscow in October 1917. It was led by professional revolutionaries and resulted in a vicious and bloody civil war. When the Red Army emerged victorious in 1923, they drove an entire generation of Ukrainians from the Crimea and the port of Odessa. Millions escaped to Paris and other European cities and North America. Ukrainian refugees were forced to start their lives all over again.

Sigi had been born, half Jewish and half Ukrainian Orthodox, near Odessa in 1874. As a young man he studied chemistry in Vienna, traveled to Brazil, and met British army officers who recommended him in 1896 to Britain's Secret intelligence Bureau (SIB). By now, Sigi displayed signs of the courage and audacity that would mark his career. He also developed a healthy skepticism toward the promise of authoritarian rulers to protect Jews and those of divergent political beliefs. In 1899 he received the code name of Sidney Reilly. By 1901 Sigi was working in a variety of British undercover operations.

In 1917, when Communist revolutionaries seized control in Moscow, Sigi quickly spotted a fraud. He saw that the coup was not a grass roots uprising to save Russians and Ukrainians from the tyranny of the Romanov Tsars. Rather, it was the imposition of another brutal tyranny, this time by ambitious adventurers who used manipulative lies to obtain power and rule through force over a bewildered and mostly illiterate population.

Sigi was appalled by the foreign Communist ideology and the ruthless government forced on Ukrainians and Russians. In 1918, he and a fellow Secret Service envoy were sent to Moscow to kidnap Lenin and Trotsky, and almost succeeded. They were betrayed by a Communist army officer, and Sigi was forced into hiding with a huge price on his head.

Now known as Sidney, his exploits caught the attention of Winston Churchill, and he became one of Churchill's most admired secret agents. The rest is history.

Author's Note

The Greatest Spy is a work of history. All the characters in this book are real people, and I have used their actual names throughout. References to archival sources can be found in the Acknowledgments.

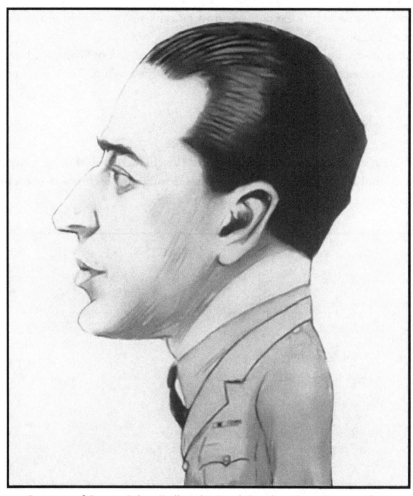

Caricature of Captain Sidney Reilly in his Royal Canadian Flying Corps uniform (SIS collection 1919).

THE GREAT GAME

1
The Great Game

WILLIAM MELVILLE—KNOWN SIMPLY AS 'M'—gazed from his seat beside the open roll-top desk at the new young candidate for the job. He had applied as a confidential agent for Britain's Secret Service Bureau. He was still a mystery to the Chief, who had placed a sheet of lined paper and a newly sharpened pencil in readiness at his elbow.

But where had this man named Sigmund Rosenbloom really come from? And what was the significance of his arrival in England at that particular time? All that 'M' knew at that moment was what little he had been told by the founders of Britain's Military Intelligence. They included Colonel Kell, who was known as 'K,' Major Thwaites, and Sir Henry Hozier. It was a fairly new game for them too, in which complete secrecy was felt to be the wisest course at all times. In any case, William Melville was a skeptic who knew well enough not to believe anything they told him, since all three army officers were masters of subterfuge themselves. This was "The Great Game" at play between the British and the Russians for military domination—not to mention the Germans. But they were more interested in conquering Europe than the Afghan border and India.

The youth appeared to be taller than he was, because of the self-confident and alert way he held himself, although he was very young. Melville searched for the right word to describe his features: *exotic* perhaps? And, he thought, slightly sinister. But he possessed a charming veneer, like a chameleon, but with a more polished skin. There was something androgynous about his handsome features which 'M' could well understand might be engaging to either sex. The Chief noted that he was always alert, watching his interrogator as he himself was being watched, but with a very slight and disconcerting smile of superiority at the corner of his sensual mouth, which had cautioned 'M's military colleagues not to believe everything he said.

"Where did you find him?" 'M' had asked the Colonel sceptically on one of his rare visits to St. James's, where Kell paced like a frustrated lion in his immaculate office which he used rarely in between assignments. He never visited 'M' in his anonymous den close to Victoria Station. Melville worked separately, and there was an understanding that, as far as they were concerned, he did not even exist.

"Top secret," 'K' had remarked with a breezy smile and a nod of respect to the large framed picture of Queen Victoria on his wall, as he passed her. She had been young then.

He added helpfully. "I *can* tell you his name is Sigmund Georgievich Rosenbloom. He was born in South Russia, not far from Odessa, on March 24 in 1874. If true, it means he is only twenty-two. But a find! He says he is the son of a wealthy Polish-Jewish landowner and contractor from Grodno, Poland, which, as you will know, is part of the Russian Empire."

There seemed to be considerable secrecy about the candidate's early background that Military Intelligence either did not wish Melville to know or did not know themselves.

"In any case," the Colonel said, "I leave it to you to find out in your own way, since you are the one who will control him."

For some reason known only to Military Intelligence, they had decided that Sigmund, Sigi, Schlomo, or Soloman Rosenbloom was the right man to handle the highly complex and confusing situation that Britain's government found themselves in at this particular moment in its rich and varied history. So 'M,' the pragmatic chief of its Secret Intelligence Bureau, had recognized he had no choice, since he had no other bilingual agent on his payroll. Efficient and effective spies were hard to find. Indeed, from his own experience, there was no such thing as a real professional spy. It was all trial and error that, more often than not, ended in failure.

William Melville was quite sure that Germany's secret agents and German money were behind the fractious transport unions, the threatened strikes in the coal mines, the volatile Irish and Indian problems, the discontents and sabotage in industry, the more stormy clashes between the ruling political party and the Liberals. Even the women suffragettes had increased their own pace of violence with extremists targeting leaders they disliked, attacking them physically, and burning down their houses.

Melville was the first director of Britain's Secret Intelligence Bureau (SIB), which was set up to counter anarchy at home, and sometimes even abroad. He was forty-seven, and had previously worked for the Special Branch and the Special Irish Branch at Scotland Yard. He was not an army officer like the others.

Although he appeared on the surface to be more or less typical of an English civil servant of the times, in fact William Melville was very different. For one thing, he came from County Kerry in Ireland. For another, he had worked as a baker on arriving in London, before joining the Metropolitan Police force. He had been selected as one of the founding members of the Special Irish Branch, created to prevent Fenians and anarchists from causing trouble in London with their bombs.

He had since been assigned to protect the Shah of Persia during his state visit to Britain, and had then been called upon to protect Britain's Royal Family. He had already put plans in place to foil the anticipated "Jubilee Plot" against Queen Victoria. And he had begun to plan an aggressive campaign against anarchists by destroying their clubs and their underground printing presses. But he needed the right type of hard men as agents to do so effectively before matters fell out of control. Britain's foreign adversaries were violent, whereas the nice young army officers who volunteered for Military Intelligence were too decent and naïve even to be able to imagine what they were up against.

Melville was a determined no-nonsense man—a laconic interrogator and briefer who seldom wasted a word—with impassive features, receding hair, and an efficient-looking clipped military moustache. Secretive, suspicious, and often silent, he operated in quiet anonymity to preserve his cover in a general business agent's premises in London's Victoria Street.

He already possessed a reputation for finding suitable agents, but there were not enough of them to deal with the increasing disorders. His mission was to keep a close eye on what foreigners were up to—largely meaning Germans, French, Russians and Poles, and Irish troublemakers, who were always plotting some destructive mischief. The required credentials for the right man now was a knowledge of several languages.

Britain's Intelligence Services had, so far, found that most young but dedicated army officers possessed the wrong attitude for the job. What they preferred instead were strong-minded rogues, scoundrels, cheats, and mavericks, who got things done. They were skilled in finding them and keeping them under control. That was why Melville had asked few questions of his army colleagues. He preferred to listen silently to their recommendations and watch them with care, then spring into action in his own way. They were like sporting falconers—he, Colonel Sir Henry Hozier, Colonel Kell, and Major Thwaites—training their birds of prey and releasing them to perform their next assignment.

Melville thought he might obtain more information from Thwaites, who was always helpful and somewhat less competitive. He knew he would learn nothing from Hozier, who was the oldest of the three in Military Intelligence. He had been in the Secret Service from the beginning as a young Captain who had signed his official documents with a capital 'C' for Chief—thereby instituting a tradition to be followed by all his successors. He was now nearing sixty.

'M' never saw Hozier, who was also a bit of a mystery to him. All the press knew about him was as a business man associated in some way with the shipping insurance firm, Lloyds of London. It was excellent cover for a man who was always travelling somewhere on a different secret mission. Melville believed he was now in Panama, where an important canal was being built. All three had risen in the ranks through merit, but Hozier also appeared to have aristocratic connections with the ruling classes through his marriages to an Ogilvie and a member of the Lyon family.

Major Thwaites agreed to meet Melville for a brisk walk in St. James's Park, where they could talk privately while admiring the ducks in the stream from the little rustic bridge.

"This new recruit," the Major said, "is far too valuable to be stuck in a routine administrative post. Here is a young and energetic man who not only knows Russia and Germany, but can speak at least four languages almost perfectly. His German is flawless and his Russian hardly less fluent."

"Is that your unanimous opinion?" 'M' asked cautiously. "You all think he is the right man?"

"Each of us interrogated him independently and thoroughly. Then we cross-checked with each other afterwards for any omissions or lies. We all vouch for Rosenbloom."

"As far as anyone can vouch for a spy," Melville said dryly. "What's he look like?"

"You'll see soon enough," Norman Thwaites replied. "I'd describe him physically as; complexion swarthy, a long straight nose, piercing eyes, black hair brushed back from a forehead suggesting keen intelligence, a large mouth, figure slight, of medium height, always clothed immaculately. He is a man who impressed me with a sense of power."

In no way did the candidate concur with William Melville's own idea of an Englishman. But people in the burgeoning industrial cities, and certainly in London, were becoming more accustomed to mixing with foreigners. And Melville had sensed, even then, that chameleon-like quality of a breezy diplomat with an engaging and ever present smile of friendliness, which might enable young Rosenbloom to blend himself into whatever surroundings in which he might need to operate.

"Your father?" the Chief enquired politely of the candidate, pencil ready in hand, as if he'd only just been told and neglected to make a note of it.

"My father is a colonel in the Russian army. Fortunately, well-connected."

Melville noted that the young man possessed a slight speech impediment rather than an accent when pronouncing a particular letter in English.

"In what way connected?"

"The only way that counts—the Tsar's court."

"And your mother?"

"Russian. Of Polish descent."

"Your father's family?"

"Landowners of the minor aristocracy. Catholic."

So already, 'M' thought, this self-assured and somewhat arrogant young man possessed two different identities—each with a different father; one Catholic, the other Jewish—apparently only one of which was known to Army Intelligence. And in order to join the groups of subversives in London and Manchester, he would require a third persona to fit in. An Irish one, since the priority of the moment was to infiltrate the bomb-throwing Fenians who had recently set a time-bomb in one of the lavatories of police headquarters at Scotland Yard. Fortunately, no one had been sitting on it at the time.

William Melville, Chief of Britain's Secret Intelligence Bureau (SIB), known as "M," to whom Reilly reported.

Of equal priority was the circle of Russian émigrés whom Melville had been watching only from the outside until now. That was how he had known when this young man had sought them out on arrival in London less than a year ago. He appeared already to know several of its members, including the main two suspects. She was the novelist Ethel Lilian Voynich. He was her husband Wilfred Voynich, alias the forger Kelchevsky. 'M' was well aware that Russians always had several different identities which they changed whenever it suited them to be someone else.

Now he had to find out who this young man really was before he could risk trusting him.

Melville locked eyes with him. "What made you come to us?" he asked, innocently enough.

"Several reasons" the young man said equably. A rueful expression flickered briefly across his face. "I'll do my best to explain."

Melville said nothing while the applicant

Known as "K," Sir Vernon George Waldegrave Kell was founder of MI5 and first Director General of the British Security Service.

Colonel Sir Henry Montague Hozier. What Hozier did for the British Secret Service is still Top Secret. His caricature in *Vanity Fair* in 1883 mentions that he was Secretary of Lloyds of London—good cover for his clandestine activities.

gazed for a moment into the middle distance, as if attempting to pinpoint a moment in time when he had come to an important decision. Even so, he did not blink or remove his gaze from Melville's.

"I expect it began when I was only sixteen," he said with an engaging smile. "*Possibly* soon afterwards. Or perhaps at university in Vienna."

Melville was a good listener. He waited patiently for the story to emerge, as if ready to believe every word he was told.

"You must understand," Rosenbloom said tentatively, "that I could see everything changing around me."

"In Russia?"

"Elsewhere, too." He paused to find the right approach. "In a word, industrialization!" He elaborated: "Imperial tyranny can no longer survive with industrialization. It is only a matter of time. Meanwhile, my father represents the oppressive forces of the Tsar."

"So you became a revolutionary?"

"A Social-Revolutionary," he said cautiously, "yes."

"Go on."

The young man shrugged, almost without being conscious of it; but Melville knew it was affected, even though Rosenbloom was a persuasive storyteller. "There was a family row."

"About politics?"

"No. We had already established our differences. We were already wary of each other."

As Rosenbloom described it, the row was triggered soon after a family photo was taken in 1890, when the sixteen-year-old Sigmund Rosenbloom fell violently in love with his first-cousin Felicia Rosenbloom. She was the daughter of his Uncle Vladimir. Both families were horrified, and firmly forbade the match, which young Sigmund wished to make permanent. Already a self-opinionated and rebellious youth, he had abruptly left home and severed all connections with his family, to go abroad.

"That was when I attended the university in Vienna."

Sigi had found himself comfortably at home as a student in the cosmopolitan atmosphere of Vienna before the turn of the twentieth century. The Viennese Dr. Rosenbloom apparently kept a watchful eye over him, without his yet being aware that the medical doctor was his real father. He still thought of himself as the colonel's Catholic son and part of the Imperial Russian establishment. That version of his formative years would be questioned later on.

2
The League of Enlightenment

UNFORTUNATELY FOR SIGI—OR GEORGI, as he was more often known as a nineteen year old student in Vienna—he became involved in the typical half-formed and only shallowly understood political life of other students, in which they questioned why there was such a huge gap between rich and poor and why there was so much injustice. Searching for explanations, he joined a fairly harmless socialist society at the university which was named "Friends of Enlightenment." As with all such revolutionary societies in despotic countries, extremists joined and turned the society to violent protests and terrorism.

Hearing that Georgi was about to leave for Russia to visit his very ill mother, a member of the League asked him to deliver a letter to Odessa first. He said the letter was urgent and the Russian customs officials must not find it and prevent it from being delivered. So young Georgi sewed it into the lining of his coat—no doubt feeling important and heroic.

"Even earlier, I suppose," he said sheepishly, "we all enjoyed that popular thriller by Jules Verne. You may know the one I mean? *Michael Strogoff: The Courier of the Tsar.*"

A formative book for that generation, Melville had thought, so of course he'd read it. Evidently Rosenbloom had identified with the hero of this exciting adventure story who dared to perform feats of extraordinary heroism that others could not do, because it required unusual audacity and courage. 'M' said nothing, barely nodding for him to continue.

"I was arrested by agents of the *Okhrana* secret police on arrival in Odessa, and placed in a cell. The police accused me of being involved in a conspiracy by revolutionaries. I continued to insist that I was innocent for a whole week in solitary confinement, and claimed I had no idea what was in the letter. I didn't even know the person it was addressed to. As it turned out "The League of Enlightenment," as it was also known, was listed by the *Okhrana* as a terrorist organization."

Although his family's influence prevented him from being exiled to Siberia, his mother was dead by the time he returned home.

At his mother's funeral, Georgi found that his family were shocked at the disgrace he had brought on them by being arrested and imprisoned. He found the Colonel, whom he had thought of as his father, tight-lipped. It was only then that he learned from his uncles that the Colonel had adopted him to avoid a much earlier disgrace of being exposed as Dr. Rosenbloom's and his own wife's bastard son.

Now, with his mother dead, he was on his own. It was then that the ultra-sensitivity of his character revealed itself, not only in shame that he was illegitimate, but also in shock that he was not a devout Roman Catholic as he had always thought, but Jewish. It meant he was no longer part of the Russian establishment. He had lost his identity.

That, at least, was how Sigi Rosenbloom explained his troubled youth. What was true and what was false would come to light later on.

It did nothing to ally himself with his natural father whom he had always admired until then, but for whom he now felt contempt for the doctor's adulterous affair with his mother and the way his stepfather had been shamed. On top of all that was the embarrassment and inconvenience of having his life suddenly turned upside-down.

In a state of shock at being abandoned by his dead mother and his stepfather, he went into denial of the whole situation and decided to start his life anew without any ties. In a panic from the emotional crisis, he faked suicide by leaving some of his clothes abandoned on the seashore. Then he left the family home in order to post the mysterious letter in Odessa, as he had agreed to do. Once there, he substituted his well-cut suit for a workman's clothes, and took a steamship for South America. He gave his real name on board ship, not his adopted one, as if tentatively trying out another identity to replace the previous one. He was no longer the Colonel's Catholic son but a Jewish bastard called Sigi Rosenbloom.

According to him, his next three years in South America—mostly in Brazil— would be a training station where he developed many of the skills he would need as a British secret agent.

Melville had encountered similar situations before and concluded that rebellion started in adolescence when young men and women resisted the authority of the father. He had also come across rebels who were motivated by a fantasy of being born to grander parents, as a result of parental indifference or neglect. Even if a child only feels he is neglected, when he misses the love of his real parents, or regrets having to share them with his siblings, he finds relief in the romantic idea of being an adopted child whose real parents are noble or princely. In that way he feels special, as a man of destiny must.

It was left for Melville to decide how much of what the young man told him was fantasy, and what might be true. Evidently the rejected young man was searching for a new family.

Rosenbloom had paused for reflection.

"Go on," Melville said politely to bridge the sudden silence in his office.

Rosenbloom attempted, not very successfully now, to depict Mother Russia and the Austro-Hungarian Empire as degenerate. He described the social and political scenarios of both as sick and decaying cultures with out-of-date traditions that imposed injustices on the masses, as the empires rejected modernity, progress, and industrialization of the economy. He described himself as a modern and progressive individual of a new and more democratic generation, to whom a backward-looking escape into the past had to be resisted and overcome.

"You in England," he said with some envy, "were fortunate to enjoy a great age of Victorian aspiration and exploration, and economic growth, which the rest of Europe missed because of its backward regimes. British adventurers and explorers discovered new territories and new tribes and nations unknown to white people. They were generally young army officers seeking excitement and glory, while often also working to map particular territories for British Intelligence. They made notes of the terrain, its resources, and the inhabitants and their lifestyles. In fact, *you* would be the most likely person to know why Army or Naval Intelligence had sent them there."

He paused again, as if he had lost direction and was inviting Melville to agree heartily, or at least show a flicker of interest.

In fact 'M' had no idea what he was talking about. Perhaps Hozier, Kell, or Thwaites knew. And this young man appeared to imagine they had conveyed some such information to Melville which they had not. But 'M' did not allow his ignorance to show by as little as a blink of an eyelash.

Rosenbloom seemed momentarily confused, and hesitated for a moment before starting on another tack.

"You must know about the expedition to Brazil to explore the Amazon about two years ago?"

"Why not give me *your* version?" Melville said non-committedly.

"I was told they were the first white people to chart the Amazon Basin," he said hesitantly. "No European knew the terrain or its resources before then. Nor even the extent of the massive jungles that spread along both banks of the Amazon River."

Melville reflected for a moment on the Amazon Basin, as he was intended to do. He imagined that, with the enormous length of the river, it must be one of the largest drainage basins in the world. He had some idea it ran through four different South American countries: Peru, Brazil, Colombia and Ecuador. He would look up the exact information as soon as possible to satisfy himself, as he always did when introduced to new intelligence information. He would find it covered an area of over 2.7 million square miles.

"When I lived in South America," Rosenbloom continued, "I learned to speak fluent Portuguese. New languages come easily to me. People called me Pedro. Then three British army officers arrived. They discovered I spoke English, and hired me to cook for the expedition. Major Fothergill was the leader. I could tell he was a wealthy man, accustomed to having his orders carried out."

"How did you survive in South America until then?"

"Mostly from labouring jobs. Like on the docks, and the ship-building yards at *Rio de Janeiro*."

Rosenbloom stopped as if surprised that his interrogator would want to hear his story all over again.

"Tell me about the expedition," Melville said. "What exactly happened?"

3
The Amazon Misadventure

"WELL," ROSENBLOOM BEGAN HESITANTLY, as if collecting his thoughts, "it was an ill-fated exploration from the start." He drew in his breath and began again. "The territory was hostile, to begin with—tropical diseases, poisonous snakes, belligerent natives who could not be trusted not to kill us, and dangerous wild animals."

He paused to assure himself that his interrogator was satisfied, and continued at what he interpreted as a nod of approval.

"As for the safari, our bearers were soon persuaded to desert by local tribes who could attack us more easily on our own. A native guide was essential, otherwise we would be entirely at the mercy of the heat, lack of drinking water, and prone to get lost in the jungle, where we would be killed by the poisoned darts or arrows of one of the jungle tribes. Whatever we possessed was a priceless treasure to them. We couldn't hope to survive for long."

Melville had read several accounts of hazardous Victorian expeditions. Now he felt some momentum might be gained by making a minor contribution to encourage the candidate, who had paused as if unsure which trail of thought to follow.

"The usual retinue of women, children, and slaves, I suppose?"

Rosenbloom nodded while recollecting what had happened. "Porters, soldiers, other paid staff . . . We ended with nearly double the number of what was originally planned."

"How many?"

"Was eighty—grew to over two hundred."

Melville recalled that the famous explorers—both Burton and Speke—had suffered from stupefying bouts of fever and other illnesses that reduced them to varying degrees of helplessness during their journey to the source of the Nile. Unable at various times to walk, to see, to hear, or even to talk, they had returned to England emaciated shells of their former selves. Soon after, an entire expedition of some geographer or other had disappeared while searching for a lost city in much the same area that the candidate described. Evidently Fothergill's exploration of the Amazon Basin was threatened with the same types of hazards. He studied the candidate's face searchingly.

"Our bearers deserted us," Rosenbloom told him grimly. "Our native guide vanished after another few days. It was a region of malarial swamps and yellow fever. The British officers went down with a tropical fever that made them completely helpless. It was an opportunity for the natives to kill the officers while they slept and make off with their guns and equipment and all the stores."

But, according to Rosenbloom, he had slept lightly and heard the sounds of natives crawling through the bushes towards them at night. Although still half asleep, he took hold of a service revolver and stopped the attack with his marksmanship in which he made sure that every bullet counted.

"One officer died of fever and we buried him in the swamp. But I managed to lead the other two back to *Rio*. Major Fothergill gave me a cheque for £1,500 for saving their lives. He also had the mysterious ability to provide me with a British passport and bring me with him to England. I realised by then, of course, that he must be connected with British Intelligence."

'M' stole another look at the notes he'd made. "And Fothergill was?"

"An assumed name."

"Any ideas?"

Rosenbloom raised an outspread hand to stop him going any further. "Can't discuss—top secret."

"Fothergill" sounded to Melville like Hozier. Colonel Sir Henry Montague Hozier had been decorated with the title of Knight Commander of the Most Honorable Order of the Bath; one of the oldest British orders of chivalry, which was instituted by King George the First in 1725. Hozier fought in the Second Chinese War in 1857, the Abyssinian War, the Austro-Prussian War of 1866, and was awarded the decoration of Knight of the Iron Cross when attached to the Prussian Army. But whatever he achieved for Britain's Secret Service was still top secret.

Young Rosenbloom sounded like a good man to have at one's side in a crisis—if anything he'd claimed was even half true.

Now in London, and back to being Sigi Rosenbloom again, with his good looks, charm and self-confidence, and his aristocratic airs, the twenty-two year old became an elegantly dressed man-about-town with plenty of friends. The private clubs of St. James's appeared to be his natural *milieu*. Rosenbloom told anyone who asked him about his surname that he was German. His new friends began to call him Sidney.

Kell had assured 'M' that the unlikely scenario of this former dock labourer dining at the best restaurants and hotels in London and playing for high stakes at the gaming tables, and winning more than he lost, was all true. Gambling and young women were Sidney's escape from boredom. He enjoyed living on the edge. Even so, he knew that banks always win over time, and his capital could not last much longer. The Major invited him to make a visit to Russia for British Intelligence. But the idea of returning to Russia was still too painful for him: it was associated with his disgrace and alienation from his former family.

Thwaites had added a footnote to the Brazilian trip and Rosenbloom's arrival in London, about which 'M' was curious but sceptical, since boasts about women and passion were foreign to him.

"Sigi" Rosenbloom, most probably age 20 or 21.

"Evidently, with his last money, young Rosenbloom threw himself into another love affair with a woman a few years older than himself who was just beginning to make a name in London as a writer. She was born in Ireland but married a Russian. Her married name was Ethel Lilian Voynich."

After a brief pause, 'M' had remarked thoughtfully, "There's still something you are not telling me."

"Lots, dear boy!" the Major said with a knowing grin. "It's up to you to find out. But I can tell you the loving couple went off to Italy on Rosenbloom's last £300. Once there, he was back under the influence of the Roman Catholic Church. He was a sensitive, emotional, and romantic young man."

The affair apparently gave the young

Rosenbloom greater confidence in himself when he returned to England. The last thing Thwaites had told 'M' before he glanced at a gold fob watch from his pocket like the White Rabbit in *Alice*, and hurried off in the direction of Buckingham Palace as if he might be late for the Queen, was; "Voynich published a novel that revealed his early life, which she called *The Gadfly*. It became a best-seller in Russia."

4
Home is the Hunter

Now, AS 'M' GAZED AT THE RELAXED YOUNG MAN seated in a thoroughly self-possessed posture before him, he was reminded of the famous writer of adventure stories, Robert Louis Stevenson, whose death had only just been announced in the newspapers. It was something to do with the eager thrust of his chin. The author's own words were carved on his tombstone: *"Glad did I live and gladly die."*

Rosenbloom was one of those peculiar men of destiny, Melville thought. But his name would have to be changed. His own wife's maiden name seemed somehow more appropriate—it was Reilly. He nodded impassively as he considered this immigrant to England assuming a new identity as Sidney Reilly. He could draw up all the documents to make it legal. But he hesitated. He wanted more information, but knew it would be unreliable. The question was how far could he trust this Rosenbloom, if at all?

The others had endorsed him, and expected Melville to agree to take him on as an agent. But still he hesitated. On reflection, he decided the hurdle in his mind was a cultural one involving the traditional tyrannies in Europe where he came from, on one hand, and Democracy as it was played out in America, which at times seemed to the British to be more like unrestrained mob rule.

"But Europe is not like America," the newcomer calmly explained. "America will take care of itself in its own way. The dangers to Britain come from all the backward countries on the Continent of Europe with their old ethnic hatreds and their determination to kill each other."

His remark struck Melville as being something more than a common-sense observation, perhaps because it echoed his own distrust of foreigners.

Rosenbloom added earnestly, "I simply cannot understand why some people will go to such lengths to dig themselves into a hole, and yet not stir to dig themselves out of it."

Melville waited watchfully for the young man to elaborate, but the candidate evidently felt he had made his point. It seemed to his interrogator to be the truest and most heartfelt statement from him yet. And it transformed 'M's perception of him from that of a slow and observant chameleon focused solely on securing the basic needs of life, into an agile-minded fox—a sensitive and constant hunter of prey.

'M' recalled a phrase used by Kell when they'd leaned casually over the rails of the tiny bridge in the park. 'K' said they were Hozier's words after he'd interviewed Rosenbloom and expressed his own observations on their candidate: "A burning and ruthless ambition has been sown."

What had Hozier meant? All he'd apparently told 'K' in explanation was that young Rosenbloom had sent him a long and detailed report of the political situation in Italy, before he'd returned to London, leaving Ethel Voynich behind in Florence.

"Europe has always been plundered and raped by unjust and oppressive regimes," Hozier had remarked to 'K.' "Although Napoleon is dead, he's still a figure of hope for romantics like Rosenbloom who despair at injustice and look for someone to take charge. They dream of how it might still be possible to lead an army against the forces of tyrants."

Young men of the times read and were inspired by the memory of the young liberator Napoleon Bonaparte in popular novels, like Stendhal's *The Red and the Black*. It was a study of the mind of a provincial young man of the same age as Rosenbloom, who was searching for his own identity and destiny, and caught between the power of the ruling classes who used the Church and the Army as instruments to oppress the people.

Hozier had read Reilly's account of the complicated political rebellions and counter-rebellions taking place in Italy, which the young man had sent to British Intelligence. The old secret agent who played the Great Game so elegantly was impressed by Reilly's report. It was of extraordinary value to the Secret Service, since the chaos in Italy and Sicily was difficult to place in its proper perspective and otherwise impossible to understand from Britain, which was fortunately separated from Europe.

There was also the financial crisis and banking scandal which resulted from Italy's political instability. This intelligent and worldly young man understood its importance to international currency markets.

According to his detailed report, which was read carefully also by others in British Intelligence, Italy's problems appeared to have come about because of fierce attempts by Sicilian Fascists to overthrow the traditional liberal left government, and attempts by the military to restore it. 40,000 Italian troops were rushed to Sicily, which was now in a state of siege. Anarchists, Fascists, Republicans, and their student sympathizers, were crushed by the Italian army, and summary executions were carried out on-the-spot.

Sir Henry Hozier and his military colleagues instantly recognized Reilly's assets as a shrewd observer and analyst of current and foreign affairs, and his self-assurance and audacity in taking valuable risks to acquire intelligence information.

They now found that his attitude towards Russia had changed. It seemed that his experiences of the chaos in Italy had stirred up his own political or romantic longings and turned them into zealousness. That was probably what Hozier had meant when he'd said, "A burning and ruthless ambition has been sown."

"How can we use your skills?" Hozier had asked Sigmund Rosenbloom during their interview.

Rosenbloom told him, "I want to return to Russia in an official capacity. Then I'll do whatever I can to ferret out useful information and convey it to the Chief of Britain's Secret Service."

That was when Sigi Rosenbloom was introduced to 'M.' They studied each other in William Melville's Spartan office for the first time, almost as adversaries. Yet each wished to befriend the other. What each began searching for was a key to the other man's character. Now, 'M' was finally convinced he had found the key to the stranger's character and motivation: he was distressed at the unfairness and injustice in the world. He had been drawn to Britain's Intelligence Bureau because he hoped to find justice there.

Rosenbloom had met Englishmen before, like the man he had known as "Major Fothergill" and his younger officers. Englishmen in the late Victorian era were different from almost everyone else. They set themselves above the baseness and pettiness that drove others to envy, meanness, or hatred. Compared with the corruption on the Continent of Europe, the British must have seemed a more amenable family to belong to.

"Loved and reviled," as Czech author Karel Capek wrote of them, "if you get to know them closer, they are very kind and gentle; they never speak much because they never speak about themselves. They enjoy themselves like children, but with the most solemn, leathery expression; they have lots of ingrained etiquette, but at the same time they are as free-and-easy as young whelps. They are as hard as flint, incapable of adapting themselves, conservative, loyal, rather shallow and always uncommunicative; they cannot get out of their skin, but it is a solid, and in every respect excellent skin."

That observation may have been more measured than one perceived through more sentimental Russian eyes like Sigmund Rosenbloom's. Another elegant writer, George Santayana, wrote of the archetypal Englishman of the time;

"He prefers the country to the town, and home to foreign parts. He is rather glad and relieved if only natives will remain natives and strangers, and at a comfortable distance from himself. Yet outwardly he is most hospitable and accepts almost anybody for the time being; he travels and conquers without a settled design, because he has the instinct of exploration. His adventures are all external; they change him so little that he is not afraid of them. He carries his English weather in his heart wherever he goes, and it becomes a cool spot in the desert, and a steady and sane oracle amongst all the deliriums of mankind. Never since the heroic days of Greece has the world had such a sweet, just, boyish master."

Britain's MI5 and MI6 did not exist when Reilly joined Britain's Secret Intelligence Bureau, so they had to be invented. The original Military and Admiralty Intelligence Services, generally known as SIS, were formed not long before Reilly was hired to infiltrate terrorist organizations in England, and then sent abroad as a secret agent to acquire top secret information in Germany, China, Russia, Japan and the United States; so that he made a significant impact on the development of Britain's Secret Service.

Melville's conception of an Englishman for Rosenbloom to use as a role model in England, would have been little different from a description written by a highly observant and articulate English philosopher: "Those who write of the English are generally favorably impressed. Those who find fault with the English usually condemn qualities that the English themselves condone—such as their coldness, which the English praise as reserve; their hypocrisy which they call compromise; their snobbery, which is decorum; and their stubbornness, of which they are justifiably proud."

It was this coldness which had first caused Kell, Thwaites, and Hozier, to be hesitant about Rosenbloom's sentimentality. That and his passion were considered inexcusable in their circles, and also in Melville's. The leaders of British Intelligence were motivated more by their own hard-headed Anglo-Saxon common sense; none of this emotional nonsense which could be a weakness resulting in failure.

Nevertheless, it is recorded that William Melville recruited young Solomon Rosenbloom as a confidential agent in 1896 for several assignments in Britain's Secret Service.

Since Reilly was to inform on an organization that Melville suspected was involved with Russian anarchists and revolutionaries, no doubt he could easily fit in by being himself, as well as with the Russian bourgeois group, which he knew Rosenbloom had already penetrated in London. He'd had him watched from the moment he had stepped off the boat on arriving in England the previous year. It was how he knew that Rosenbloom had gone straight to his old mistress, Ethel Voynich.

Britain, in its open-hearted way, had welcomed fugitives from war-torn countries to find safety within its shores, and there were always some revolutionaries who intrigued, or even sought revenge, plotting and bringing their own foreign values to work in London with guns and bombs, and obtaining secret information for use against Britain by a foreign power.

Melville had his own personal connections with the German Secret Service, since he would have to prevent a plot to assassinate the Kaiser at Queen Victoria's state funeral, which was expected soon, in London. He advised the Spanish Government on anarchists working on their own turf. Working secretly under an alias, he also operated counterintelligence and ran foreign intelligence missions abroad, sometimes turning up unexpectedly to clinch a deal with a counterpart.

Since Britain was balanced precariously at the peak of its wealth and power, with an Empire comprising over a quarter of the world's population, troublemaking rebels could not be ignored, either inside the Empire or anywhere in the rest of the world. Territorial power created envy. Envy caused discontent. And discontented individuals joined disaffected groups formed to create uprisings against authority.

Nor could the British be ignored by the other three-quarters of the world, although Englishmen attempted to look unconcerned and feigned indifference to their success. Despite that, 'M' believed there was more than mere chance in Reilly's arrival in England at that particular moment in Britain's history. He knew very well that although the aristocracy were still the top layer of society, revolutionary undercurrents were stirring that could topple princes, monarchs, and even empires.

He was also well aware that, ever since the French Revolution in the previous century, no aristocrat, or prince or monarch, had been safe from the frustration and anger of the masses. And yet the royals had still not learned to change their arrogant, indifferent, or contemptuous attitude, or their resort to prison cells and executions for their subjects. Nor had the masses, with their hysterical mob riots and random assassinations, been interested in civilizing themselves. But he did not believe in philosophizing or in political solutions. He was a man of action. That was why he relied on his colleagues' endorsement of this foreign spy.

Most Englishmen had not been mired in the barbarism and hatreds of the Continent of Europe, but their classical education had taught them the profound truths about the eternal frailty of the flawed human condition. Melville had learnt it at first-hand with the murderous hatreds of Catholics and Protestants in Ireland. Reilly had experienced the corruption himself in Mother Russia. Those who had been confronted by it knew that among all the tremors underlying society, the difference between those caused by idealists or criminals, heroes or traitors, partisans or terrorists, was impossible to separate; they were all troublemakers. Every one of their actions caused a reaction. Every tremor rebounded and continued to echo from down the centuries, creating conflicts between the elites and the masses, and leaving the foundations of the major European empires cracked and trembling.

That was the fragile volcanic background of conditions on the European continent into which young Sidney Reilly was thrown by his own fateful circumstances that would cause him to conspire with Britain's Intelligence Service.

He had emerged from the huge Russian Empire of the Romanov dynasty of Tsars. But the same situation applied to the massive Austro-Hungarian Empire and the smaller but more powerful German Empire; not to mention the sick and crumbling caliphate of the Ottoman Turks. All of those societies were about to collapse.

5
Young Sparks

"EDDIE IS A VERY UNUSUAL YOUNG MAN," said Winston's aunt firmly. "One of those youthful sparks who burst into flame when their talents are needed. Well-read and already acknowledged as an expert of Greek and Latin poetry . . . He has written for the *Cambridge Observer* on the French novelists."

"Heavens, not another child prodigy!"

"Evidently so."

She had not exaggerated: Eddie Marsh was already acknowledged as a classical scholar. Winston knew from his own scholarship that nine-tenths of the traditional classical education was rubbish, but the remaining one-tenth was priceless.

He glanced up and peered across the drawing room to study Eddie Marsh's features. What he saw was a somewhat foppish youth, still coltish, tall and lanky with broad shoulders, his fair hair brushed well off of an intellectual forehead. Eddie engendered an air of natural superiority. But Winston thought it not at all difficult to achieve in this high society salon, which he found sterile. But he was intrigued, and now understood why his aunt had insisted on his attending the *soirée*. He liked to have intelligent and original people around him who stimulated his own ideas, and he loved an intelligent audience for his sudden histrionic outbursts of oratory and wit.

More to the point, Winston was the newly-appointed Under-Secretary of the Colonies under Lord Elgin, and Mrs. Leslie, his aunt, had evidently invited him to scrutinize Eddie for the vacant position as his Private Secretary. Winston was one of the youngest Ministers ever to be appointed to the House of Commons. Now he needed a dependable assistant whom he could work with on affairs of state. And, as usual, the female members of his family, with their scores of social contacts, were a great help to him with introductions and recommendations.

"I must tell you what has happened," Eddie wrote soon after to his friend Pamela Lytton. "It's so thrilling for me—the man who ought to be Winston's Private Secretary is very ill and can't come back to work for six months or so—and W. has asked for me! I've just been dining alone with him, he was perfectly charming but I can see what he will expect from his P.S. and it's simply terrifying —all so utterly beyond my capacity . . . I expect I told you how much I admire him, so I shall do my best."

Winston always made up his mind very quickly about people and never wasted a minute on anyone with a mediocre mind. He'd learnt to be discerning as a soldier fighting at the front in the Sudan, in India and Afghanistan, and in the South African war, because there was no time to natter when you might be dead in seconds and instant action was called for to prevent it from happening. He'd seldom been wrong.

He'd told Eddie over dinner, "Academics like you are still kept as sheltered from real life as ever, pointlessly pondering over unproven theories. You will never enjoy a life of action. But I will, because I am compelled to be at the very centre of it. And I can take you with me."

Was Marsh a Nancy-boy? He could certainly be described as precious, as well as *precocious*. But Edwardians were modern men and women who accepted facts without questioning them. Respect for the privacy of others was considered far more important in England's code of good manners. In fact, Eddie sublimated his sexuality in close and warm friendships with creative young men who were poets, painters, or playwrights. Wrote one of his friends to him after a party, "It's not fair on young women that such an irresistible young spark like you should be about."

Eddie's appointment with his new chief began in 1905. He and Mr. Churchill had worked together and become friends ever since. While Winston energetically pursued his political ambitions, Eddie stayed in the shadows and watched history being made by the movers and shakers of the world.

Eddie, with his classical scholarship, and his chief with his sense of military history, were conscious of Britain's leadership in world affairs. Both envisioned the Colonial Office as central to a panoramic view of historic and current events. They sensed that Winston was about to play a pivotal role. And Eddie, if he behaved himself, would accompany him.

Eddie Marsh was immediately thrown into the drama of politics, and was expected to keep up with the workload and pace of his new chief, who was about to contest the Conservative seat in North-West Manchester, which was known for its cotton mills and warehouses. He was particularly sensitive to the problems of working class industrial neighborhoods. When they walked to his hotel in a poor neighbourhood, and he pointed with his cane at the rows of grim and

Private Secretary Eddie Marsh (standing) with his chief, young Winston, in Africa (1907).

tiny row houses, he couldn't help remarking to Eddie with compassion, "Fancy living in one of those streets—never seeing anything beautiful, never eating anything savoury, never being educated enough to think or say anything *clever!*"

Marsh served him well in his first test as confidential assistant to the new Minister, with the defeat of the Conservative opposition, and it gave him confidence to stay the pace. One of his functions was to hear Winston rehearse the delivery of his political speeches privately and advise his chief of his reactions. He proved to be a perceptive and critical audience, and a sounding board for his chief's ideas. But it was only when he read his chief's newly published biography of his father, Lord Randolph Churchill, that Eddie realized he was not only working for an influential politician but also for a man of letters with literary panache.

His new chief's realpolitik ideas and experience were far broader and more profound than Eddie's romantic notions of life, glimpsed from the accounts of Herodotus and classical history at Cambridge. While Eddie knew poetry and literature, Winston already knew the real world, had defied death on several battlefronts, and was an intimate of world leaders.

What Eddie Marsh did not know was that his chief's mind had been distracted at that moment by dramatic and confidential information which had only just been passed on to him by Sir Henry Wilson, the Director of Military Operations and Intelligence at the War Office. Wilson had warned him of his suspicions that Germany was preparing for war against England.

Winston gave himself time, as he always did, to consider all the factors and their possible consequences. He finally admitted to his Private Secretary,

"I have not, so far, seen any signs of war from Germany myself. On the contrary, when I was invited by the Kaiser to review his Prussian troops on manoeuvres only two years ago, I felt there was a lot of out-of-date posturing and pageantry with the cavalry, but nothing to be alarmed at."

Young Clementine Hozier, now Mrs Churchill.

"How did you get on with the Kaiser?"

Eddie's Chief smiled indulgently. "Frankly, I found the Emperor's vainglorious preening and posturing quite laughable."

His P.S. gazed at him with interest. "Did you get to know him well?"

"Well enough to be touched by his princely self-aggrandizement. And, what I thought of at the time as his stumbling ineptitude."

"And now?"

"I was younger then," Winston admitted almost ruefully. "Not burdened with the somber responsibilities of the Home Office, as I am now. I was more focused on what political elements made for an orderly society in peacetime, like insurance and pensions. Bismarck had already established such things in Germany, you see. He was an extraordinary Chancellor."

German officials were always scandalized by the familiarity between Eddie and his chief. They expected Herr Marsh to snap to attention and click his heels and bow stiffly whenever addressing his superior, as they always did with their own superior officers in a military society in which even ladies were expected to step off the kerb of a pavement to allow an officer to pass.

Eddie did not accompany his chief to Germany on that occasion, but remained in London to forestall his chief's creditors.

"I shall be back Oct. 8 and not before; but if that does not satisfy them let me know and I will pay them at once . . . Will you send me the copy of Clemenceau's speech against Socialism." His chief was staying as a guest in Switzerland of the King's closest friend, Sir Ernest Cassel. Evidently he had visited Paris on the way.

"I have today bought a lot of nice French books."

The "nice books" turned out to be the complete works of de Maupassant, Balzac, Musset, Voltaire, Lamartine, Chateaubriand, Michelet, Sévigné, the correspondence of Louis XVI and Marie Antoinette, and *Manon Lescaut* by Prévost. Marsh added them to his chief's already extensive library on arrival, to be eagerly devoured by his erudite chief on his return. Winston was always greedy for information, knowledge and ideas, and could never get enough of them.

While Winston bought books in France, Eddie Marsh bought contemporary paintings and drawings at London's more modest art galleries.

"My dear Brooke," he wrote to a new friend from Cambridge; " Or may I say Rupert and will you do likewise? I have just heard of a superb John drawing which I shall have to buy if I can go and see it before it is snapped up—I have only got one, and *must* have another before you come, or you will think my collection stick-in-the-mud."

But the main delight of Eddie's leisure time was still the enchanting social life that his chief scorned.

"Beware of the Smart Set!" one of Eddie's more outspoken friends warned him. "You can't imagine how funny you look floating around the dance floor to the gramophone and fluttering your hands in the air."

His friend Conrad went even further in his criticism: "The life you lead simply strikes me dumb . . . When you write to me 'Lady X is a dear little woman' I feel very nervous. Because I know she is a vulgar old bitch with the brain of a squirrel."

Although the darling of gossips in London society, Eddie Marsh was faithfully silent whenever conversations turned to high political issues, and loyally pretended to ignorance, with an impassive face, if ever the names of his chief's intimates appeared on anyone's lips. He was completely trustworthy: there would be no leaks on his watch. Eddie Marsh had worked in the Colonial Office since 1896, and achieved a prim-and-proper reputation for harshly criticizing senior colonial officers in his despatches for any alleged injustices. He had been promoted in the spring of 1900—the dawn of the Edwardian Era—because he was so punctilious and likeable, and dedicated to quality.

Marsh had already developed a reputation as a connoisseur, even a patron, of the arts, particularly of poetry and painting, but also theatre, when his chief was appointed Home Secretary in Asquith's coalition government. The previous Conservative Prime Minister Campbell-Bannerman had just died.

"He could be described," said Winston, "as one of the last gentleman leaders to perform a selfless service for England before the inevitable onslaught of careerist politicians who will focus instead on their own personal ambitions."

When Eddie Marsh was called into his chief's office, six years after they had begun working together, he found him sitting anxiously forward from behind his desk, wide-eyed with a rueful yet impish expression. Winston had already become accustomed to being blamed as a maverick for everything that went wrong, even if it had happened before he was born. It had all been his own mischievous fault, according to the political opposition or the newspaper press. Now—to judge by

the theatrical expression on his face and the telephone receiver still in his hand
—evidently something else had happened that shouldn't have, and he expected to
be blamed for it once again.

6
The Siege

"WHERE DID IT ALL GO SO TERRIBLY WRONG?" his chief asked from the seat
on the other side of the desk as he hooked the earpiece of his telephone
solemnly onto its cradle: "For England, I mean—not for me."

Eddie gazed at his chief's grim features, the downturned lower lip and determined chin. He was about to reply with a specific date, as was so often the case in
researching for his chief's books or speeches in the House, when Winston abruptly
apprised him of what he had just heard about the violent affray in London's East
End. He had only just been informed by Scotland Yard.

Somehow, the fact that a violent riot had broken out in London did not sit
comfortably with Eddie's foppish gestures or his somewhat castrato tones caused
by a disabling schoolboy illness.

But Winston recognized the news as a milestone of sorts in Britain's history,
and elaborated on what he had just been told:

"Three police sergeants shot dead by rifle fire when they called at a house at 100
Sidney Street, to investigate a burglary of a jewellery shop in Hounsditch."

"The East End?"

His chief nodded, paused for reflection, and said "Stepney."

"Is it in the newspapers yet?"

"Apparently only in the stop-press news so far. They call the incident "The
Siege of Sidney Street." And describe it as a political act by a Russian *agent provocateur* who is holed up in a house with other anarchists."

"You mean it's still going on?"

"Even as we speak. Can you imagine what the press will make of it when they
set the size of the headlines on the front page?"

Eddie was aghast. "It sounds like something out of *The Secret Agent*."

His chief nodded again, somberly. "I know."

Improbable foreign conspiracies aimed at undermining society in London
had been described in a popular novel by Joseph Conrad only three years earlier.
Winston had read it, too. The story had been inspired by a real French anarchist
named Martial Bourdin, who had foolishly detonated his bomb by accident and
killed himself on his way to blow up Greenwich Observatory.

Conrad, originally a Pole, wrote in elegant English. He had evidently sensed what was happening in London because he supported Polish nationalists fighting for independence from Russian domination. And, since the British Empire was the greatest empire in history, and London was its operational hub, this was the place where subversive elements of all sorts eagerly undermined Great Britain, as if every problem in the world could be laid at its doorway.

"We are being dragged into the nihilistic and violent era of the twentieth century," Winston said solemnly. He made up his mind as Home Secretary in that instant, by reaching decisively for the telephone again and calling out the Scots Guards to assist the police.

When he hung up the phone and rose in sudden haste from behind his desk to reach for his winter overcoat on its hanger, Eddie raised a nervous hand to warn him not to act impetuously by appearing personally at the scene of the shoot-out.

"My dear," Eddie warned him hesitantly and with a nervous stammer, "the press will c . . .crucify you . . . and so will the C . . . Conservatives."

No gentleman would wish to draw attention to himself in the newspapers. It was considered even more vulgar than boasting about oneself, since it revealed a shallow and insecure character that could not be trusted. The Conservatives already scorned Winston for deserting them and resented being beaten by him at the polls. They were out for his blood and would not be satisfied until they trampled his face in the dirt. Why give them an opportunity?

That was not his chief's reaction. "It's better to be crucified for doing something than for doing nothing," he growled.

"I'll order a carriage," Marsh said instantly.

So Marsh accompanied Winston to the scene of the shootings in London's East End.

They arrived in Stepney by noon, with Eddie Marsh at his chief's heels, both wearing heavy overcoats. It had been a cold night. Snowflakes fell gently but steadily on the helmets of the uniformed police who had already surrounded the house in Sidney Street. The Home Secretary and his assistant were greeted on arrival by a hail of bullets from automatic pistols that shot two more policemen dead.

Shootings in London were such a rarity that Britain's police constables were not equipped with firearms on their regular patrols. All they had to protect the public and themselves was a wooden truncheon.

The fire brigade had been called out, but Winston restrained them from breaking in or they would certainly have all been shot dead. A plainclothes man from police headquarters at Scotland Yard, with a walrus moustache, stood by in an anonymous raincoat and a crushed Trilby hat. The scene was illuminated by gas lights as it grew darker. Now, in addition to the nineteen Scots Guardsmen, seven hundred and fifty uniformed policemen were called out. The guardsmen used a Maxim gun, and Winston agreed that a couple of field guns should be summoned from the Royal Horse Artillery depot in St John's Wood. This was war!

At the first sign of the expected news photographers, Eddie concealed himself by edging behind his chief, to remain anonymous.

Winston knew he would inevitably be criticized by the opposition party as a publicity seeker, because of the unusual media coverage of the incident. He could imagine the eight-point type of the stop-press news at the bottom of the back page transferred into bold headlines as front page news in the evening edition. Nevertheless, he already knew more about the affair than the journalists and politicians who would criticize or ridicule him. And it evidently needed his military experience to direct the fire from the guardsmen against the gang of anarchists who had broken into the store. Someone had to restore law and order.

So far, neither the newspapers nor Parliament had any idea of the sudden rise in crimes and violence from outside sources and inside saboteurs, whereas Melville's military security bureau and the police had kept the Home Secretary informed. 'M's secret agent, code-named Reilly, had infiltrated a whole variety of gangs of malcontents, subversives, and other troublemakers in Britain. The incident in Stepney was not just another commonplace burglary, but a counter-espionage matter that represented a watershed moment in English history.

The house finally caught fire and was burnt down. The so-called gang leader —whom the press named "Peter the Painter"—would turn out to be a secret undercover agent from Tsarist Russia's *Okhrana*; most likely Peter Straume from Riga. He had infiltrated a group of anarchists and incited them to break in to the store in order to alert the police so that they could all be eliminated.

According to one newspaper report, the episode had begun when "police found a pistol, six hundred cartridges, one hundred and fifty *Mauser* bullets, and numerous 'dangerous' chemicals" in a Mr. Moroutzeff's house in Gold Street. Although Straume was known to be connected, his defence counsel at the trial had him released on a matter of mistaken identity.

Winston knew from his own military and political experience that, while routine life continued without much change from day to day, as reported in the popular press, nothing was as it might seem on the printed page. It was not that the news was intentionally false, but that an undercurrent rippled quietly and unseen beneath the surface and influenced events in strange and unforeseen ways.

"A dark current," Winston elaborated on for Eddie Marsh's benefit after the fire had gutted the building. "Few people even know about it as they pursue their own self-absorbed interests."

The worst difficulties from which Britain suffered—or so Winston expressed to his Private Secretary at the time—"do not come from outside the British Isles, they come from within. Our Intelligence reports show that such activities do not come from the homes of wage-earners, but from a peculiar type of subversive intellectual."

"I always think intellectuals are so colourful."

"That may be so, but they drain Britain of its strength."

Active subversion by disloyal nationals, or their subversion by foreign spies, was the main reason why Winston had supported the secret gathering of useful information by Britain's infant Secret Intelligence Bureau. Not only had he authorized wireless cryptography—which was something entirely new with the recent invention of the new wireless technology—he also obtained intelligence in any other way possible through the initiative, the special skills, and bravery of British secret service agents. One of them was William Melville's new agent, whose detailed reports of subversion he read with special care. He knew the agent's name was Reilly.

He had not yet met Reilly face-to-face, although he and Colonel Hozier had been instrumental in having him hired by Melville. And there was another individual who would have almost as much to do with the cataclysmic events that followed. The third man was a Social-Revolutionary in Russia named Boris Savinkov.

Savinkov was described by one of Britain's secret agents as "the most remarkable man I have ever met. He has the prosperous looks of a lawyer, but is actually a terrorist. He organized several assassinations in Russia only six years ago. The first was Russia's Minister of the Interior—a man named Plehve—and the Grand Duke Serge a year later."

When Winston finally met Savinkov face-to-face for the first time, he would write of his first impression of the alleged assassin, "I had never seen a Russian Nihilist except on the stage, and my first impression was that he was singularly well cast for the part. Small in stature, moving as little as possible, and that noiselessly and with deliberation; remarkably grey-green eyes in a face of almost deathly pallor; speaking in a calm, low, even voice, almost a monotone; innumerable cigarettes . . . Savinkov's whole life had been spent in conspiracy."

Winston, Reilly, and Savinkov, were more or less the same age and had much in common, but were as different as the legendary "Three Musketeers." They would have an extraordinary influence on world events when they finally met and agreed to support each other as comrades-in-arms.

What led to their combining their talents in a deliberate attempt to restore law and order in Britain's suddenly chaotic society and political life, and also in international affairs, was the unexpected turnaround from public satisfaction in the restraint and orderliness of authority, to mass discontent and self-destructive disobedience of the laws. The Siege of Sidney Street was only one of the first symptoms of how the world had shrunk with the advent of the new industrial technologies—the telephone, the wireless, railroads, and steamships. Everyone's problems were being dumped onto Britain's lap; which meant the Home Office, the Foreign Office, the Colonial Office, the War Office, and the Admiralty.

Until then—as Winston explained to Eddie Marsh, as if dictating one of his history books on momentous affairs, as soon as they returned to Whitehall;

"Most English people felt they had reached acceptable solutions for the material problems of life. Our political principles had withstood every test. It was necessary only to apply them in an orderly fashion."

He added almost wistfully while lighting up a new cigar; "It seemed that at last the world had escaped from barbarism, superstition, authoritarian tyrannies and wars. Naturally, there were plenty of differing opinions to quarrel about, but surely that should not affect the life or foundations of society? At least, that was what most of us thought."

And yet, suddenly, as it seemed, forces of discontent arose from every quarter. It appeared that the very nature of industrialization was contrary to the spirit and way of life of free individuals. The stresses and strains of neglecting the more natural lifestyle of a rural society and an agricultural economy, suddenly set everyone at each other's throats. Some said it was the result of increased densities of populations living check-by-jowl in ever-expanding cities. Whatever it was, opportunities for further advances in liberalism, wealth distribution, and living standards, now disappeared beneath the welter of complaints and subsequent turmoil, with a desperate need to restore law and order.

"Time," Winston intoned somberly, as he puffed away steadily on his cigar, "with its tense spring and its clockwork mechanism, has suddenly reversed itself and retreated from hope, aspirations, and adventure, to the tribal envies and hatreds and dark superstitions of the barbaric past. Criminality is in the air that everyone breathes. I fear we will be dragged once again into a European war."

Ethel Voynich, author of the best-selling novel in Russia, called *The Gadfly*, which they filmed.

Eddie knew enough not to interrupt his chief's dramatic flow of words which translated his emotions into a global epic, without worrying too much whether he

Home Secretary Winston Churchill takes charge as snow falls and police are killed by Latvian
anarchists in London's East End in the "Siege of Sidney Street".

was exaggerating or not. Indeed, Eddie Marsh knew by now that his Chief loved
war. He was a soldier and been trained for it.

"And now," Winston informed Eddie with exasperation, "we have a bloody
railway strike on our hands as well! The trade unions are determined to test our
resolve in protecting the economy."

'It would be very interesting to know," Eddie mused, "whether there is any
German money behind all our troubles."

Eddie now lived a life of contrasts between his chief's solemn affairs of state and
his own lighthearted entertainment with the Smart Set, dancing after-hours to all
the new modern steps, like the "Turkey Trot." Inspired by Eddie's encouragement
that "London is getting quite amusing," and "Everyone is very pretty this year,"
and audiences who returned again and again to a theatre where a new musical
called *Hullo Ragtime* was playing, Winston wondered what he was missing by not

socializing, and accompanied Eddie to a *soirée*.

In the parlance of their set, everything was "too wonderful!" But the small-talk was so full of tiresome clichés that they invented a game by standing in sight of the entrance to the ballroom and rated each young woman for her beauty as she came in. Their scoring was based on Marlowe's quotation; "Was this the face that launched a thousand ships, and burnt the topless towers of *Ilium*?"

Eddie would say grudgingly, "I wouldn't even launch a hundred little fishing boats for her," or "Only a small gunboat for that one, my dear!"

The beauty of only two women warranted their full thousand ships that night. They were the greatly admired and envied beauty Lady Diana Manners, and Colonel Sir Henry Hozier's adopted daughter, Clementine. Clementine was a tall and slender young woman with startling blue eyes and bright red hair. She would have been an ideal model for one of Botticelli's lovely redheads who repeatedly appeared in his paintings.

Boris Savinkov. former Assistant War Minister in Imperial Russia's provisional government under Kerensky before the October Revolution.

Unknown at the time by Winston, his mother had invited Clementine as a suitable wife for her restless son. When introduced to her at dinner, Winston—who always had so much to say for himself—was suddenly struck dumb.

Marsh had already met Lady Randolph Churchill at Blenheim and, like everyone else, adored her. Now, when he accompanied his chief to Malta, to sort out two bickering Orthodox archbishops demanding union with Greece, she wrote him a personal little note; "Look after my Winston—he is very precious to me."

7
The Fox Knows Many Things

THE RULING CLASSES THROUGHOUT EUROPE were apprehensive of change, unlike the self-made men of the newly-created United States, who knew how to initiate changes to their advantage and the best way to exploit them. The reason why Britain's leading wealthy families still qualified for leadership in government was because they were not influenced by the taint of sordid ambition and greed that drew others to political life. The English milords were still popular, for a little while longer at least, because they believed in honor, service, and duty.

That was the background to the arrival of Sidney Reilly, who began to operate as a paid spy infiltrating society on behalf of Britain's Secret Service, to discover what was happening to subvert it at home and undermine British power overseas.

From the shabby but respectable neighborhood of Bromley in London, for example, the exiled anarchist, Count Peter Kropotkin, claimed, "The progress of mankind is being held back by those who have a vested interest in the existing system. War or revolution is needed to galvanize people out of their ruts and on to new roads."

His view was shared by the revolutionary Bulkanin, who said, "I have drawn up a little list of undesirables we should do away with. It includes priests, monarchs, statesmen, soldiers, officials, financiers, capitalists, money lenders, and lawyers."

Every rebel had his own list of victims for execution the moment he achieved power. It was spoofed by The Doyley Carte Opera Company, which gave repeat performances of the popular Gilbert and Sullivan comic opera called *The Mikado*. In it, Ko-Ko the executioner gleefully persuaded audiences that "there will be no difficulty in finding plenty of people whose loss will be a distinct gain to society at large."

He assured everyone, "I've got a little list! And they'll none of them be missed."

Audiences roared with happy laughter, not realising the seriousness of the situation, while dissatisfied rebels, anarchists and revolutionaries waited in anticipation for the birth of a new order when their wishes could come true. It commenced with the death of Queen Victoria on January 22, 1901.

It was a time when the sharp eyes and even sharper wits of Sidney Reilly were carefully studying the appearances and motivations of England's ruling classes, as well as the rebels and anarchists, the revolutionaries and terrorists, and other malcontents working quietly underground to undermine Britain.

As Home Secretary, Winston knew that London's anarchists were mostly Russians, Poles, Italians, and other exiles from their own countries which were in turmoil. But Eddie was appalled—this was not *his* England.

"But where do they live? Where do they go? I never see them. What do they do?"

"Of course, you won't have heard of the *Autonomie Club*" in Windmill Street. Bourdin—that anarchist who blew himself up with his bomb by accident in Greenwich Park—frequented the *Autonomie*. Others live in poverty in Whitechapel and the poorer neighbourhoods in the East End, like Stepney."

"My dear, how do you know that?"

Winston smiled archly over his cigar. "I have my spies."

"No, really?"

"Eddie, my dear boy, there are at least two anarchist magazines published openly. As well as Kropotkin's *Le Révolté*, there's *The Torch*, and *Freedom*."

"I've never been sure of the difference between anarchists and socialists," Eddie admitted with bemusement.

"Nor are most people. Anarchism's one advantage over Socialism is thought to be that it is not authoritarian. They are protesting against authority, Eddie. Fortunately, most Britons prefer our splendid isolation from Europe to continue by avoiding the meaningless ideologies of romantic and unpractical foreign intellectuals, God damn them all!"

"That's my impression too," his Private Secretary agreed cautiously. "Surely the working classes can't want to lose a system that allows them to be free and live in relative comfort. Ours is far superior to any society on the Continent."

"Yes, you would imagine they realize it took centuries of struggle to improve and achieve our success. But who knows what goes on in their minds? It certainly doesn't prevent them from complaining and protesting they are entitled to more and more. But that's the human condition for you, Eddie, people are naturally greedy. And since we are a democratic nation, we must respect their vices as well as their virtues, and try not to be too judgmental."

Perhaps the most annoyed at the complacency of the English in their splendid isolation were their former English colonists in North America who had fought their own revolution to become a separate breed. The English ruling classes watched the antics that democracy had brought about there since the American Revolution, and feared the same thing might happen in Britain.

"Democracy is a very tricky system." Eddie remarked thoughtfully. "It appears to be just another name for mob rule."

"Ah," Winston said with a wicked smile, "but Speaker Reed in the United States has recognized that American politicians would be wise to give the majority what they want in order to stay in power. That is the subtle difference between mob rule and Parliamentary Democracy."

The British public knew nothing about the ongoing undermining of their nation by foreign spies. Nor did they know of the clandestine activities of their own secret service. Instead, they read persuasive and scary fiction that appeared in bookstores, like *England's Peril: A Story of the Secret Service* by novelist William Le Queux, and *Kim* by Rudyard Kipling, which was considered to be one of the greatest spy stories ever told. *The Riddle of the Sands* featured heroic young British Army officers always ready for a lark, a bit of adventure, or a stake in heroism and a medal to prove it. It predicted a German invasion of the British Isles with grim reality, compared with typical popular adventure novels of the times.

Public alarm caused former Lord of the Admiralty, Lord Selborne, to say, "We must look into the possibility. I want a report to see if such a plot is actually feasible."

British agents were sent to examine the Frisian coast, in case it turned out to be a launching venue for German troopships. Their report confirmed that the Frisian Islands and Borkum were located off of the north coast of Germany, more or less opposite the outlet from the Kiel Canal, where it entered the North Sea to face the east coast of Britain. But neither Naval Intelligence (NID) nor Military Intelligence (MID) considered that there was a real threat of invasion by German troops.

Despite that, the ageing British military hero, Field Marshal Lord Roberts, warned, "Britain is not ready for war."

He called for conscription. Alfred Harmsworth who owned Britain's first mass circulation newspaper, the *Daily Mail,* agreed with his sentiments. Harmsworth believed in stirring up friction between opposing views. "People buy newspapers when they get angry," he explained to Le Queux, and paid him to write an invasion serial called "The Invasion of 1910."

"Make sure you provide enough facts to make your story seem realistic," he advised him.

Le Queux and Oppenheim managed to stir up war hysteria in Britain at the very moment when the German Kaiser really did begin planning and organizing an arms race in preparation for war against France, Russia and England.

Although the German spy hysteria was not nearly as widespread or effective as the novelists and journalists claimed, the threat from Germany turned out to be a real and insane desire to conquer the world. The key to world power at the time was thought to be by achieving supremacy in controlling the high seas.

8
A Race for Naval Supremacy

B RITAIN WAS STILL THE MAJOR NAVAL POWER in the world. But the Kaiser was determined to compete by copying the plans of the new British *Dreadnought* class of battleships, and adding additional German innovations to modernize and enlarge the German Fleet.

"Why would he want to do that?" young Eddie March had asked his chief. "It makes no sense."

Prussian power always came from its well drilled and disciplined army. Its enemies were not seagoing nations, but landsmen living across the other side of its frontiers.

Winston grinned in reply. "Because he's an emperor. It's his duty to assert the importance of the German Empire. Bismarck taught him that if he wants to keep the love and admiration of his subjects, he must be their champion."

Eddie gazed at him in amazement. "You mean international politics can be reduced to the whims and notions of one man?"

"The short answer, dear Eddie, is *yes*. And I agree that to be in the hands of one man is not a nice thought, in spite of his admiration for us. You see, Willi is convinced we mean to do him harm."

"And do we?"

"Of course!" Winston said with a mischievous smirk. "The King can't stand him. We have just upped our order for new *Dreadnought* battleships from four to eight."

Despite his composure, lack of solid intelligence information gnawed at Winston. When Major Edmonds became head of MO5, which ran the 'Special Section' of the War Office, he had discovered that its records contained only a few irrelevant documents about the South African War, some scraps about France and Russia, but absolutely nothing about Germany.

The admiralty had employed only three or four secret agents a couple of years back, and now searched for agents to spy on Germany. They also began modernizing the Secret Service. It was divided at first into military and naval sections, with Major William Thwaites heading up a German section at the War Office. But, significantly, the few German spies who were detained in England were interested only in naval espionage. German military intelligence functioned in France and Russia but had no spy ring in Britain, and no plans for wartime sabotage. But the German Navy did.

"Why?" Eddie wanted to know.

"Their reason," Winston patiently explained to his Private Secretary, "is Admiral

Mahan's book, *The Influence of Sea Power on History*. It gave the Kaiser the notion that Germany's destiny lies in controlling the seas."

Mahan had also influenced the admirals in the Japanese Navy. And Secretary William White of the US Navy had agreed with its arguments even before them. It was, they thought, a revelation. Mahan had decided, after studying the great battles of history, that control of the sea was a significant factor in the superiority of Britain's empire which had never been strategically appreciated before, since it had come about almost by accident and with little or no planning.

Winston elaborated for Eddie's benefit; "All three nations want to build their own modern navy at least on a par with ours. A *superior* fleet of battleships could provide any one of them with overwhelming might to dominate the major sea lanes and coastlines of the world."

Marsh was well aware by now, from working closely with him, that his chief was deeply motivated by an almost maternal passion to protect the British Isles from its enemies, whereas his own sociability had begun to annoy more of his friends, who chided him on drinking too much champagne.

Champagne had come into its own as a fashion for the Smart Set. It was a moment of truth for Eddie, who recognized he was working for, not only an over-achiever, but a man with an overdeveloped sense of responsibility for others. Eddie had thought himself free to continue behaving like an irresponsible student after working hours, and yet he was two years older than his chief. But such was the genuine warmth between university friends that he could not quite bring his romantic nature down to earth. Eddie loved everyone, and was showered with affection by his friends in return. He was still a social butterfly.

His new-found friend Rupert Brooke from Cambridge—whom everyone adored the moment they met him—had just published a volume of poetry that Eddie was thrilled with. It was at that moment when he decided to encourage some of the others by having their poetry published at his expense. It was not an act of charity, nor of entrepreneurship, since it was a non-profit enterprise. He could afford sponsoring them from a trust fund set aside for him by his great-great-grandfather. It was known familiarly as "The Murder Money."

Eddie Marsh's first book was a collection of Georgian poets, including Brooke, Robert Graves, Siegfried Sassoon, and D. H. Lawrence. It sold remarkably well and encouraged further editions.

The Georgian poets were Marsh's invention, influenced partly by his reading of St. Augustine, who had remarked "One flaming heart sets the other on fire."

Eddie was enabled to become a patron because of the murder of Prime Minister Spencer Perceval back in 1812. The PM had been carrying his red leather despatch box through to the lobby of the old House of Commons on Monday, May 11. As the door was opened for him to enter the lobby, a pistol shot was heard. An almost inaudible voice gasped out, "Oh, I am murdered!"

A body was heard to fall on the floor. The Prime Minister was carried to a sofa in the Speaker's room, where he was found to be dead. According to official records, "the intruder offered no resistance." The emotionally unbalanced assassin, named Bellingham, had nursed a grievance against the government.

In the sympathetic outpouring of the moment, Lord Castlereagh made a proposal in the Commons which was seconded, giving the grieving widow a thousand pounds a year for life and a sum of £50,000 granted in trust for the twelve surviving children and their descendants. On the death of Marsh's uncle, Eddie found he had inherited one-sixth of the grant. He began to use it to help support hard-up young poets, including the penniless but lovable tramp, W. H. Davies.

At the same time as Eddie Marsh was launched as a patron of the arts, the first head of Britain's military intelligence section was appointed. Not surprisingly, it was Captain Vernon Kell. Unusually for a British Army officer at the time, 'K' spoke fluent French, German, Russian and Chinese. He had qualified as an interpreter in the first two languages and travelled to Moscow and Shanghai to learn the other two. His section would later become the home department of the Secret Service Bureau and the future MI5.

After the incursion of a German gunboat into French Moroccan waters at Agadir in April 1911, which caused a political crisis with expectations of war, 'K' kept his eyes focused for other signs of war preparation by Germany. The Secret Service Bureau had been formed to provide intelligence in precisely that sort of situation. But it was *The Times* which reported that the German High Sea Fleet had begun its annual summer cruise and that one of the German squadrons had passed through the Kiel Canal to the North Sea. It clearly demonstrated that Germany was now ready to wage war against Britain.

It had taken several years for Germany to widen the canal to connect the Baltic to the North Sea, into which German battleships could now pass with ease, making the east coast of the British Isles vulnerable to salvoes from heavy German naval cannons. It brought to mind the predicted—although fictional—military invasion by boarding parties in German boats, in the novel called *The Riddle of the Sands*, a decade earlier.

The foreign section of the Secret Service Bureau was now responsible to the Admiralty, which was its principal customer, although they also continued to supply intelligence to the War Office. The original vision for a secret espionage agency was to counter German planning for invasion as a sudden "bolt from the blue."

It was understood that Admiralty and War Office intelligence would now be directly controlled by a Chief who would coordinate the work of both. His name was Mansfield Smith-Cumming, the admiral with a monocle over one eye, a wooden leg, a hearty laugh, and an addiction to Gilbert and Sullivan comic operas.

'K' noted that, as well as building a modern fleet in readiness for war, Germany was also practicing war manoeuvres with its army close to the Belgian border. The price of flour had suddenly risen because of Germany's heavy purchases of wheat in anticipation of shortages. Kell's reports also revealed that Germany's secret service was focusing its own intelligence searches on Britain.

Although all information the SIS garnered was secret, it was a sign of early success that General Henry Wilson, the Director of Military Operations, supported proposed salary increases for Cumming and Kell for having done 'excellent work.' Admiral Alexander Bethell spoke highly of them, and noted that Cumming had spent considerable sums out of his own pocket and was most economical in restraining overhead costs.

That note at the very beginning of the SIS revealed the penny-pinching which would continue to annoy those who used intelligence the most, as if its aim were frugality rather than to obtain useful information of possible threats to the nation. It was a part of the amateurism which British institutions favoured, to demonstrate that no one was profiting from public service or public funds.

Winston considered penny-pinching was a defeatist approach to a serious and vital enterprise, claiming that, "If SIS agents get the idea that they may be thrown over at any moment, for the sake of a limited budget we cannot expect to find them."

'C's budget was increased to send the two agents to investigate the Frisian coast, although Winston had argued for fifty percent more to avoid jeopardizing the quality of information. Eddie listened to his anxieties as he took dictation from his chief, and drafted notes and memos and letters to particular authorities, warning that, "It could take a year to find and train suitable new agents in an emergency."

Eddie's chief claimed that the man he learnt most from was General Wilson, the Director of Military Operations. While unburdening his anxieties on to his Private Secretary, he went to great lengths to justify his admiration as he thought aloud, cigar in hand:

"He has extraordinary vision and faith. He has already acquired an immense and, I expect, an unequalled amount of knowledge about the Continent. He knows the French Army intimately, and even the secrets of the French General Staff. He has been laboring with one object, that if war comes we should act immediately on the side of France."

"Do you really think it will come to that?"

His chief nodded sagely. "Sooner or later. All the strings of military information are already in Henry's hands. The whole wall of his small office is covered by a huge map of Belgium, across which he has painted every possible road on which the German armies can march to invade France. He spends all his holidays examining those roads in person, and the surrounding countryside with binoculars, or on foot, or with a bicycle."

As Home Secretary, Eddie's chief was invited to a special meeting of the Committee of Imperial Defence, with principal officers of the British army and navy and all the Ministers who would be involved in time of war. They sat all day listening, first to the army's views in the morning, and then the Navy's in the afternoon. While General Wilson displayed his maps, he discussed the War Office's opinions of Germany's plan for invading France—firstly in the possible event of a war between Germany and Austria, and then, alternatively, with France and Russia.

First Sea Lord Sir Arthur Wilson gave the Admiralty's views of the situation at 3 p.m., while displaying their own maps. He explained what they believed should be their own policy if Britain became involved in a war. He kept the Admiralty's strategic War Plans and tactics secret but, of course, they included the traditional blockading of enemy ports.

It soon became clear that the two armed forces viewed the situation differently, and that a small British army would be swallowed up by overwhelming forces on the Continent, so that Britain's response should rather depend on its Navy.

It was because of the disagreements between the War Office and the Admirals that Asquith appointed Winston to the Admiralty to coordinate their activities. The Prime Minister had great faith in Winston's military knowhow and warlike abilities. Winston felt that the army's mistaken views arose from Britain's General Staff, who placed too much faith in the support and strength of the French military.

By the time the conference ended, it left a miasma of apprehension behind it. Churchill let off steam by confiding to his Private Secretary how unimpressed he was with the professional hierarchy of the Royal Navy:

"It is bound by bad traditions it has never even attempted to improve. It is altogether unadventurous. And hardly endowed with initiative or intelligence."

Winston was also involved as Home Secretary in the growth of military intelligence and policing departments of the Secret Service Bureau. He arranged for all Chief Constables to seek Kell's help in the case of undesirable aliens and anyone suspected of espionage in Britain. He approved Kell's secret register of aliens from expected enemy powers like Germany. He also made it easier to apprehend espionage or sabotage agents by introducing the interception of a suspect's correspondence, to provide evidence for their arrest and also for discovering other foreign spies in England.

Famously known as "C," the jovial Captain Sir Mansfield Smith-Cumming, Chief of Britain's Secret Intelligence Service (later to become MI6).

That was how 'K' discovered an extensive network of German secret agents ferreting out naval information, mostly in London, but also in Britain's dockyards and ports. He initiated a number of spy trials that eliminated some German spies by deporting or imprisoning them.

Kell brought several German spies to justice himself, including the first German spy to be tried under the 1911 Official Secrets Act, Heinrich Grosse, and Schultz, Salter and Bunn. Then there was Karl Graves and others. Although there was a popular spy scare, most German spies were quickly rounded up, since they were uninformed amateurs. The last two to be brought to trial and convicted before the war were Wilhelm Klauer, and Frederick Adolphus Schroeder who was the most successful German spy.

It took 'K' three years to round up the entire spy ring. Most were spying for money. And although the greatest fear was that they might commit sabotage, most were simply attempting to gather useful information for Germany about Britain's Navy.

One result of the Agadir Crisis, in which Germany sent the gunboat *Panther* to French Morocco—although soon brought peacefully to an end—was that it initiated Prime Minister Asquith's decision to appoint Winston to head the Admiralty, which he proceeded to reorganize, modernize, and thoroughly shake up in readiness for war.

The foreign section of the Secret Service Bureau had been founded in October 1909. It was the nucleus of the future SIS and MI6, and headed by Commander George Smith-Cumming, who would sign himself in green ink as the presiding "C."

The old soldier, Hozier, who had been the original "C," had come to his end in Panama.

9
A Man of Property

JUST AS 'M' HAD SURMISED, Sidney Reilly was a polished actor and a quick learner, with a repertoire of different faces for different places, and a variety of identities to match every change or challenge. He could mimic the correct manners and speech to merge with the English, who wore masks of their own to confront every situation. He knew instinctively how to ingratiate himself with the patrician class, to obtain whatever privileges he sought. At the same time, he possessed the gift to infiltrate the underground dens of malcontents and rebels who sought to undermine Britain's society and its economy.

Having established a position and a reputation for success in England, Reilly was given a new assignment in the following year.

"Your main objective," 'M' told him, "is to find out if Russia had any ambitions towards Persia. Tentative surveys indicate huge deposits of valuable and much sought for oil. Its particular significance for Britain is that British battleships are still powered by coal, but could be modernized to be fueled more efficiently with oil. It would require an agreement for the British Government to acquire oil wells in Persia."

'M' immediately found that Reilly required only the barest of directions to proceed freely on his own initiative. Point him in the right direction and he was off at an extraordinary pace.

In his capacity as a secret agent for Britain, Reilly discovered that Russia was already developing oil wells in Baku in the Caucasus. Persia's geology across the other side of the border was almost identical.

Reilly reported back to 'M' to say that, "Russia will be happy to acquire a fair share of the oil, and should be allowed to do so."

He provided a detailed report on the new Trans-Siberian Railway which, he informed the British Secret Service, now ran as far as Lake Baikal.

Reilly also acquired a new mistress named Margaret Thomas. She was an attractive redhead of twenty-three who evidently appealed to him, although she had recently married a minister of the nonconformist church of Wales who was sixty years old. The result of such a huge gap in ages was that she had become bored with being little more than his housekeeper and bed companion.

Reilly observed and noted that the Reverend Hugh Thomas was unusually wealthy for a clergyman. He made the couple's acquaintance and accompanied them on a European tour. Apparently the minister slept very soundly and, although naturally possessive of his young bride, suspected nothing.

Reilly rented rooms in Holborn on their return, while the Thomases returned to their house at 6 Upper Westbourne Terrace in Paddington.

Westbourne Grove was becoming an unfashionable London neighborhood. Although fairly central, its eyes seemed closed to the outer world and was dimly lit inside with gas mantles that created an otherworldly glow. Perhaps it was because it was hidden away in a nondescript area somewhere between the Edgware Road, with its unattractive street-walkers plying their trade at the eastern end of Sussex Gardens, and dubious Notting Hill Gate with its tiny theaters and the Coronet music hall on the far side. The interiors of its terraced houses were still rather gloomy and cluttered, as most Victorians evidently liked them to be, and not yet modernized in the lighter and brighter Edwardian shades of colors that were enlivening more appealing homes. Or perhaps the distant sound of steam engines shunting in and out of Paddington Station annoyed residents on otherwise quiet nights. The effect was one of shabby respectability.

Soon after Reilly's first overseas mission for the SIS, 'M'—still chief of Britain's Secret Service Bureau and pleasantly satisfied with Reilly's performance and his detailed reports on the oil reserves in Russia and Persia—found another assignment for him. They met again in Victoria Street.

Reilly immediately told him, "I'm sorry, but I must take time off."

"How long?" Melville asked agreeably, expecting to have to approve a weekend, or seven days at most.

"As long as it takes."

Normally an urbane individual whom nothing surprised, Melville was astonished when Reilly insisted he was too busy to take on other business at the moment. 'M' was furious at the time he had so far spent on training his bird of prey, but never showed himself to be in the smallest bit perturbed.

Reilly was currently involved in an assignation with Margaret Thomas, a fact which he did not share with his chief. He had become a frequent visitor to the Thomases' house; even more so when her husband became ill. With great concern for the Reverend's health, Reilly, who had studied chemistry in Vienna, had a local pharmacy concoct his own special medicine.

When Hugh Thomas's condition failed to improve, he left everything to his wife in a will on March 4, 1898. Then they and Reilly prepared to take another trip together to Europe. They packed and left. But Thomas became so seriously ill before they could board the cross-channel steamer at Newhaven that he died in a hotel there on March 13. The local doctor gave the cause of death as heart failure, which was a common diagnosis found on any number of death certificates at that time.

Margaret Thomas inherited the Westbourne Terrace house and what was a considerable amount of money in those days from her husband's life insurance policy. She and Reilly were married only five months later, on August 22. His name on the marriage certificate at the Holborn Register Office was Sigmund Georgievich Rosenbloom. He described himself as a consulting chemist and his father as a 'Landed Proprietor.' Margaret entered her father as 'Edward Reilly Callahan, deceased, Captain in the Navy.' Margaret lied, since, prior to her marriage to Hugh Thomas, she had been his maidservant at the house in Upper Westbourne Terrace, and her father had been a common seaman.

To Melville's surprise, Reilly waited a year after he had offered him a new assignment, before phoning for an appointment. 'M' saw him the next day, when Sidney Reilly apologized for the delay and explained the circumstances candidly to his chief before they discussed the possibility of any new business.

"I'd like to be sure you are aware of the changes in my circumstances."

"Yes?"

"I had no wish to offend you. But I felt it important to provide myself with enough money and a respectable background as cover for any further confidential work"

"I see."

"I am a married man now, with a British-born wife who came into some money when her husband died. We have rented out the house she inherited to boarders and moved to more modest rented rooms located more centrally in Caxton Street, Westminster."

'M' knocked out the cold ashes from his favourite pipe and reached for the tobacco jar at his elbow. "So you are taking in lodgers now?"

"It provides additional income."

"Also equity. A good plan!"

So Reilly was no longer an impecunious foreign immigrant but a man of property, and he wants me to know it, 'M' thought to himself.

"I thought so. Now I can afford to accept the poorly paid work of an agent in the Secret Service."

'M' was startled but did not show it. "What do you mean?"

"I know how hard-up the civil service is when it comes to budgets; always cutting costs. I mean you won't have to pay me from now on."

Melville revealed his surprise at this turn of events by raising his eyebrows theatrically. "You mean you want to work for us without being paid?"

"Just expenses, so I'm not out-of-pocket. No offense intended."

'M' filled the bowl of his pipe equably. "None taken."

"I also want to assure you that you can be confident of my wife's security where confidential or top secret information is concerned,"

"Any reason why I shouldn't be?"

"None at all. Women love to gossip, of course, but you can be sure there would be no leaks of information from that quarter."

Melville locked eyes with him, wondering what lay behind Reilly's claim. "What makes you so sure?"

"I have . . . How can I put it? Margaret wouldn't dare to repeat anything confidential because I have a kind of hold over her, if you understand what I mean. So there's no risk."

Melville waited to hear if any further explanation was forthcoming, as they gazed at each other's expressionless features. But Reilly said no more about it.

'M' had already been impressed by his agent's professionalism in carrying out his previous missions, compared with the general standard of mediocrity demonstrated by most agents, whom he didn't trust. Although he had been disappointed when Reilly had turned down his previous assignment, now he was fascinated, even awed by Reilly's candid description of his unusual but practical domestic arrangements. It was all one to Melville whether Reilly kept his wife locked up in a room, or threatened her with violence to keep her quiet.

As for the poor pay given to employees, 'M' managed because he was naturally parsimonious and lacked interest in leisure pursuits or in acquiring material possessions. His wife was frugal because she had grown up with the same attitude towards achieving a purpose in work, and saving money instead of spending it; so he never felt himself to be short of funds. Nevertheless, he knew that an agent's recompense was pitifully poor. Few stayed the course, and many who did either fiddled their expenses or indulged in additional paying pursuits in secret – to which he turned a blind eye.

One result of that uncharitable attitude towards agents was that it was difficult to find good ones who could also be trusted. Some were army or navy officers who drew their regular pay. But, although they might possess a spirit of adventure or patriotism, they were likely to be gentlemen, with a code of honor that assumed their enemies were gentlemen to whom they owed some kind of loyalty. Spying on friends for information, stealing military secrets, or committing sabotage, were viewed with disapproval by young British officers who were reluctant to do anything underhand, such as blatantly lying or deceiving, or stealing plans.

As far as Melville was concerned, that amateurish attitude was no longer acceptable in the present state of the world, in which Victorian morality and decency had been swept aside.

But this Russian-born spy was no English gentleman, William Melville thought, as he lit his pipe with a wooden match and puffed briefly to keep it alight. He scrutinized Reilly from the other side of his desk. He was satisfied that Reilly did whatever had to be done for the success of his mission in a highly professional manner.

He was still unsure of what his colleagues had told him, or hinted at, about Sidney Reilly's background. Melville was deferential to society leaders like Sir Henry Hozier, with their cool and self-assured ways, who had now gone. And the other founders of British Intelligence were in a class above his own modest one. He was just a policeman. It was why he worked endlessly to become indispensable.

On reflection, 'M' was not completely convinced that Reilly's motives for not accepting pay were philanthropic. There was bound to be a catch somewhere, and he wondered what it was. But the fact was that Reilly spoke seven languages fluently and knew Europe intimately. He was also a first-rate pistol shot. And from his showing on his last mission, he possessed the attributes required of a professional spy. So, despite their difference in background and values, Reilly was too good for 'M' to lose.

Melville had provided him with a British passport in the name of Sidney Reilly in 1899, when the saga of Britain's master spy took a more earnest leap. After being engaged to inform on local terrorists and having showed himself to be the most unusual, competent, and audacious of all British spies, he undertook several fairly unimportant missions on the Continent. And in between assignments there was Margaret and gambling.

He was in Holland during the Second Boer War, speaking German—since he did not speak Dutch—and reporting on any Dutch aid to President Kruger in South Africa. When the Secret Service chief offered him an assignment to Persia in 1902, it involved oil resources again, and he was sent back to the Caucuses.

But despite Reilly's continual successes, 'M' was still not completely convinced that his motives were genuine. Something still bothered him about Reilly, and he was unable to place his finger on exactly what it was.

10
Oil Mania

THE OIL FIELDS OF BAKU IN RUSSIA were now a famously going concern, whereas exploration in a similar geological area in adjacent Persia had only just begun. The Rockefeller oil interests were growing in the United States. Several farsighted companies and European countries that appreciated the value of oil, including Britain, France and Russia, were particularly anxious to exploit the oil reserves in Persia. It meant there could be a clash between Russian interests and those of the other Great Powers. But, fortunately, Reilly had maintained useful contacts in Russia and could discuss arrangements with them as a Russian patriot.

Mount Morgan Gold Mine of Australia was one of the competing mineral resource companies. It was owned by an American named William Knox D'Arcy, who had already made a fortune from mining gold. He persuaded and funded the Shah of Persia to provide him with sole concession rights for oil exploration in much of Persia.

Britain's Admiralty was still interested in oil as a more efficient fuel for their battleships, and Britain's First Sea Lord, the forceful Admiral Fisher, was actively spearheading the change of fuel to modernize Britain's fleet. When young Winston was appointed First Lord of the Admiralty, he developed a close working relationship with the Admiral, who became known as an "oil maniac," because oil was part of his program to modernize the British Fleet with a more effective and economical fuel, instead of the more laborious, filthy, and wasteful coal.

"What I want to know," Fisher demanded of the Secret Service, "is when meaningful quantities of oil will be discovered for exploitation in Persia."

'M' was requested to make a report for the Admiralty. In view of the possible diplomatic friction from Russia, and the fact that Reilly had been involved in reporting on oil exploration in the area before, he appeared to be ideally suited to undertake the mission.

Melville assured Reilly that they had no wish for conflict with Russia.

"Your job," he said, "is to discover and sift the truth from the rumors which seethe in Teheran. And to advise what action, if any, the British Government should take to circumvent trouble with St. Petersburg."

"Has the Admiralty read all the reports reaching the Foreign Office from embassies and legations abroad?"

"Your investigation must be entirely independent of the Foreign Office. They can't be trusted. They have their own biases that conflict with the Admiralty's wishes."

"My cover?"

"Your cover for the mission," said 'M' as he scrupulously filled his pipe, "is to travel to Persia as a manufacturer and distributor of patent medicines - cheap cure-alls for the subjects of Shah Mozaffer-ed-Deen."

Having some knowledge already of the terrain, Reilly knew that Persia was ruled locally by tribal chiefs or elders. He let his thoughts run aloud for the Chief's benefit;

"It's important to remember that the country is a barren plateau with hardly a road going through it. It's plagued by smallpox. It was so hot when I was there last that the temperature reached 110 degrees in the shade by seven a.m."

'M' smiled in sympathy while lighting his pipe. "Fortunately, that is your problem, not mine."

Using his new cover as a patent medicine salesman, Reilly travelled by camel on a desert caravan route to Chia Surkh, where drilling for oil had already begun. After talking with the men on the spot, he confided in his report that they knew the oil business and its geology. Reilly was a visionary and an entrepreneur, like D'Arcy, and could imagine the worldwide effects if enough oil flowed. His first report described the appalling working conditions there with locusts, sunstroke, smallpox and a shortage of water.

"But they are determined to find oil, and I am certain they will."

He charmed his way through the embassies and legations, and took orders for his patent medicines to maintain his cover. After departing from Teheran and arriving back in England, he fulfilled the orders he had received, out of his own funds.

Melville wondered whether Reilly was treating his assignments as a sideline for something more rewarding. But, when back in Melville's office, he observed Reilly's excitement with interest, as his agent enthusiastically predicted the future of oil.

"What the Admiralty should do," Reilly advised, "is buy D'Arcy's concession."

"What about Russian interests?"

"Russia will be satisfied with a division of Persian oil between them and Britain. I'm convinced that a satisfactory alliance could be arranged between Britain and Russia over the oil wells, with no political friction."

"Arranged by whom?"

"By me. I explained that in my report."

His detailed report was noted by the Admiralty and the Foreign Office, but no action was taken. Nevertheless, it was not lost in the filing cabinets. The situation would take several more years to mature, and Reilly's report and recommendations would reappear when needed.

While the oil situation was slowly incubating, 'M' offered Reilly a new assignment in China that directly affected Russia too.

As Melville explained in his briefing, "Russia has taken a lease on the Liatung

Peninsula. They intend to convert it into a naval base. Know where it is?"

Reilly nodded. He was invariably ahead of the game.

"You will be provided with suitably detailed maps. What we want is regular detailed reports, continually updated. According to our information, you could be there for quite a while. I'll give you your local contacts. Any questions?"

"Yes. Margaret."

"Problems?"

"Only that I need to keep a close eye on her. She gets lonely." He made a motion to describe her drinking habits.

'M' nodded understandingly. "Take her with you. An appearance of family stability will provide good cover for your activities in China."

Reilly obtained a position in a Russian shipping company in Shanghai. And, after only six weeks, had persuaded them to appoint him as their manager in Port Arthur, which was the location of Russia's Far Eastern Fleet. It was where the Russians were constructing fortifications for their new naval base. Having established himself there, he became a managing partner in a firm of timber merchants named Ginsburg & Co. The entrepreneurial young Ginsburg had entrenched himself firmly and built up a considerable number of influential contacts and customers. Reilly also became the manager of the Danish *Compagnie Est-Asiatique*. Now he developed influential contacts from each source.

As Germany was at the forefront of industrial development, whereas Russia had lagged behind, Reilly obtained technical information from the biggest armament companies in the world, which were German; like Blohm & Voss, Krupp's, and Schneider, who sent their representatives from Germany to supervise the development of the defenses for the Russians.

From small and seemingly innocent pieces of information he obtained from his sources, he was able to put together a complete picture of their intention, which he reported to 'M'. And, despite Russian counter-espionage agents protecting the security of the fortress, he managed to borrow plans which he photographed at his new home with Margaret before returning them.

Reilly was always sharply focused on his work to ensure the very best results, and planned meticulously to avoid anything possible going wrong. But he soon realized that his wife wanted more and more attention, since she felt unsafe and alone in such foreign and chaotic surroundings. She was uneasy and anxious in an unstable foreign country which was being exploited by several major powers that were temporarily in charge of parts of China. The continental land mass was being cut up by foreign nations, and was disintegrating piecemeal between foreign troops and local Chinese warlords fighting each other for territory and resources.

Conflict was mounting in particular between Russia and Japan. Reilly kept

Britain's Secret Service Bureau informed of new developments by code.

Margaret had no idea what Reilly was up to. Every time she asked him, he always told her it was top secret.

"Do you know what the penalty for espionage is in this part of the world?" Margaret warned Sidney with a shiver.

"Yes I do," Reilly said stonily. "It's crucifixion."

They quarrelled constantly. She became hysterical with fear for herself and him, and her drinking was soon out of control. He knew he could not relax his guardedness for a single moment in case she suspected what he was doing and mentioned something that might warn the authorities that he was exposing their trade and military secrets to Britain.

Britain and Japan's alliance, from 1902, created a further complication that his reports to Britain's Secret Service might end up in Japanese hands at a time when Japan was Russia's enemy. Reilly was a patriotic Russian, as well as a British officer who admired the British Empire as a unique work of extraordinary philanthropy. But with all the international complications which might go either way, Reilly was always remarkably cool and collected, appearing to know exactly what was happening ahead of time and precisely what he was doing.

Whenever Margaret protested, and drank to assuage her fear, appealing to him time and again to get out before everything exploded, he would begin to quote a saying of the Chinese sage Tzo-Lim which appeared to calm him like a mantra.

She would interrupt furiously with, "Yes, I know—*That which is escaped now, is but pain yet to come.*"

It always failed to calm her, filling her with fear and anxiety instead. But his intuitions were sound, since the Russo-Japanese war would erupt only two years later.

Back in London, Winston explained the complex situation in Manchuria to Eddie, in his usual somewhat ponderous way, as if the whole world were listening in to admire his oratory. It was a declamatory style of speech borrowed from an admired literary predecessor, Samuel Johnson, who had invented the English dictionary.

"My dear Eddie, our statesmen have more penetrating eyes than any other nation in Europe. We measured the martial power of Japan and found it had gained remarkably in strength and security in the industrial revolution. And we decided in our wisdom that Japan should be our new ally. Japan will triumph over Russia because Russia belongs to the past and Japan represents the future."

"But what on earth can Manchuria mean to *us*?"

"It means, my dear, that now we can safely bring back home all those bloody British battleships in the China Seas to protect us against an attack by Germany."

Reilly, at the sharp edge of the Russo-Japanese conflict, hurriedly sent Margaret back to London when he sensed danger of an imminent Japanese Naval and land attack on Manchuria. Japan was Britain's ally and he was in the pay of Britain's intelligence service. So his job was to remain behind and see the situation through to the end.

Reilly had been contacted personally beforehand in St. Petersburg by the Japanese General Akashi Motojiro, to provide information to Japan's Secret Intelligence Service. Apart from earning money from the arrangement, he also acquired information from Japan and other nations that he passed on to British Intelligence. 'M' was duly grateful, in anticipation of an expected war.

The Russo-Japanese War erupted in February 1904. And, typical of the world of espionage, its agents often had advance warning through their knowledge and razor sharp instincts. Reilly's instincts about world affairs were generally correct, as a result of his accumulated information from all quarters. It was demonstrated by the letter he wrote a year earlier, in December 1902, that "The Manchu's are finished. It is only a matter of time before China becomes the playground of the great powers."

The greatest power in the East, Japan, was now industrialized and well-armed for war.

Even so, there was considerable shock in the West when Japan made a surprising pre-emptive attack on Russia's Pacific Fleet at Port Arthur without a formal declaration of war. Unbeknown to the West, such a warning of intent would have seemed insane to the Japanese navy, and entirely against their warrior-class principles of *Bushido*. Japan's military culture favored, instead, an unexpected strike with overwhelming force to demoralize and, hopefully, utterly destroy their enemy's capacity to fight.

In spite of the element of surprise, it was a costly victory for the Japanese Navy against the Imperial Russian Fleet, and the war ended in a treaty between the two nations.

The only question remaining was who had stolen the harbor plans to guide the Japanese Fleet in? And not only them but Russia's defense plans, and the plans of Russia's minefields. All were passed to the Japanese beforehand to enable them to invade the peninsula. No evidence of Reilly's involvement was ever found. The theft of the harbor defense plans was attributed to a Chinese engineer named Ho-Li-ang-Shung who, most likely, passed them on to Reilly by previous arrangement.

That had been the whole point and end result of his assignment on behalf of Britain's Admiralty. Both he and Ho left Port Arthur shortly after the attack, and after Reilly had made sure to erase any evidence that might incriminate him. Carefully covering his trail was one of the skills that made him such a masterly secret agent.

But then, he took leave without permission from Melville and disappeared into the uncharted areas of the Chinese hinterland for several months. No one knew where he had gone.

When Reilly finally returned to England, he discovered that Margaret had vanished a year earlier and taken with her all the funds in their joint bank account. Apart from his valuable collection of Napoleana, he had only a few hundred pounds left.

In spite of his quarrel with the Chief over taking leave without permission, Reilly had proved himself to be far too good at espionage to dismiss or ignore. Nor did Reilly wish to alienate the Secret Service which he now thought of as family. His skills in deception and subterfuge to acquire secret information were needed by them more than ever in this time of world crisis. Both he and Melville were well aware that they depended on each other.

So Reilly made contact with 'M' to request another posting to Persia, where oil had since been found. The Chief, who had imagined Reilly had retired from work and was living a gentlemanly life of leisure, gave him a mission in Germany instead. He would work at Krupp's, where the industrial arms race had become even more of a priority than oil.

11

Anna

'M' could be forgiven for imagining he had lost his former spy to the attractions of luxury, gambling, and idleness, since Reilly appeared to be financially well-off, and was as immaculately dressed and self-confident as ever. But leisure pursuits had no value for Reilly unless they were a means of introduction to influential people. Nor could he tolerate idleness. Although he enjoyed any opportunity for gambling and womanizing that his job provided, it was only in short bursts to unwind by clearing his mind of the residue of his previous missions. He was easily bored and needed the challenges of intellectual stimulation that his more dangerous assignments gave him. He was addicted, not to leisurely pursuits, but exciting ones.

Although 'M' still speculated on what drove his agent—was it really a search for justice, or wisdom? He could not read Reilly's impenetrable mind to discover what he was really after.

"Know anything about Krupp?" he asked his agent when they met.

Reilly's eyes came alive with interest. "Only that it's thought to be the biggest industrial conglomerate in the world."

"Think you can find out?"

"It's certainly the biggest industrial enterprise in Europe," Reilly answered cautiously. "They call it "The Colossus of Essen." It's said to be bigger than Skoda, Vickers-Maxim, Schneider-Creusot, and all the other European combines, mergers, and conglomerates put together."

The new cycle of economic activity in Europe, which resulted in his assignment at Krupp, had never happened anywhere in the world in such gargantuan proportions before. The industrial revolution had spread from England to Germany, Japan, and America. It turned out to possess a momentum of its own. Armament manufacturers could not stop their assembly lines and governments that bought from them dared not stop building up their arsenals. Although Russia's industries were underdeveloped, Germany's were already overdeveloped.

"Your mission is to discover if all that's really true, and how well-organized they really are. There's no doubt that Germany is bursting with vigor and bulging with material success, but your job is more specific and detailed than that."

'M' briefed him on the background and reason for his particular task: "Germany's national income had doubled in about twelve years. Its population has increased by about fifty percent. Its railroads have increased in length by about fifty percent. The development of its electrical industry added thousands of new jobs. So does I. G. Farben's chemical, pharmaceutical and synthetic dyes industry, and the coal, iron and steel industries in the Ruhr. As Germany's wealth burgeoned, so has employment. And so has German pride, which has become swollen out of all proportion."

Reilly smiled and nodded in agreement. "They really have become odious, haven't they?

"To everyone!"

"So what's your point?"

"The point is," the Chief explained, "that by expanding Germany's armed forces and embarking on an arms race, they have to increase the size and number of German ship-building yards and munition factories."

Reilly listened carefully as Melville explained how he had placed a British agent in the Krupp's factories.

"But, after he sent us several reports, there was a sudden and ominous silence from Germany. Either his reports were being intercepted, or he had been somehow exposed and arrested. Even worse, the Germans might have quietly murdered him after extracting information about our Secret Service organization. You see the problem?"

"You want me to replace him—is that it?"

'M' instructed Reilly to become apprenticed to a factory in Sheffield for several weeks to prepare himself by learning a new trade as a welder in a ship-building industry.

When Reilly arrived in Germany with the cover name of Karl Hahn, he had cropped his hair shapelessly with scissors, displayed roughened and grimy hands, shabby clothes and worn boots, as a German industrial worker from the Baltic. He described himself as a Russian national from Reval, with a cover story that he had worked as a welder in St. Petersburg at the Putiloff shipyards.

Labor was in great demand with German industry growing so rapidly, particularly in ship-building, so that Reilly had no problem being hired as a welder at Krupp's, the biggest industrial conglomerate in Germany.

Back in London, Winston explained to his Private Secretary how foreign affairs worked, not through diplomacy or politics, but as a result of psychological factors. "The rest is bosh. Whoever it was who said that history is made in the bedroom was closer to the truth."

"Using which psychological attributes?"

"Flattery."

Eddie laughed in disbelief. "My dear, you can't be serious?"

"No one's immune. Imagine you were brought up from childhood—like the Kaiser—to believe you were appointed by God to be the ruler of a mighty nation. You are solemnly told that the inherent virtue of your blue blood raises you far above ordinary mortals. Now, imagine feeling the energetic and single-minded German race bounding beneath you in ever-swelling numbers, strength, wealth and ambition. And imagine on every side the tributes and unceasing flattery of sycophants. "You are," they say, "the All-Highest. You are the Supreme War Lord who, when the next war comes, will lead to battle all the German tribes at the head of the strongest, finest army in the world. It is up to you to renew on a still greater scale the martial triumphs of 1866 and 1870!"

His voice had risen at the most suitable dramatic moment, as if he had been orating to a spellbound audience in the House. Eddie, like most of Winston's friends listening in awe to his after-dinner speeches, regarded his chief in amazement, unable to hear his rhetoric without being thoroughly convinced he must be right.

"But what about Germany's new-found prosperity? It puts more money into the pockets of German consumers than ever before. Why should they want war?"

"In spite of that," Winston assured him, with a nod of understanding and a raised oratorical finger to emphasize his point, "the German Army is still an object of worship. Germany's common people will do what they are told."

He explained that Germany was now thought by many to be too pushy and ambitious, while they viewed others as their enemies. "Their arrogance arises from self-congratulation at their new-found wealth and greed from the power of money."

Reserve army officer Churchill when invited by the German Kaiser to watch the annual autumn maneuvers of his Prussian army near Breslau, Silesia in 1906. (Wroclaw, Poland).

"The typical nouveau-riches symptoms," Marsh agreed with a knowing shrug.

"You see," Winston continued; "Germans believe they are the most industrious and civilized of all peoples, that they were chosen by Providence to occupy the supreme place in history, and be acknowledged as paramount by all other nations."

"I read a remark by that modern composer Richard Strauss. He was quoted as saying that "It's a thoroughly good thing the strong should triumph.""

"If so, he was only repeating what Bismarck said. People are becoming increasingly irritated by Germany's claims to superiority," Winston assured him. "Not only in industry, but in music, the arts and literature. Some people find their craving for power at any cost is unnatural and morbid. They are in love with death - as in Wagner's *Gotterdammerung*."

"The destruction of everything," Eddie echoed thoughtfully. He smiled at the irony. "Perhaps it's time for Germany's *hubris* to be punished by the Gods."

Reilly's new work at Krupp's was hard and demanding with its long hours, but he had a clear purpose in mind: it was to obtain plans of the workshops under construction and those in the planning stage, and also details of the types of plants or machine shops they were designed to contain. They were like pieces of a jigsaw puzzle that he would put together to find out what Germany was up to. Like his efforts at Port Arthur, he enjoyed solving mysteries and boasting of the success of his operations to the Secret Service chiefs.

But German industrial security was elaborate and efficiently planned for almost any eventuality. It was well organized by officers dedicated to Germany's expanding armament and ship-building program. Reilly continually stumbled over guards and day-and-night watchmen who appeared to be posted everywhere, whereas Krupp's paid him to work on a project which was limited solely to a specific place in his own working area. Each time he left it to investigate the rest of the workshops, he would raise suspicions and have to return to his own place.

When he read a request posted on one of the notice boards for volunteers for a fire brigade, he realized it would present opportunities to explore the rest of the premises legitimately, particularly on night shifts when he would be expected to patrol the corridors of the workshops. So Reilly volunteered to work in the fire brigade.

In his new capacity, he now found himself able to move around at night and examine what was going on in the factories. With a specially shaded torch and equipment he had brought with him to pick locks, he investigated several of Krupp's drawing offices. He discovered a great many finished plans carefully stored in their special places, and unfinished ones on drawing boards. After making several night-time explorations, he was able to select which plans were most likely to interest Britain's Admiralty. Then he had to find the best and safest way to copy them.

He did not care to risk taking plans back to his rooms, one at a time, in order to make copies, since that would create too many opportunities for exposure. Instead, he attempted to copy some onto tracing paper on the spot. But it was far too time-consuming, leaving him open to discovery for long periods. Then, it suddenly occurred to him that the works firemen should have a complete set of plans of the entire premises in case of fire.

"Hasn't it ever occurred to you," he warned the officer in charge, "that the whole place could burn down if we in the fire brigade don't know exactly where every fire hydrant and fire extinguisher is located for use in an emergency?"

It took time and a little hard thought for the officer to realize it was a flaw in an otherwise efficient system.

Reilly offered him a cigarette. "Smoke?"

The foreman thanked him and took one. As Reilly lit it for him, he accidently dropped the match on the wooden floor. The man gasped, and Reilly deliberately trod out the spark.

"You're lucky I'm here. Imagine what would happen if I were a saboteur and the old wooden planks caught fire—you'd be the first one to be shot by a firing squad!"

Reilly needed to use little more persuasion for the foreman to be convinced that the plans were essential for the fire brigade to do their job efficiently in times of danger and possible sabotage. The plans he needed were immediately provided for him in the foreman's office, which was freely available to all members of the fire brigade.

Nevertheless, his first stumbling attempts to investigate the factories and workshops were met with suspicion. And although he felt he had talked his way out of each situation that arose, he was uneasy about staying in his job for too long and risking being found out. Instead of waiting for his inevitable exposure, he made up his mind to steal the most important plans and disappear as quickly as possible.

Two days after deciding that his time was almost up, he bought a train ticket to Dortmund. Reilly had a key to a safe apartment which had been arranged for him there by one of 'M's agents. Money and clothes, and a different passport, were waiting for him to use. Everything he needed for his escape was there. He planned to reduce the risks by having several large envelopes in which he intended to place the plans after he had stolen them, and mail them to London, Paris, Rotterdam and Brussels, in case one or other of them was intercepted.

He had already identified where each of the security guards would typically be. Even so, there was no simple plan to avoid having to kill one or two of them in order to steal the plans and escape. In the event, he had to strangle and tie up one of the guards before he could reach the drawings he wanted. Then he tore each plan into large pieces in case some did not reach their destination, and placed them in the stamped and addressed envelopes he had concealed in his overcoat. He had to attack another unsuspecting guard on the way out of the main gate, and tie him up and gag him.

Reilly mailed all of the envelopes in a letter box at the Essen train station. In no time at all he was seated in a train *en route* for Dortmund. He travelled on to Paris the very next day.

After sending his report to the Chief from Paris, he decided to remain there and relax for a few days after all the tension he had experienced in the Krupp's works. He had booked in at a luxurious hotel on the Rue de la Paix. And, comfortably dressed in a civilized suit, instead of his work clothes, he enjoyed a moment of leisure by strolling along the boulevards in the fresh spring weather and glancing at shop windows on the Rue St. Honoré. Gazing with interest at one of the elegant young women coming out of a shop, he was surprised and shocked to discover that it was his half-sister Anna.

According to what he told friends, Reilly followed Anna in a daze, not knowing, and even fearing, what he might find out. It was a shock to his system to be reminded of the past so unexpectedly, when he had made every effort to erase it, and now lived a different life with an entirely different identity.

What he learned, from talking to Anna, was that she had become highly-strung after the death of their mother and his own disappearance when he was still a teenager. She had believed that he had drowned himself, just as he had intended at the time, and had become deeply depressed in her loneliness. What allowed her to carry on with life was her love of classical music, which she played well on the piano. She had studied the piano rigorously as a child, and showed great promise to be a professional concert pianist. She had taken seriously the idea of a career in music, and continued to study the piano in Vienna and Warsaw. The reason she was in Paris was that she had been invited there to be taught by the celebrated musician Paderewski. Her life now revolved around piano rehearsals and her ambition to be a celebrated international concert pianist like her famous teacher.

Playing the piano had filled a deep gap in Anna's life. But she felt incomplete and, only recently, a man had fallen in love with her and followed her to Paris. He was a Polish officer. Although she admitted to Reilly that she did not love the young officer, she described him as a kind man who had proposed marriage to her. After some doubt, she had finally accepted his proposal, but she confessed to Sidney that she now had reservations about the whole idea, and was nervous at the prospect of marriage to a stranger. Who knew how it might turn out?

Reilly was pleased to meet up with his half-sister, whom he loved. He decided to remain a little longer in Paris as a consequence. So he was shocked to learn, only a few days afterwards that Anna had just killed herself by jumping out of a window from the top floor of the hotel in which she was staying. She left a note addressed to Georgie, saying that she had made up her mind not to marry the Polish officer after all. But the stress of being challenged by the exactitude of continual piano rehearsals, loneliness, and her uncertain emotional problems and indecision, had been too much for her to handle. Apparently she had not been able to live with it.

At least, that was what he told his friends to justify her appearance and her even more sudden disappearance. In reality, both Reilly and Anna had parted with the truth, as they had so often done throughout their lives, in order to conceal their real relationship. For the young woman he had introduced as Anna had been pregnant, and he knew that

Admiral of the Fleet Lord Fisher.

she and her child could be in danger. Her very name was a cover for her real identity, as most of Reilly's identities always were. Its objective was to protect not only the individual in this case, but their child.

Whether she was Anna or just plain Ann, Johanna or Annie, made no difference, providing it distracted attention and covered their trails by concealing her real identity. The young lady he called Anne was as mysterious as "The Dark Lady of the Sonnets." She had to be, since she was Reilly's *real* wife, and had been for some time.

She had turned up unexpectedly in Paris, pregnant with her and Sidney Reilly's daughter. Taken by surprise when he'd been drained of energy after the climax of his extraordinary episode at Krupp's and his escapade from Germany, he'd had to concoct a story on the spur of the moment to put any watchers off the scent and get her out of Paris in a hurry.

His quick thinking not only succeeded in confusing foreign secret services who had him watched but, hopefully, everyone else for years to come. The lady—always vulnerable to watching eyes—had turned up. She had to be made to look like someone else. And her pregnancy had to be instantly concealed, or she and their child could be in danger for the rest of their lives from Reilly's watchers. So the lady was immediately made to vanish.

12
The Royal Fleet

BACK AGAIN IN LONDON, Reilly called on the Chief for a debriefing, and drew his pay. He was now on the payroll of the Secret Service, since Melville had wanted to be sure to hang on to his best agent by treating him more generously than other agents. But, although 'M' congratulated him earnestly on completing the secret mission at Krupp's, Reilly obtained no pleasure from the praise that had previously buoyed him up. He felt deflated instead. Although cool in most circumstances, he was not immune to shocks to the system.

He continued to rent rooms in St, James's and spent several months leave in gambling and womanizing to keep him occupied in London's West End and not dwelling on something or someone he felt was missing. Or perhaps it was the new weight of his responsibilities as the father of a new little daughter. He would have to take more care to protect them both. He did not bother to enquire about Margaret.

When he finally sat down with the Chief to discuss new business, 'M' filled him in on changed events that would influence his future assignments.

"We've talked about oil before," he said, watching for the flicker of interest he expected would illuminate his agent's memories of the oil fields which he had been so optimistic about in previous years.

"What happened to D'Arcy?"

"Hopefully, he's still our friend."

For some time now, the heads of the Admiralty had argued back and forth about the merits and demerits of using oil instead of burning coal in furnaces, with sweating human stokers endlessly shovelling more and more into them to be rapidly consumed by the flames. It was dangerous too.

The Royal Navy had already modernized itself with various new technologies since the days of wooden hulls and sails, which they had replaced with steel and smokestacks. Fisher had improved the types and power of cannons used on battleships, too. Now he was determined to have oil, and had organized an Oil Committee. Unfortunately for the British Admiralty, the British Isles possessed no underground oil. On the other hand, the United States possessed plenty of oil wells, and the fastest-growing naval fleet in the world. It was watched with apprehension and suspicion.

"I'm sure you know D'Arcy's company struck oil in Persia," 'M' said. "But it is not gushing in sufficient quantities to make it economically viable. Some of the first oil wells have already run dry."

Reilly looked searchingly at the Chief for more news.

"D'Arcy invested most of his personal fortune in the oil company," Melville continued. "And he's earning nothing from it to pay off his bank loans. So the banks have taken over his shares in Mount Morgan Mining. Some of the very biggest financiers in Britain, like King Edward the Seventh's friend Sir Ernest Cassells, and the major caterers Joseph Lyons and Company, no longer view D'Arcy's oil wells as a profitable investment."

"He must be desperate," Reilly remarked with fellow feeling for the American's predicament.

"He's anxious enough to seek investments from foreign banks in Europe. That's a red flag for the Admiralty—they are concerned about the Royal Fleet. It needs oil. And Persia seems to provide the best opportunity to supply it."

"Not just the best, it's the only available source."

"Exactly! That is why Admiral Fisher's Oil Committee has begun searching for investors for D'Arcy's company. That's what you recommended yourself. Your mission now is to ensure that if D'Arcy sells his oil company as a going concern, it will be to no one else but Britain."

Seeing Reilly's contained anger, he added, "I know what you must think. The whole process has been far too slow. But you and I have no control over that."

"But now, from what you say, it looks like D'Arcy's company will be lost to other bidders."

"Not if you can prevent it."

"How? They should have come to an agreement with Russia when I recommended it."

"It's not like you to be defeatist," 'M' said. "And it's not the Russians but the French whom D'Arcy is dealing with. Your earlier recommendation were not forgotten. The Cabinet is considering your advice at this very moment."

"Better late than never, I suppose."

Reilly was partly consoled but still truculent.

"You are going to have to be particularly diplomatic and most confidential in your dealings with D'Arcy. We don't want the French to know how desperate the Admiralty is for oil. If the French Government discovers that the Admiralty sent an agent to D'Arcy, they would intervene and prevent the transaction taking place."

Reilly nodded almost reluctantly. And 'M' had all the arrangements made for him to be booked into the *Ritz Hotel* in Paris.

But Reilly learned on arrival that D'Arcy was already negotiating a deal with the French branch of the Rothschild banking enterprise. And they were not in Paris. D'Arcy was staying with Alphonse de Rothschild in the South of France.

Reilly now felt challenged to display his own skills against the worldwide Rothschild family firm of financiers. They were justifiably admired for their brilliance in finance, as indeed were many Jewish bankers—both admired and envied for their judgment and shrewdness. Reilly must have wondered if his own recently acquired Jewish hallmark provided him with similar financial skills. His own judgments were generally good, and he made up his mind swiftly and decisively.

In his own scheming imagination, he could see himself being handsomely rewarded if he managed to negotiate a deal with D'Arcy on Britain's behalf. And if he brokered an *entente* with the Russians, perhaps even the Tsar might be impressed with Reilly's skills—just like the heroic courier of the Tsar in the popular novel about the fictional Michael Strogoff, which had thrilled him as a romantic and adventurous teenager.

Whether delusions of glory could trigger bizarre new ideas, or if it was the other way round, a histrionic plan was already forming in Reilly's fertile mind. He knew—or imagined he knew—how he might achieve victory over Rothschild. So he bought his stage props and disguise for his adventure during a shopping spree in Paris, from where he took a train at the Gare de Lyon for Nice.

By the time he arrived in the South of France, he had changed his clothing into that of a Roman Catholic priest. It was as good a disguise as any in a Catholic country; perhaps the best of all. He would not stand out, and yet be respected in his wide-brimmed black hat and cloak. In Reilly's mind, at least, he had overcome the problem of being recognized as a British agent, since Britain's Secret Service would hardly be likely to hire a priest to approach D'Arcy and negotiate a complex financial deal with him involving shares in oil wells.

As part of his cover when he booked a room in the hotel in Nice, Reilly dropped hints that he hoped to obtain donations from rich tourists on holiday, for a resettlement program for orphans. He claimed it was his favorite charity. And those donors would be found in some of the splendid luxury hotels on the *Côte d'Azur*. Merely mentioning the famous Rothschild name elicited the information he needed—that there was a party of Rothschild's family and friends gathered on holiday in Cannes, where Alphonse de Rothschild's yacht was anchored near the biggest quay.

Reilly moved out of his hotel in Nice and travelled further along the Mediterranean coast to Cannes, where he took a room, this time in a modest *pension*. Once settled in, he strolled to the quay at the edge of the harbor where numerous luxury yachts were idling at anchor. The huge and luxurious vessels formed a wealthy community across the way from the colorfully canopied smart restaurants, with their outdoor tables and chairs for tourists, beside patisseries and boutiques, and other shops facing the harbor.

He familiarized himself with the area over several days, still dressed as a priest and getting the hang of his pose, while carefully studying people coming and going and boarding Rothschild's yacht. He had established himself as a regular customer in and outside a fashionable restaurant, almost immediately opposite where the yacht was anchored, and sat, making his observations over numerous cups of coffee, croissants, brioches, and glasses of water.

After waiting impatiently for two days for D'Arcy to come ashore, without success, he strolled closer to the yacht to take a better look at the guests, and recognized D'Arcy's burly figure from photographs that 'M' had shown him. But D'Arcy continued to remain on the yacht. Evidently he was sleeping on board. In that case, Reilly realized, a deal might already be in the process of being negotiated and signed, while he was waiting outside. He had to get aboard the yacht as quickly as possible to talk with D'Arcy, whom he observed strolling back and forth for exercise and fresh air on the deck.

Reilly was an ardent admirer of Napoleon's first principles for victory; "audacity, audacity, always audacity!" So he wasted no more time, and boldly stepped onto the gangway and boarded Rothschild's yacht. Then he strode self-confidently towards several passengers on the deck, beside D'Arcy, with an outburst of French, while he waved his arms in an appeal for funds for his charity.

Taken by surprise at his sudden appearance, they watched him wordlessly at first, but were fascinated by this eccentric priest. Small groups of guests discussed with each other whether to offer him a donation, while Reilly continued to hold their attention by speaking effusively in French—which he knew the bewildered D'Arcy did not understand. But he managed to take D'Arcy's arm and lead him further along the deck before he could protest.

As soon as they were out of the hearing of the others, Reilly stopped talking in French and spoke to him more confidentially in English.

"Please forgive this intrusion Mr. D'Arcy. I am on a mission for the British Government. They have given me a confidential message for you. It amounts to a generous offer for your shares that you wouldn't want to refuse."

D'Arcy stared at him with surprise and open suspicion.

Fearing rejection and even hostility, Reilly hastily added, "The British Admiralty may even be prepared to pay you twice what the French or Rothschild might offer for your company or the oil concession."

"How can I be sure of your authenticity?"

"If you will meet me at the *Grand Hotel* at 7 p.m. this evening, I promise to show you all the credentials you need."

He looked questioningly at the American. As soon as D'Arcy nodded, Reilly turned away and hurriedly left Rothschild's yacht.

13
The Côte d'Azur

D'ARCY WAS ASTONISHED at the secretive and unconventional way he had been contacted by the British Admiralty, but met Reilly as arranged. Seated in the *Grand Hotel* with D'Arcy that evening, Reilly told him that the British Government were presently discussing a plan to provide him with all the finance he required. He explained the oil situation. D'Arcy promised not to sign any deal with Rothschild for ten days, to give Reilly time to provide written assurance of an offer from the Admiralty.

Reilly was able to return to 'M' in London and report that he had been successful in preventing D'Arcy from signing a deal with anyone else. But he warned, "A written offer from the Admiralty is immediately necessary."

The Right Honorable E. G. Pretyman was a Civil Lord of the Admiralty and a Member of Parliament. It was he who wrote a formal letter to D'Arcy on the appropriate letterhead to explain that the British Admiralty requested an opportunity to acquire his oil interests. It invited him to London for immediate negotiations with Britain's Oil Committee, and asked him to suspend discussions with Rothschild.

A Concession Syndicate was formed and financed with the assistance of the Burmah Oil Company, enabling continued exploration for oil in Persia. D'Arcy's interest was protected if oil was found.

As a result of the satisfactory discussion that followed in London, the Committee arranged with the Burmah Oil Company that they should investigate the prospects of the Persian Oil Field. They agreed to form a Syndicate and develop it.

'M' had switched, meanwhile, to a Military Intelligence Investigation Branch in the War Office, which was a forerunner of MI5. And, conveniently for the negotiations to succeed, a Mr. and Mrs. William Melville booked in at the local *Grand Hotel* during that crucial time frame when D'Arcy's various discussions fluctuated. He was being badgered by one of the banks, which asked for the oil concession as security for his loan. So that, D'Arcy stayed at the *Grand Hotel* talking sometimes to Melville and at other times with Rothschild.

Six months later he was involved in discussions with Burmah Oil. When D'Arcy returned to Rothschild, the situation was more or less as it had been before, except that the Melvilles were no longer needed in Cannes. 'M' had passed negotiations on to Reilly, who became more directly involved again, but without his theatrical disguise, since the British Admiralty feared that the concession might fall into foreign hands if D'Arcy was left to muddle through on his own. He needed firm guidance to fall in with their plans. And who better to provide it than Reilly?

Discussions fluctuated once again when Rothschild came upon a report which doubted the commercial success of the Persian oil venture. Coincidentally, just up the coast at the picturesque fishing village and vacation resort of St. Raphael, a Mr. and Mrs. Reilly were registered at the *Continental Hotel*. It is recorded that Reilly wrote a letter there, dated June 30, which referred to "a most useful report that had helped him to turn the tide."

However it was that Reilly caused Alphonse de Rothschild to lose confidence in D'Arcy's scheme, Rothschild now doubted the financial benefits of the transaction, and his discussions with D'Arcy collapsed. By the time Darcy's agent cabled the bad news to him, D'Arcy was already happy with the British Admiralty's discussions and proposals. His deal with Britain was signed on May 20, 1905. Oil gushed in Persia three years later, when the developers found it on May 26, 1908. This time the well did not run dry. The Anglo-Persian Oil Company was formed the following year.

But, instead of feeling pleased as the success of his mission, Reilly found himself disappointed and frustrated. He felt that his remunerations were not enough to pay for his skills, his diplomacy, his advice, and his quick witted reactions.

14
Rumors of War

T HE MENACE OF A POSSIBLE INVASION by German troops was a constant topic of conversation by politicians, newspapers, and the public. But what dominated daily life was that England had undergone a change in attitude from its gentlemanly past with the obligations of its ruling class to take care of others, and the leadership of the aristocracy after the death of Prime Minister Campbell-Bannerman. He had been a much beloved man who believed in duty and honour, and in giving his services to Great Britain without recompense. The mood of the country became even more quarrelsome when it took to violence at the arrival of the twentieth century, when Asquith became Liberal Prime Minister of Britain.

The waves of rebellion that arose took the establishment by surprise. Leaders lost control and watched helplessly as revolutionary events took place before their eyes without being able to do much to avoid them. Prime Ministers became mere time-servers, while other classes of people were intent on taking over the country and replacing the ruling class and the Liberals in government. The stability of Britain's society with its former liberal attitudes came undone.

Evidently the new Prime Minister Asquith was not the right man to lead the country at such a critical time. It was said he had the sort of character which is often found in the Senior Common Rooms of Oxford and Cambridge, in that "he was almost completely lacking in imagination or enthusiasm." Dons and Ministers preferred to order their lives in an easygoing manner, with "the idle pleasure of the library, of the palate, of conversation or intrigue."

Others felt that at least "The most important thing was that Mr. Asquith was felt to be *safe*."

No one had expected the troubles that arose by 1910 and continued to disturb the peace for the next four years and beyond. It was the end of an era of *noblesse oblige*, in which the British aristocracy had ruled the British nation as wisely as they knew how. But they had not been appreciated and were now outnumbered by people who could not agree with anyone else.

There were continual clashes between all sorts of factions in Britain during the following years which were marred by the rise of violence. In short, there was hostility and conflict between the classes and between the sexes.

David Lloyd George had now become Chancellor of the Exchequer. Winston Churchill was President of the Board of Trade at age thirty-four. They were known as "The Terrible Twins." Both were impressive politicians who enjoyed entertaining and manipulating their audiences in the House of Commons. They loved words and turned them into rhetorical magic that stirred people up and, one way or another, initiated desperately needed reforms to the less privileged members of society.

Since it was thought that the most dangerous threats to Britain came from outside, Prime Minister Asquith offered Winston the position of First Lord of the Admiralty in October 1911. As Winston told the Prime Minister's young daughter Violet, "It is the biggest career opportunity to come my way – even though it represents a drop in seniority and salary."

The supremacy of the British Navy was the key to the security of the British Isles. And the Senior Service could give him the closest thing to military glory, which was what he craved.

Throughout the early months of 1912 Eddie Marsh spent much of the time working on the HMS *Enchantress* for his chief, accompanied by Winston's new wife Clementine. The Admiralty yacht was used exclusively by him since he was appointed First Lord and undertook continual tours of inspection of major Naval fleets and dockyards, to shake them all up. Eddie spent most Sundays on board and Winston never left off working before 8 p.m.

Now that the Agadir threat by Germany had changed his mind about the Kaiser's intentions, he recognized that the German Navy was expanding and modernizing its fleet of battleships in preparation for war. Lloyd George agreed.

Under the influence of Admiral Fisher, he immediately launched a program to replace coal power with oil, which was already being used in submarines and destroyers. But most battleships in the British Fleet were still powered by coal, even though oil was being sprayed on the coal as a booster to achieve maximum speed. He ordered the *Queen Elizabeth* class of battleships to be built with oil-fired engines. He established a Royal Commission to confirm the benefits of oil in three different reports, and confirmed that ample oil existed. He also recommended that oil reserves be maintained in the event of war.

The commission was chaired by Admiral Sir John Fisher. The delegation travelled to the Persian Gulf, and the British Government finally invested in the Anglo-Persian Oil Company, which duly became the British Petroleum Company (BP).

D'Arcy was repaid all of his cash outlay, and £900,000 in Burmah Oil shares. He was appointed to the board as a director of Anglo-Persian and became a very rich man.

But despite the success of Reilly's mission, Reilly was annoyed that he did not become rich from it himself. Although only an employee of Britain's Secret Service, he thought his value to the British Government and the Admiralty deserved greater recognition.

The thought of how very different the situation would have been if he had not taken the initiative to board Rothschild's yacht remained seething in his mind. His disappointment and frustration continued after the Anglo-Russian *entente* which he had recommended was finalized in 1907.

Reilly's resentment rose to the surface again when the British Government acquired fifty-one percent of the stock of BP and negotiated a contract for oil supplies for twenty years. It was considered to be "as farsighted as former Prime Minister Benjamin Disraeli's purchase of the Suez Canal for Britain."

Reilly had initiated each idea and advised his chief and the Admiralty to turn them into reality at each stage. And yet, his only reward had been his regular but modest pay as an employee, and the usual congratulations from William Melville for his success. But it was not the same as being congratulated and awarded a medal by the Tsar.

It was in that frame of mind that Reilly decided to resign from British Intelligence. He needed to be free to make some real money.

AIR SUPERIORITY

1
The Flying Club

REILLY SAW MONEY AS A MEANS to political and commercial power, and to be able to live in the elegant style he felt he deserved. He now possessed all sorts of different influential contacts at every political, financial and commercial level in several different countries. He had been a student of chemistry. And he had no problem in securing sufficient finance to start up a new company specializing in patent medicines. Plenty of other people were making fortunes by selling health enhancers to hypochondriacs that claimed to cure all kinds of medical conditions, many of them imaginary. But an extraordinary number seemed to work. Since the largest and most gullible market for nostrums was in the United States, of which he had no knowledge, he brought a young American named Long into his new business as a partner.

Long was to provide patent medicine formulas from the United States that claimed to cure rheumatism and restore lost hair. Typical of the long-established "snake oil" business from the days of the Wild West were pills that could enhance sexual potency. Reilly would have the recipes made up in England. Long would sell the patent medicines in the United States. And Reilly, with his contacts abroad, would sell them on the Continent as well as in Britain.

He transformed his rooms, which were now in Cursitor Street, into the offices of "Rosenbloom and Long, Manufacturers of Patent Medicines."

In spite of his enormous self-confidence and his skills, Reilly was relatively naïve in the world of commerce. Although sales proved satisfactory, the patent medicine business operated on the edge of fraud. Sugar-coated pills had long worked to cure perhaps as many as half of the patients with imaginary illnesses. But the other half resisted cure. It led to claims. There were also more costly claims for breaches of patents. Reilly was obliged to borrow more money to pay off the claims and maintain a positive flow of revenues to cover costs. He managed to keep the company afloat for four years, until Long absconded with the last six hundred pounds from their bank account.

Reilly needed more money, but no one would lend it to him. Fortunately, he was offered help by a solicitor named Abrahams, one of whose clients he owed money to. Abrahams organized the winding up of Reilly's business for him and, after paying off all of Reilly's creditors, closed down the enterprise with a final balance to his credit of £160. To Reilly's relief, Abrahams made no charge for his work.

Like many adventurous people at that time, Reilly was impressed and thrilled at the invention of the aeroplane, and the aerobatics of pioneers who were dare-devil flyers, as well as designers and experimenters, and manufacturers of the first aircraft—like Blériot in France, Farman, Dumont and others, whose early planes seemed to be made out of cardboard, canvas, string and glue, and occasionally fell apart in the air. But it was the adventure of flying, and of living on the edge, that captured his imagination. Flying was a young man's game, full of thrills and prone to fatal accidents in the fragile aircraft with simple instruments that didn't always work as they should. Danger appeared to be part of the attraction.

He was only one among many. Churchill felt the same exultation in taking command of the air, and planned to take flying lessons at Eastchurch naval station and aerodrome on the Isle of Sheppey in the Thames Estuary.

Reilly was drawn to Frankfurt for an international flying exhibition in 1910. Mixing with enthusiastic young pilots and picking up their unique jargon, he was able to forget about his failure in commerce and stop worrying about his future for a while. He easily made friends with them by showing the same enthusiasm for flying as they did. It was not difficult when he realized with excitement that they and he were pioneers of a new age of flight, as they took control of the air.

One pilot he could not help noticing was a Welshman named Jones who, at previous flying exhibitions, had shown himself to be a masterful pilot. But, for some reason, Jones had crash-landed on the first day of the Frankfurt exhibition, as if he were a beginner. Now he spent his time chatting with the other pilots and mechanics, and joking with them. Reilly wondered what he was up to, and why he was suddenly acting like a clown.

When a German plane stalled and spun out of control on the fifth day of the flying display, they all stopped talking and watched another tragedy unfold, as the nose of the plane tipped down and headed for the ground, striking the airfield. They rushed towards the plane in a vain hope of saving the pilot by pulling him from the crash. But the aeroplane was in pieces and the pilot had not survived the crash.

Jones, who was the first one to reach the wreck, immediately took charge of the situation by giving everyone abrupt commands to dismantle and salvage whatever they could save from the flying machine. Each man took back whatever he could to the hanger. Reilly noticed that Jones was interested only in the engine.

"This," Jones said in a low voice to Reilly, without any trace of a Welsh accent, "is what we need. Give me a hand to get it into the hangar!"

Once in the shelter of the hangar, Jones instructed him to separate the engine from other parts of the plane's structure.

"Keep it covered," he added, and pointed to some fabric.

Reilly took care to conceal the engine under the tarpaulin. Then Jones had several mechanics load the concealed engine onto a trolley. Turning confidentially to Reilly and still speaking without a Welsh accent, he said, "I was sent by 'M.'"

Before Reilly had adjusted to the implications, Jones added, "What I need you to do is distract the mechanics while I study the engine on my own. Give me five minutes to remove the magneto."

Reilly remembered that the pilot who had been killed in the crash had previously boasted that the design of the magneto was superior to any others, and that the German army were interested in it.

Jones made a hurried drawing of the German magneto before replacing it in the engine, Then they took it to the hanger used by the German pilots.

Jones—who was an engineer commander in the Royal Navy—had realised that the magneto was a new and improved design. 'M's' spy appeared to know from Melville about Reilly's work as an SIS agent. Once away from the aerodrome, they discussed the possibility of war and the coming age of air superiority, and concluded that, since Germany was intent on increasing the size of its battleships and modernizing its navy, the Teutons would be ready for war as soon as they had completed their modernization program.

"Who are they most likely to attack." asked Jones, "when their army and navy are big enough and powerful enough to win? France or Russia?" It appeared to be a rhetorical question, to judge by his witty smile.

Reilly said he was sure it would be Britain.

"You should go back to work for the chief," Jones said. "He's certain to welcome you. In fact I know he will."

Reilly realized that 'M' had put Jones up to the oblique invitation to rejoin the SIS. So he made contact with the Chief as soon as he returned to London.

'M' told him his next mission was in Russia, where Reilly would have a free hand in his own country, where Melville knew he had considerable influence and would be accepted as a compatriot.

"Your mission is not to spy on Russia" 'M' said. "It's to obtain intelligence information about Germany's military and naval power there. This information is not for the Admiralty but the Foreign Office."

Typically in peacetime, the Treasury had cut back on intelligence gathering, and the British Secret Service was miserably short of funds. Although Reilly was short of money, too, he found himself unable to accept the meager salary which was all the chief could manage to offer him.

"All I need," Reilly said, "is £600 for expenses to establish myself in St. Petersburg. I can easily find a cover job to provide me with more money."

'M' briefed him carefully on his new mission and provided whatever Reilly asked for.

The only idea in Reilly's head when he arrived in St. Petersburg was to organise an international air display and make sure that the Germans would receive an invitation. It could put him in contact with German aviators, and probably provide him with information about the German army. Moreover, it would establish him as a local celebrity, and the publicity could bring introductions and invitations to other senior German officials, embassy staff, or politicians.

Feeling comfortably back at home in St. Petersburg, Reilly took a stroll down the *Morkaya*, which was one of its main streets, and dropped in for lunch at the *Kuba* restaurant. It was considered to be one of the finest, and certainly one of the most famous restaurants in Europe. It claimed to have been praised by the Russian poet Pushkin.

It was decorated in an elaborate French style which ensured comfort with upholstered armchairs for each customer. The chefs were French and the waiters were Tartars. Its greatest advantage for Reilly was not what was on the menu, but who he might usefully meet there.

He had only just entered and stood for a moment to look round and enjoy the warmth and tantalizing smells of cooking in the foyer, when he recognized an old friend and called out "Boris!"

On his very first day he had ran into Boris Savourin from his Port Arthur days. He accepted the invitation to Boris's table where, eating *hors d'oeuvre* with him, was his friend Alexander Ivanovich Grammatikoff, known familiarly as Sasha.

Savourin was a journalist and the son of the owner of one of the leading newspapers in Russia, *Novoe Vremya*. He was a local personality and another admirer of England. Sasha Grammatikoff was a barrister, descended from Greeks who had been invited to the Crimea from Turkey by the Empress Catherine, after it had been added to Russia at the end of the eighteenth century. Reilly knew little more about him. He was a man of mystery, and always an entertaining conversationalist.

Soon after placing his order with the waiter, Reilly introduced the exciting topic of the pioneers of air supremacy who had conquered gravity by designing aircraft, and the pilots who risked flying their aeroplanes. He found plenty of interest at the table, particularly from Savourin the newshound. In no time at all, an idea emerged for organizing and promoting a competitive air race.

"What route?" Boris asked excitedly, wondering immediately of the publicity his newspaper could obtain by sponsoring it.

Reilly had already worked out the route beforehand. As usual, he left little to chance.

"I think it could be flown in stages from St. Petersburg to Moscow. It's 390 miles away"

The three friends were mesmerized at the novelty of the idea and ended up by enthusiastically supporting a new flying club to be known familiarly as "Wings." Their only competitor would be the Imperial Aero Club. It was soon agreed that Reilly would instantly visit the President of the other club to obtain his support for a joint flying week. They would invite foreign aviators. It would lead up to a race between Russian pilots as a climax. Savourin would take charge of press publicity, and work with Grammatikoff to obtain enough finance to turn it into a success.

In the event, ten aviators competed in the race. But only Vasilliev finished. Reilly greeted him at the end to the flashing of lights from Boris's cameraman, and felt satisfied that he had done something for Russia. Most importantly, the publicity for the "Flying Week" established him in St. Petersburg society.

The downside was that, as soon as the news of the aeroplane race was published in newspapers in Europe, Margaret read it and discovered where Sidney was. She had been drinking their money away in Brussels, and thought she recognized an opportunity to get Reilly back now that he was successful and probably rich. Since the social scene in St. Petersburg sounded thrilling, she decided to arrive there without warning.

Unexpected surprises were not what Reilly needed: everything had to conform with his own plans. But although he was angry at her sudden arrival, he allowed her to stay with him in St. Petersburg. His unusual behaviour seemed to be out of character. But, if Reilly thought he held some kind of threat over Margaret to keep her in line, it was equally possible that the same threat might apply to him as a possible accomplice. In any case, she set up home for herself and Reilly in Potchtamsky Street.

Margaret continued drinking. But that did not stop Reilly from achieving another triumph, which would be described by Britain's Vice Consul in Moscow, Robert Bruce Lockhart, as "one of the most brilliant coups in the history of espionage."

2
Reilly's Mistresses

WOMEN COULD BE POTENTIALLY DANGEROUS to audacious espionage agents like Reilly, since they might accidentally reveal secrets to the wrong people. That was why he had reported his marriage to 'M' and assured him of Margaret's security. So a game was constantly played by most spies to separate spying and secrets from their domestic life. It rarely worked, although some managed fairly successfully to live separate lives simultaneously with two families. Reilly's approach, instead, was to use his mistresses as part of his network, choosing those who—because of their husband's influential position, or their affairs with other men—could provide him with useful information, effective cover, assistance, or security.

Reilly was generally skillful in managing to enjoy the company of several mistresses simultaneously. There were always women who were attracted to him—a quality that 'M' still attributed to his androgynous features and his powers of command. Women were not an addiction, nor a vice, with him. His sole vice appeared to be the eternal one of gambling, which he enjoyed at the *Koupechesky Club*, known also as the "Merchants' Club," where he frequently met rich and influential people.

As cover for his activities in Moscow and St. Petersburg, he took a position with a previous employer named the *Compagnie Est-Asiatique*. He built up a circle of influential friends and contacts in St. Petersburg, and was often seen at the best restaurants and hotels in the city, where he could meet new and influential people as well as old friends.

He played his spying game with thought and precision, like a game of chess, in which he first set his pieces in readiness for a battle of wits on which he gambled everything. Now he was seen in St. Petersburg as a man of mystery, an apolitical business man whose leisure pursuits were gambling and women—while all the time he focused on his real objective; it was the Russian Fleet of battleships.

Russia's navy had been almost entirely destroyed in the war by the Japanese. It had to be rebuilt and enlarged. The Russian Government had already approved a five year construction program which had been agreed upon by the Tsar. Its operational date was scheduled for 1911. A great deal of money would be spent on it. Since Russia's own shipbuilding yards and armament factories were limited to handling only about a tenth of the shipping they needed, most of the construction orders would be given to ship builders from other countries.

France was Russia's military ally, so that the French Government considered they were in a privileged position to acquire the contracts to build Russia's fleet. Their naval attaché had lived in St. Petersburg for many years and knew who had to be bribed to obtain the orders. On the other hand, the British were the acknowledged leaders in ship building and considered they should have the biggest share of the business. Their naval construction companies worked independently of each other, but Vickers possessed a team of agents who were led by the millionaire Basil Zaharoff. He was a Turk or a Greek—who knew? He was known as "The Mystery Man of Europe."

But there was another important competitor after the contracts for Russia's new Fleet: it was Germany. The Germans had extraordinary influence at the Tsar's court and possessed a considerable number of useful business connections in Russia; so they naturally assumed it was they who would obtain most of the contracts.

Britain's Vickers won a contract to construct a new shipyard at Nikolaev on the Black Sea, not far from Odessa, in 1911. It was the same year that Germany's Blohm & Voss landed the Putilov project. Basil Zaharoff became the exclusive European agent for the American Electric Boat Company the following year, with Reilly's help. The Electric Boat Company soon secured a contract to build six new submarines for the Russian Navy in St. Petersburg. Zaharoff initiated another grandiose scheme in 1913 for a huge arsenal complex at the Volga town of Tsaritsyn, the future Stalingrad.

Success in business was still based on acquiring a monopoly of commodities, goods, or services, from a patron, like the Tsar. Russia was not yet a capitalist system with free market competition. Not only was bribery, kickbacks and commission normal practice in Russia and other countries at the time, Vickers in England was also implicated in bribery and similar practices. But for Reilly it was not all about money. He recognized that Russia was in a perilous and vulnerable position—although it possessed by far the largest army because of its vast population, it could provide only a quarter of them with weapons.

If Imperial Russia were to survive, brokering foreign purchases of weaponry performed an essential service for Russia's war effort. Otherwise Russian troops would have to be sent to the front without rifles or bullets. And there was a shortage of artillery shells. A war at that moment could result in the loss of millions of Russian men in battle in the first year alone. So, although Reilly aimed to become wealthy, he had the satisfaction of knowing he was helping his desperate homeland.

He recognized the situation was critical for Russia, with its "Lack of munitions, the painfully limited number of factories in Russia for their production, not enough railroad lines for transportation—all that simply invited defeat."

Reilly made it his business to be informed of every aspect of the situation by making contacts with all parties and collecting key influential intelligence information. He particularly met with the leaders of the Russian Admiralty, and made a point of befriending the Naval Assistant to the Minister of Marine. He was Petr Ivanovich Zalesskii. Petr was known also for his beautiful wife Nadine. Reilly charmed them both, and became a frequent guest at their home. He was especially drawn to Petr's unhappy wife, whom he recognized as the key influential figure. In no time at all, she fell deeply in love with him and was determined to have him.

Reilly believed that most of the naval construction orders would go to Germany, many of them to Blohm & Voss in Hamburg, who were about to choose Russian agents in St. Petersburg to consider tenders. But any appointments would have to be approved first by the Ministry of Marine, meaning, in effect, Petr Zalesskii.

Among the companies likely to be appointed as agents by the Germans was a moderately small firm called Mendrochovich & Lubensky. Reilly already knew Mendrochovich, It was not difficult for him to come up with a plan that involved Mendro's company.

Mendrochovich had already been successful at selling German railway goods wagons to the Russians. He was not only the brains of the business enterprise, he *was* the enterprise: his nominal partner was a burden to him. But, as a self-made and cultivated Jew in a society sullied by anti-Semitism, Mendro had been obliged to take the indolent Count Lubensky as a partner for the aristocratic image he conveyed. The Count was a front-man, and supposedly a contact man, using his aristocratic name and title as added prestige. But he was not entrepreneurial material and had been a disappointment to Mendro from the very beginning.

As soon as Reilly discovered that Mendrochovich & Lubensky was one of the three firms on the shortlist of possible agents for Blohm & Voss, and that all that was now needed was Russian approval, he visited Nadine's husband, Petr—the Naval Assistant to the Minister of Marine—and persuaded him that the only firm on the list that the Russians should consider was Mendrochovich & Lubensky.

Having successfully done so, he immediately took a droshky to Mendrochovich's place of business and, without mincing words, asked Mendro what the Blohm & Voss business would be worth to his company. His friend knew exactly what such an agency would be worth. He also knew that Reilly had befriended the Ministry of Marine. Without equivocating, he offered Reilly 200,000 roubles and twenty-five percent of the profits. When Reilly upped the offer to half the profits, Mendro was perfectly happy to agree.

It took barely two weeks before Mendrochovich & Lubensky were informed by official letter that they had been appointed the sole agent for Blohm & Voss, and that they had been approved by the Russian Ministry of Marine. Reilly visited Mendrochovich again, to remind him that although he was now the sole agent, someone was needed to negotiate the contracts. Mendro agreed to take Reilly into the firm for that purpose.

Reilly immediately sent an urgent coded message to his old Chief, William Melville, in London, requesting that 'M' send him a top agent to discuss the operation he had in mind.

The agent who arrived turned out to be the spy he had known as Mr. Jones.

Reilly explained to him that his company would be the agent in Russia for Blohm & Voss:

"Mendrochovich and I are close friends. In effect, I control the company, since he will be happy to leave everything that has to be done entirely to me. All the blueprints of the drawings and the specifications of the latest German battleships will be in my hands, so that I can present the new designs of the Russian battle-ships to the Russian Ministry of Marine. You realize what that will mean?"

Jones smiled. "You are well ahead of me this time."

"It means that Britain's Secret Service and the Admiralty could have complete knowledge of every one of the innovations and improvements in the designs of Germany's and Russia's entire new naval Fleet."

Reilly let the impact of his statement sink in before adding, "That would include all new specifications of the engines, the guns, the armor, the torpedoes and everything else."

Jones grinned from ear to ear. "Now I think I understand what you are up to."

"There's only one thing I want to know from 'M.' Would the British Government be at all concerned if the shipbuilding contracts went to German construction companies instead of British ones?

"Good point!"

Jones agreed to ask that critical question immediately he returned to London. And Reilly asked him to explain to 'M' that he would take nothing from the Secret Service as his own fees, since he planned to obtain ample remunerations from his cut with the Germans.

As soon as Reilly received a coded reply from 'M' that told him to go ahead, Reilly resigned from his cover job and officially joined Mendrochovich & Lubensky.

Reilly spent the next three years working on the contracts and plans for the German designs of Russia's new warships, while Mendro waited with a patient smile for the commissions to pour into his lap.

Reilly now mixed with important people in Moscow and St. Petersburg. He charmed them and their wives, and became friendly with all sorts of people at all levels. Nobody of any importance to him escaped his attentions. He developed a reputation as a man who could arrange complex international business deals, and was a man's man, and a lady's man, who loved parties. All who met him were mesmerized by his magnetic personality and his natural gift of having people do things for him without even asking.

He continually pressed the Russian naval staff to urge Blohm & Voss to provide the most recent innovations and improvements to all the designs and specifications of the German Kaiser's new Fleet, which was being, in effect, replicated for the Tsar.

Reilly was not viewed without suspicion by the Germans. Their agents watched his apartment as well as the office. One of his mistresses noticed two suspicious men loitering outside in the street, day and night, and remarked on it.

"It's my bodyguard," Reilly said with a knowing smile. "The government are protecting me. I am a very important man."

She had laughed at his joke. But when the numbers of contracts for Blohm & Voss continued to grow, it was considered to be evidence that Reilly was working on Germany's behalf, and the plainclothes men stopped following him.

"You see," he said one evening to his mistresses, when he glanced out of his window at the gas-lit street.

"But there's no one there."

"Exactly! My watchers—the one's you saw the other night - are gone."

She laughed as he embraced her. "You are funny!"

But neither the British shipbuilders, like Vickers, nor the French, like Schneider Creusot, were happy to see all the contracts going to German shipbuilders.

Zaharoff's professional reports made it clear that he knew Reilly and considered that he was "a very shrewd man. Part thug, part chameleon, Reilly was above all a skilled and ruthless manipulator of other people. He used women as easily as men, even in the most desperate of conspiracies."

"Whose side is Reilly on?" they asked Zaharoff.

"His own," Zaharoff replied.

"What can you do about him?"

Basil Zaharoff visited Russia to find out what was going on and why his agents at Vickers were not receiving any contracts.

When they met in secret, Zaharoff did his best to exploit Reilly's influential contacts by offering him a considerable amount of money if he would join forces with him at Vickers. He was amazed when Reilly turned down an offer which would have been more than Reilly planned to make from his deal with Mendrochovich. But Reilly was always his own man. In the shadowy world in which he operated, he trusted no one.

Meanwhile, the Germans were unaware that all the latest designs of their modern Fleet were being carefully studied by the British Admiralty in London. Although each plan from Germany was sent by diplomatic bag to their embassy in St. Petersburg, in a sealed envelope, and clearly addressed "To be delivered to the appropriate authority of the Russian Ministry of Marine," each one was taken by hand to Mendrochovich & Chubersky. It was the new name of the firm after Reilly had replaced the languid Count Lubensky. And Reilly opened every envelope himself.

Working secretly in his apartment, he made a plaster cast of each and every seal he had to break. He also used a special steam press to open each envelope in order to leave no trace of tampering. He was extraordinarily patient and careful, spending hours with a hot iron and plenty of blotting paper. He placed the blueprints between sheets of glass to make Photostat copies.

During the entire three years, he informed Britain's Admiralty of every new design and improvement in the German Navy; its speeds, armaments, tonnages, the crews of their battleships, and every other important detail. He was constantly afraid that someone would notice the time it took between the arrival of the envelopes and their despatch and arrival to the Ministry of Marine.

At the same time, using his contacts in Russian court circles, and with a woman-friend of Rasputin, Reilly managed to pass on regular political intelligence information to the British Secret Service.

The beautiful Nadine willingly cooperated in her seduction by Reilly with her husband's knowledge. Petr's marriage to her had been troubled for some time, because she

Multi-millionaire Greek arms dealer Sir Basil Zaharoff was one of the richest men in the world.

was discontented, dissatisfied and moody. Petr and Sidney became close friends and drinking and gambling companions in the evenings. Petr Ivanovich Zalesskii finally agreed to divorce Nadine for a large sum of money, so that Reilly could marry her.

Margaret refused to divorce Sidney, even when he offered her £10,000. When she threatened him with disclosure, he gave her forty-eight hours to agree or face the consequences, which he made abundantly clear. Knowing perfectly well that Reilly would carry out his threats, she hurriedly caught the Vienna Express and vanished.

Reilly made enquiries to ensure he knew where Margaret had gone to. She needed watching. He found out that she had travelled to Belgrade and then joined the International Red Cross in Sofia. If he could not lose her by paying her off, he decided at least to lose her officially. He did so by arranging for his journalist friend Boris Savourin to publish a story in his newspaper which reported the unfortunate accident of a Red Cross ambulance in Bulgaria, when it skidded and fell off of a mountain road into a ravine, killing several nurses. One of them was "Mrs. Reilly who until recently was a resident of St. Petersburg."

He persuaded his friend Sasha Grammatikoff to be his divorce lawyer on behalf of Petr and Nadine, but Nadine's divorce from Petr took much longer than anticipated. It was still not completed by the early part of 1914, when war in Europe seemed imminent.

Life in England appeared to continue much as before. But not for Eddie Marsh, who was in close contact with his Chief almost day and night during another political crisis. He wrote to his dear friend Rupert Brooke, who was abroad in Tahiti, "I remember when I last wrote I was desperately unhappy about politics."

The reason was the destabilizing effect of conflicts between all groups and classes in England, even the possibility of a Civil War. But, "Things took a better turn afterwards, and I feel much easier in my mind. I don't think there will be a 'civil war' now."

As the months passed and March 24th appeared in his engagement book, he scrawled the words WAR CLOUD. His friend Frieda Lawrence wrote later that when he visited her and D. H. Lawrence, "Eddie was late and excited and told us, "I believe Sir Edward Grey has just prevented war with Germany."

Sidney Reilly was a rich man by now, with an established position in St Petersburg's society. He sent Nadine to Nice, expecting it would be safer for her there, and planned to join her later on. Germany declared war on Russia on August 1, 1914. And Reilly would play a significant and dramatic role in the Great War that ended a comfortable way of life for a great many people in a relatively peaceful world that would disappear forever.

3

War

THE EFFECT OF WAR ON RUSSIA was disastrous in every possible way from the very beginning. The first days of battle were only the first of a series of catastrophes and disgraces before a general retreat in the spring of 1915. The generals took out their frustration at their own incompetence, the ineffectiveness of their troops, and insufficient weapons and ammunition, on a stubborn civilian population that refused to help them. Enormous tracts of land were violently laid waste as millions were driven out of the way of the armies with whips.

All that War Minister Polivanov could claim was that he placed his trust in 'the impenetrable spaces, impassable mud, and the mercy of Saint Nicholas.' In other words, Russia was caught unprepared and its generals had no idea how to fight the militant German armies, since the strategies and tactics of modern warfare were "beyond them." General Ruszky admitted that they simply could not keep up with the Germans.

One of Officer Stankevich's engineers explained the situation in his own words: "It is hopeless to fight with the Germans, for we are in no condition to do anything, even the new methods of fighting become the causes of our failure."

The Russian generals were helpless in the face of modern warfare. All they could do was call for new mobilizations of fresh recruits when their own unarmed troops were slaughtered. About fifteen million men were mobilized and filled the depots and barracks and points of transit which were overcrowded. They were stamped on, and stepped on each other's feet, while wondering where they were, why they were there, and what they were supposed to do. About five and a half million were killed, wounded, and captured, in no time at all, and the numbers of deserters continued to grow.

Soldiers joked with gallows humor of their bravery in managing to retreat.

"Poor Russia!" said the generals; "the army consists only of cowards and deserters."

Russian successes against Austro-Hungary came about only because the Austrians were even more incompetent than they were. The disintegrating Habsburg monarchy had given up long ago. Russia had only been successful in the past against decomposing nations like Turkey, Poland, and Persia. Everyone was looking for someone to blame. They attacked anyone with a German name and scapegoated the Jews by accusing them of treason.

It was said that everyone envied the Allies and hated them.

"England," they said, "has sworn to fight the Germans to the last drop of blood—*our* blood!"

Soldiers were flogged for the most trivial offenses. Russia would lose far more men in the war than any other country, partly because many had been sent to the front without guns or bullets as a consequence of the shortage of munitions and factories to produce them.

Boris Savourin and Grammatikoff saw Reilly off on the platform of Nikolai station, where the Trans-Siberian Express stood, steaming up and impatient to leave. Sidney Reilly had done his best and made a great deal of money.

Two days after his mission for the British Secret Service had ended and the war had erupted, Reilly had been offered a tempting job by a company which had been impressed by his transactions on behalf of Blohm & Voss. The Jivatovsky brothers wanted him to travel first to Japan and then onwards to the United States as a representative of their bank in Russia. He was instructed to buy various raw materials that the Russian Government needed to make explosives and other supplies for the war. Reilly was so awed by the huge salary and commission they offered him that he hastened to accept. He had no idea if or when he might return to Russia.

He and Nadine moved to Japan, which was still Britain's ally, and he became the chief commission agent for the Russo-Asiatic Bank, purchasing Japanese materiel for the Russian Army. But it turned out that Japan had little in the way of war materiel to offer, since they needed it for themselves.

He soon found himself settling down in New York with Nadine, where the fast-paced life of Manhattan suited both of them. They were not yet married, since he still had to arrange a proper legal divorce from Margaret, which Nadine knew nothing about.

Reilly was competing with German agents in America. But, after his experiences with Blohm & Voss, he was accustomed to the German way of doing business. As usual in a new city, he organized an intelligence network and soon became familiar with German commercial and political activities in the neutral United States. Meanwhile, William Melville—who was now head of the reconstructed MIIC—advised his agents in America to keep in touch with Reilly, because the Secret Service needed experienced espionage agents now that Britain was at war.

'M's main men in New York were Sir William Wiseman, chief of the British Purchasing Commission in the US, and Major Norman Thwaites. Although they urged Reilly to work for the British Secret Service again, he was happy and well-paid where he was, and felt he was contributing to Russia's war effort. Nevertheless, he provided them with intelligence material he had gathered on Germany's munitions purchasing program.

Germany was concerned at the amount of war supplies that the American Government were sending to the Allies, and organized sabotage in some of America's munitions factories. Reilly's network of agents identified the German saboteurs and he passed the information on to Wiseman and Thwaites. Although the British Government were none too happy at the wartime situation, they welcomed the German sabotage in the United States, in the hope that it would encourage Americans to want to send troops to the Western Front where they were badly needed.

Meanwhile, Nadine was impatient for marriage. So that, despite his failure to persuade Margaret to divorce him, Nadine and Reilly were married in the Greek Orthodox Cathedral in New York City in 1916. As a result of the press publicity he had arranged about Margaret's death in an ambulance accident, Reilly described himself in the documents as a widower. It would be his second bigamous marriage, possibly even his third.

American public opinion had already swung away from its traditional isolationism from Europe to enthusiasm for joining the armed forces with the British and Canadian fighting men. Nevertheless, America was still a neutral country. But Canadian forces were mounting recruiting drives with whistle-stop tours featuring entertainers who gave performances to draw crowds.

Reilly was attracted to a variety show produced by the Royal Flying Corps in New York in the autumn. He and Nadine were captivated by the dancing of a couple of artists named Fred and Adele Astaire. They were a brother and sister act.

"Their feet," he said to Nadine in amazement, "move like magic."

The show succeeded in persuading him to take part in the war.

Wiseman advised him to enlist in the Royal Canadian Flying Corps (RFC). They expected him to be transferred to England after his training, where, no doubt, he would find himself working for Britain's Secret Intelligence Service again.

He resigned from his job with the Jivatovsky Brothers bank and hugged Nadine in farewell at the train station. Their marriage had already been as troublesome with her moodiness as her previous one to Petr. He advised her to remain in New York until the war was over. Then he enlisted in the Royal Canadian Flying Corps in Toronto.

He was back in England only a few months later, facing the new Chief of the British Secret Service, Commander Sir Mansfield George Smith-Cumming, known in the service as 'C.'

Cumming was very different from Melville, and also from the average British civil servant, but somehow typical of traditional Edwardian English eccentrics. Reilly found himself gazing at a stocky fifty-seven-year-old man with snow-white hair, and a wooden leg that made him walk with a limp and a stick. Instead of concealing his self-deprecating humor behind deadpan features like most other Englishmen, he was openly witty and cheerful. He had lost his own leg in a motor car crash. It was said that he had been pinned under his car and had had to cut off his leg with a penknife, in order to free himself to try to help his son who was dying in the driver's seat.

Cumming possessed a wicked sense of humor. It was said—no doubt with exaggeration—that he would occasionally surprise a prospective agent by taking a paper-knife from his desk and sticking it into his artificial leg to see a candidate's reaction. If he showed no surprise, the job might suit him.

Sir Mansfield Cumming came from a wealthy landowning family, and had married well to a very rich lady. He was completely devoted to his job and respected by his colleagues and everyone who worked for him. Since his birthday was on April Fools' Day, he seemed to have been born for a game that was all about fooling people to get whatever was needed.

He had begun his naval career after attending Royal Naval College in Dartmouth. He was acting sub-lieutenant on HMS *Bellephron* in 1878. He spent six years patrolling the East Indies, operating against Malay pirates, and took part in the Egyptian campaign, for which he was decorated in 1882. He was listed for retirement as unfit for service as a consequence of increasingly bad sea-sickness. After his second marriage, he lived for many years on his wife's estate in

Morayshire. He was thought to have made secret forays abroad from there to seek out intelligence information. But he worked mainly on constructing and maintaining an elaborate system of boom defences at Southampton.

Like all sorts of Englishmen at the time, the new chief was a Gilbert and Sullivan enthusiast. It was their simple repetitive tunes and their witty commentaries and satires on England's current political, social, and military figures that caught his sense of humour. The foibles and follies of the rich and famous were always such fun to laugh at. It was essentially what made the British different from all other Europeans.

"Uncle Manny" to his nieces, spent much of his time sailing in Southampton Waters, where he owned a houseboat, a motor launch, a luxurious ten-ton yacht, and several other yachts. He loved motor cars, particularly his Rolls Royce, which he drove at considerable speed. He took up flying and obtained his pilot's license in his fifties.

One of his master spies in Russia during the coming revolution would be Paul Dukes. Dukes wrote of him that he appeared very severe at first meeting and his speech was clipped short. He glared at newcomers through his gold-rimmed monocle. But he had a generous heart and would melt if he took to you. He also possessed a tough and ruthless streak.

Cumming established the foreign department of the Secret Service Bureau and his own flat in 2 Whitehall Court. The building was an irregular maze of passages and steps, with oddly shaped rooms in the top level, which was accessed by a private elevator.

According to SIS records, on 15 March Lieutenant Colonel John Dymoke Scale introduced Reilly to Mansfield Cumming with the words, "He is willing to go to Russia for us."

Scale had served with Stephen Alley under Cumming during the murder of Rasputin—known by his code-name as "Dark Forces."

'C' noted in his diary that Reilly was "very clever—very doubtful—has been everywhere & done everything."

Since Reilly was to take out £500 in notes and £750 in diamonds, 'C' felt it "a great gamble as he is to visit all our men in Vologda, Kief [sic], Moscow & c."

Reilly, the so-called 'ace of spies'—brilliant, audacious and uncontrollable— was to work for Cumming over the next several years. That, in brief, was just about all the records revealed of Reilly's initiation into his relationship with the Naval Commander known as 'C,' who became his Chief—except that Reilly had met Norman Thwaites in 1917, and he was the link between him and Lieutenant Colonel John Scale. Scale, in turn, provided the opportunity for Reilly to work for MIIc.

It was said of Reilly that "He was very clever; entirely unscrupulous." It was a form of flattery, since those were the very characteristics required for the job. This incomparable secret agent who would become known as "The Ace of Spies," was initially thought of as "another of Cumming's scallywags."

Reilly would work for the new chief of Britain's Secret Intelligence Service from now on.

In Mansfield Cumming's opinion, Reilly was "a man of indomitable courage, a genius as an agent but a sinister man whom I could never bring myself wholly to trust."

4
No-Man's Land

REILLY WAS COMMISSIONED AS A LIEUTENANT in the Royal Canadian Flying Corps on arrival in England at the beginning of 1917, after which he would be involved in numerous missions behind German lines which, as one author wrote, "are unlikely to have been surpassed by any spy for sheer audacity, before or since."

Secret Service records of his activities at this time are thought to have been since destroyed. As for Reilly's own explanations, he was invariably reticent. He often used a favorite Russian proverb: "The cow that makes the most noise gives the least milk." In fact, he was sworn to be silent about his work under the Official Secrets Act.

As a consequence of his own reticence, the dismissive silence of the Foreign Office, and a tight-lipped refusal to comment by the Secret Service, exaggerated stories of Reilly's wartime adventures gradually emerged after the war. Many came from out of Germany:

"It was said that the German High Command were more afraid of Reilly, the master spy, than of a whole army."

Many of the stories that would be written about him in the popular press in the 1920s and 1930s, were bound to be invented because details of Secret Service affairs were not made public. Journalists generously filled in the gaps with any imaginative exploits they could conjure up to sell newspapers when they were urged by their editors to create news. But the truth, had it been known by the public, was more fantastic than the journalistic fiction, and plenty of readers would have refused to believe it.

According to Robert Bruce Lockhart, who had worked closely with him in Russia, Reilly was dropped behind enemy lines by aircraft many times in Germany and Belgium in various disguises—as a German officer or a private soldier, or as a French peasant. He carried a passport making him out to be a wounded German soldier on sick leave from the Western Front. He had studied the positions of German troops and sent back information to England. It was claimed that at one time he volunteered for the German army and was promoted as an officer, which made him vulnerable to exposure as a spy and eligible to face a firing squad.

According to Thwaites, he impersonated a German officer in East Prussia, where he was free to move back and forth across the German-Russian border, and sent back useful information from both sides of the lines to the Secret Intelligence Service.

One of the few incidents that Reilly himself described, later on, was the one where he posed as a driver for a German Army Colonel who was scheduled to meet the Kaiser and his Chiefs of Staff at German Headquarters close to the Western Front. He killed the Colonel on the way and impersonated him at the secret meeting, to engage in conversation with the Kaiser, Field Marshal von Hindenburg, and General Ludendorff. His mission was to discover whether the German generals were determined to continue the war, or not, after suffering heavy losses. They were short of munitions, food, and oil. That was the meeting where he learned of Germany's plans for U-boat attacks, not only on British shipping, but also to sink all neutral ships without warning, to win the war for Germany by 1918.

The Official Secrets Act prevented his true exploits from replacing the fictional accounts in popular newspapers and magazines, even if his records had not been destroyed, as it was claimed. So that much of Reilly's wartime life and most of his military exploits were still cloaked in mystery.

Those who scoffed at Reilly's alleged daredevil attributes and his own stories of them, and of their importance to Britain and the Allies, were unaware how Winston Churchill praised British secret agents who were imbedded in Imperial Russian military headquarters, so that Britain heard in advance of Russia withdrawing from the war, and in German Staff headquarters where Churchill claimed they were so efficient that he knew what was passing in the minds of the German Naval Staff even before the Kaiser did.

The main threat to Britain at that particular time was the ruthless use of submarine warfare. Even as new U-boats were leaving the assembly lines of German factories, Germany was split into two extreme viewpoints, by the arrogant Prussian Junker class in Berlin who had been born and bred for military domination of Europe, and suffered from delusions of grandeur, and also from other Germans, like Ambassador Bernstorff, who could view the situation more broadly and clearly from their diplomatic positions in the neutral United States.

Desperation had built up on both sides. The German military were as anxious not to fail as the Allies. Battles on the Western Front had been brought to an ominous halt by impassable barbed-wired trenches that extended right across the battlefronts for 440 miles, from the English Channel in the west to the Swiss Alps in the east. They faced a vast sea of mud named "No-man's Land," that stretched far and wide, and waited impatiently for the design and production of enough tanks to bridge the trenches in safety, and the improvements still needed to manufacture safe and effective aircraft to provide air superiority. It was madness to attempt a crossing until then, since no one could reach the German lines alive.

The Allies had finally learnt they could no longer advance directly into rapid machine-gun fire and Howitzer shells as they had been doing. The Battle of the Somme had resulted in sixty thousand British casualties in a single day, and the Allies and the enemy had lost more than a million officers and men in only five months from attempting to confront the enemy head-on. It was suicide.

Germany's military party had concluded since 1915 that Germany could not win the war on land. So the German Navy intended to starve Britain into submission by torpedoing all merchant food carriers and other shipping. Then, with the land war kept going to drain the Allies' strength, the U-boats would finish them off.

It was when Britain's most audacious and effective spy, Sidney Reilly, sought Intelligence information at the enemy's military headquarter behind the German lines by impersonating a German colonel, so that he could assess the true facts and figures concerning the factory output of submarines and their planned U-boat attacks in wolf-packs on unarmed allied shipping bringing food to the British Isles.

Now a new fleet of U-boats was ready for use, and Germany's navy was eager to show off what they could do with them. The question posed by German Ambassador Bernstorff was the same as American President Wilson's: "How can the war be halted?"

Wilson seemed to be focused on his own legacy and isolated from reality. Like most men with almost unlimited power, he would not listen to anyone who did not agree with him. He was waiting for the November presidential election to confirm him in office. Then he planned to make his bid to achieve a settlement between the warring parties instead of involving America in the war.

But Germany wanted all the territories it had so far invaded and now occupied. They stretched across Europe from the English Channel to the frontiers of Russia, and from the Baltic Sea to the Black Sea. They occupied Poland, Rumania, Belgium, Alsace-Lorraine, and industrial France as far as Reims. The empires of their allies were still intact, with Austria-Hungary controlling the Balkans from Italy to Greece. Turkey was still in control from Baghdad to Jerusalem.

Germany had drafted a treaty on the basis of partitioning Russia, annexing three-quarters of Belgium, and incorporating as part of Germany the French Coast from Dunkirk to Boulogne. Those were their terms for peace.

German officials, like Ambassador Bernstorff, Chancellor Bethman-Hollweg,

Sidney Reilly, alias George Bergmann, using a German passport dated
September 1918.

and Secretary of the Foreign Office von Jagow, believed they could now obtain the best terms for peace if they could stop the militarists taking to the U-boats and sinking all foreign shipping. Jagow directed American Ambassador Gerard to return to Washington and persuade President Wilson to intervene before the U-boat onslaught was ready. But Wilson was imprisoned by his own fantasies and, anyway, had to wait for the outcome of the presidential election.

American Ambassador Joseph Grew wired Wilson from the Berlin embassy to inform him that numerous U-boats had just left Kiel with enough food, water, and fuel for three months at sea. Two weeks later Grew met with Chancellor Bethman-Hollweg, who was now aged and weary from stress and anxiety over the intended U-boat war and its unintended consequences. Bernstorff added his own urgent request to Wilson to intervene before it was too late. Wilson brushed them all off.

Britain's Prime Minister Lloyd George was not interested in a settlement either. He was determined that the Allies would make the "knock-out blow" to their enemy. He believed in the power to win of the last man standing and the last bullet to be fired.

In fact, the Allies were in no position to negotiate a favorable armistice. They were helpless after the Battle of the Somme, and powerless to find a way out of No-man's Land. Turks continued to murder Armenians by the million. Poland was a wasteland with no livestock to eat or a stick of firewood left to cook it on. Belgians were still being shipped like cattle into Germany as slave labor. But Wilson remained neutral and refused to send American troops to the war Front.

On January 10, 1917, the three German Chiefs of civil, military, and naval cabinets, met at Supreme Headquarters in the Castle of Pless, to advise the Kaiser of events and decisions. His majesty was described as "pale, irritable, and excited."

Admiral von Holtzendorff rose to define unrestricted warfare, "in the course of which every enemy and neutral ship found in the war zone is to be sunk without warning."

He claimed that German U-boats "could force England to capitulate before the next harvest."

The opportunity, he said, "would never be as favorable again." He added that if they failed to exploit it, there was no way to guarantee Germany's future as a world power. He even guaranteed personally that the U-boat war would result in victory. He required only three weeks' notice in order to commence on February 1.

An official statement to launch the attacks was already prepared for the Kaiser's signature. So was the pen to sign the document: "I order the unrestricted submarine warfare to be launched with the utmost vigor on the first of February . . . Wilhelm IR."

President Wilson was re-elected soon after on an anti-war ticket.

It was then that Germany's Foreign Secretary, Zimmerman, drafted instructions to Ambassador Eckhardt in Mexico to form a triple alliance between Germany, Mexico and Japan, to attack the United States. In return, Mexico would "recover" its lost territories of Texas, New Mexico, and Arizona.

Zimmerman was unaware that Britain's wireless cryptographers in "Room 40" had immediately intercepted his telegram and

Admiral Sir William Reginald "Blinker" Hall, Director of British Naval Intelligence (1914-1919), developed Britain's top secret "Room 40" into an intercepting enterprise of eight hundred wireless operators and seventy or eighty cryptographers and clerks who listened day and night to the military, naval, and diplomatic secrets of the enemy.

decoded it. "Most secret," it began. "For Your Excellency's personal information and to be handed on to the Imperial Minister in Mexico by a safe route."

It clearly dated the commencement of submarine warfare and Germany's intention to keep America out of the European war by distracting it in other directions.

Admiral "Blinker" Hall was the Director of Britain's Naval Intelligence. He saw the German blunder as a lever to drag America into the war on the side of the Allies. But it was a sensitive tactic that required careful thought and diplomatic planning, so he placed the Zimmerman Telegram in his safe.

On February 5, Admiral Hall unlocked his safe after deciding to disclose the contents of the Zimmermann telegram to Britain's Prime Minister Balfour. Balfour instructed Admiral Hall to reveal the message to the American embassy.

Hall met with the liaison officer at the embassy, who immediately realised that publication of the Zimmerman Telegram must trigger a war between America and Germany. They left for Grosvenor Square to inform the American Ambassador, and a formality was arranged in which Prime Minister Balfour officially handed the decoded telegram to Ambassador Page.

"It was," said Balfour, "the most dramatic moment in my life."

President Wilson was so incensed at the German deceit that he immediately released the telegram to the morning papers. It appeared with eight-column headlines on Thursday, March 1, in *The Times* and the *World*. At eight-thirty on April 2, the President advised Congress to "declare the recent course of the Imperial German government to be in fact nothing less than war against the government and people of the United States."

The Senate voted for war against Germany by eighty-two to six on April 6. On America's declaration of war, President Wilson's aide, Colonel House, wrote to Admiral Hall, "I cannot think of any man who has done more useful service in this war than you, and I salute you."

The problem now was the inevitable delay in training and arming American troops and shipping them to the Western battlefront. They were needed immediately to replace Allied troops rushed to Italy in a crisis when the Italian army was overwhelmed by German and Austrian troops and risked being completely destroyed at Caporetto.

5
Revolution

"The weariness of war can be seen everywhere," wrote the director of the Russian police department in his report on the progress of the war against Germany. "There is a longing for a swift peace, regardless of the conditions upon which it is concluded." It was October 30, 1916. In only a few months, police, deputies and generals, land representatives and physicians, and former gendarmes, would insist that the revolutionaries had killed patriotism in the army. They complained that "The Bolsheviks snatched a sure victory out of our hands."

Despite their shortage of weapons and ammunition, the appalling battlefront conditions, and heavy losses of life, the Russians still believed they could have held off the German armies. When the October Revolution erupted a year later, in 1917, it was too late.

The Russian Revolution was one of the most cataclysmic events of the twentieth century. And yet, in Germany at least, there was no visible sign of it that January. Winston Churchill was Minister of Munitions when it erupted suddenly several months later, and resulted in Reilly being sent to Moscow in May of the following year.

The despotic Romanov dynasty of Tsars had ruled Russia for three centuries. Tsar Nicolas the Second had followed their example with a God-given right to rule and treat his subjects as his private property. Most Russians were illiterate and superstitious peasants who stoically coped with their privations and the cruelty of the Tsars' army and secret police, until their final release in to a more compassionate existence that the Russian Orthodox Church promised them in heaven. The aristocracy lived a separate privileged life. As far as they were concerned, their subjects were little more than farmyard animals who would end their days being slaughtered if they did not starve to death in the meantime.

The same thing could be said of Germany with its Prussian military class under the self-absorbed and arrogant young Kaiser. And of the sad old self-centred Austro-Hungarian Emperor, whose impulsive declaration of war against Serbia had forced the Allies and the Central Powers to mobilize their armed forces. Russia was even more backwards—a vast agricultural nation which had resisted modernization and industrialization for too long and made itself vulnerable to wholesale slaughter by the highly-trained and well-equipped modern German army.

The main difference between the German Kaiser and his cousin Nicholas II was that Willi was always impulsively keen to meddle in anything that caught his attention, whereas Nicki was "a narrow, rather dull-witted young man of no vision and only one idea: to govern with no diminution of the autocratic power bequeathed by his ancestors." His views were petty and he was indifferent to affairs beyond his understanding:

"One reads about the strange things that happen in the world," he remarked with amazement, "and shrugs one's shoulders."

The Kaiser's attitude towards life in general and his subjects in particular, was demonstrated by the advice he gave his new army recruits: "If your Emperor commands you to do so, you must fire on your father and mother."

"It is shocking," Winston agreed long afterwards to his Private Secretary, when they discussed the Kaiser, "to reflect that upon the word or nod of such a limited individual, to whom all Germans were obedient for thirty years, the forces of war could devastate the world whenever released."

It is often said that the Russian Tsar's downfall was due to choosing the wrong advisers. But even the right ones would have been overruled by his autocratic arrogance as a leader who had been chosen to rule over his subjects by "Divine Right." Tsar Nicholas was the pivotal figure in a self-centered court which was isolated from most of the Russian people.

He was also out of touch with the war against Germany, which was going badly and with far greater losses of life than any other nation drawn into it. Russia's armed forces, although brave and fighting well, were still ill-equipped, ill-treated, and war-weary by the time they mutinied in 1917.

Civilians starved while queuing up for bread in the cities and even in the countryside, through lack of leadership, disorganization, incompetence, chaos, and indifference. It had been a backward nation when it had declared war in support of its Austrian Allies, and was unprepared for modern warfare. Although the Tsar continually changed his ministers, none could alter the destructive course that the Tsar himself had set by his limited worldview and his overbearing attitude towards his courtiers and other subjects. The Russian Imperial Army still held. But it was a recipe for revolution.

According to Winston's view of the war from first-hand experience as Minister of Munitions visiting the battlefronts to take orders for armaments and ammunition from the generals in the field, "Russia had weathered the assaults by German troops despite its shortages of munitions and equipment, and the depots were filled with sturdy troops. General Alexeyev directed the Army and Admiral Kolchak the Fleet." Both were dedicated patriots.

He described the situation to Eddie Marsh as he saw it.

"All that was needed was to lean heavily on the far-stretched Teutonic line, in order to hold off the weakened enemy on the frontline—in a word, to *endure*. That was all that stood between Russia and victory. Despite setbacks, the Russian Empire possessed a far bigger and better equipped army in 1917 than it had started with. In March, the Russian Empire and people stood. The Eastern Front was safe. And victory was certain."

Unfortunately, only a few days later, on March 11, riots erupted in Petrograd, and spread like lightening to Moscow. Four days later a new Liberal Government was formed, headed by Prince Lvoff. It included Constitutional Monarchists and Social-Revolutionaries.

The Tsar abdicated next day when he was blamed for the army's defeat by Germany. One of the worst influences on the Tsarina, the infamous Rasputin, had been murdered secretly a few months previously by patriotic officers. Now his body was dug up and burnt as a scapegoat.

Nevertheless, the war continued against the Germans by patriotic Russian officers. But they were being assassinated by their own troops, one-by-one, on the Eastern Front.

Now there were signs that Russian revolutionaries in exile abroad had begun to return and seize the opportunity to exploit public discontent and resentment, including Bolshevik propaganda leaflets that were openly being distributed in factories and on the streets, announcing they would stop the war against Germany.

The Social-Revolutionaries were led by Kerensky, who held power in a new Government for only a brief moment before he made the fatal mistake of continuing the war when the majority of the Russian population wanted it ended. That was the real moment of crisis.

Boris Savinkov was Assistant War Minister in the Provisional Government at that time.

"You know what I regret," he told Winston and Reilly some time afterwards; "that I didn't have Kerensky assassinated. It would have prevented him from making way for the Bolsheviks to sweep parliamentary democracy aside to take over the nation in a military coup."

Bread queues in Moscow grew ever longer. Russian troops on the Eastern front lacked food as well as sufficient weapons to fight with. Their discipline deteriorated. As military defeats continued against the German war machine, Russian troops continued to murder their officers and desert from the battlefronts.

The Russian Empire fell on March 16. Three weeks later, the United States entered the war.

Lenin, the revolutionary leader of the Bolsheviks, returned to Petrograd at the end of the following month. By September, the horses that pulled the carriages through Petrograd's streets were falling dead in their tracks from starvation. At the same time, committees of private soldiers at the Front deprived some fortunate officers of their ranks instead of murdering them. The main objective was to end the war. They formed committees directed by the overall Military Revolutionary Committee of the Soviets, which was a Bolshevik and a Menshevik organization.

As for the Russian aristocracy and the rich, they looked for ways to make money and replace it with something easier to take out of the country when they had to flee, like diamonds.

Kerensky's liberal interim government made a last effort to save the country, but it had already crumbled by November 8, as Lenin and his followers seized Petrograd first, and Moscow several days later. Lenin's Soviet Government was now in power with a commitment to make peace with Germany.

All order broke down during the following months, and society in Russia was turned on its head. Private soldiers became generals overnight and railway porters found themselves commissars. Bands of anarchists roamed both town and country, pillaging and murdering at will, as criminality became a normal way of life.

As men and women fell dead from starvation in the streets of the cities, Russian troops who were still loyal to Tsarist generals fought the Bolshevik forces while they continued to battle on against the German armies.

Lenin's initial aim was to make peace with Germany. But there was a difference of opinion between him and the revolutionary Léon Trotsky, who wanted to spread communist revolutions all over the world. He was as histrionic and self-regarding as the balding Lenin, but with a mass of wavy black hair and the bushy

Russian revolutionaries in 1919. In the center, Stalin, Vladimir Lenin and Kalinin.

moustache and beard of an arrogant intellectual. Both were icy in their disregard for other people. Trotsky saw himself as a military commander and wanted to continue the war against Germany by forming a Red Army.

British and French governments and politicians were astounded and confused. Most had little idea of the geography of Europe, despite fighting a war there. It was almost impossible to find anyone who spoke Russian in England, even in London's Foreign Office. But Robert Bruce Lockhart had been Britain's Acting Consul-General in Moscow before the revolution, so Prime Minister Lloyd George appointed him to head a special mission to enter into discussions with the Bolsheviks.

"We need Russia to continue as our ally," Lloyd George told him. "Your primary task is to keep Russia in the war. If we fail, all the German troops on the Eastern Front will be freed to overwhelm the Allies fighting German forces on the Western Front."

Lockhart spoke fluent Russian and knew Russia and all classes of the Russian people. He immediately established friendly relations with the Bolshevik leaders, and Trotsky in particular, who—contrary to Lenin's claims—wanted to continue the war against Germany. Lockhart decided that the only way to prevent a separate peace between Russia and Germany was to cooperate with the new Soviet

Government. But Britain's war cabinet were convinced that both Lenin and Trotsky were German agents, so they stalled for time and instructed Lockhart to find evidence.

German troops advanced on Petrograd in February 1918. The economic situation in Russia was so desperate that Trotsky was forced to agree reluctantly to peace terms with Germany at Brest-Litovsk, while the Bolsheviks moved their government to Moscow.

According to the views in Whitehall, Bruce Lockhart was considered to be pro-Bolshevik, so that his advice from the front was considered biased and soon ignored. He was nearly recalled back to England.

Prime Minister Lloyd George, who had personally taken the decision to send Lockhart to Moscow, was playing a double game, since the War Cabinet had already agreed, early in February 1918, against recognizing the Bolshevik Government. Instead, they

Professional revolutionary Léon Trotsky in 1921.

offered funding and arms to anti-Bolshevik groups to continue fighting the Germans as well as the Reds.

It was an ambiguous situation. Churchill was fanatical about getting every shred of information to analyze political and military circumstances to get at the truth. He felt frustrated at knowing that Lockhart was the best person to provide it, but was now almost isolated from communications in Moscow.

By February 25, the Bolsheviks were pulling Russia out of the war against Germany, and views in Whitehall now turned more forcefully to military intervention against the Soviet Government.

Churchill realized that, unless the Bolsheviks were stopped now, their ideology with its debased values would spread like a plague beyond Russia's borders, as far as Trotsky could take it by initiating rebellions throughout the British Empire and beyond. He was adamant when arguing with Lloyd George, "Everything must be done to crush the Communist Government at birth."

With a feeling that their backs were to the wall, Britain's War Office consulted the Secret Service. Cumming's view was that, "if any man could engineer the downfall of the Bolsheviks it is Sidney Reilly."

He sought Reilly's opinion and informed Prime Minister Lloyd George, "Reilly wants to launch a counter-revolution to get rid of Lenin and Trotsky."

6
Riff-Raff

REILLY POSSESSED A PERSONAL HATRED FOR THE BOLSHEVIK LEADERS. He felt that his country had been stolen by criminals, mere riff-raff. To his mind, they were either Georgians, Armenians or Poles who were intent on destroying Mother Russia. Until now, he had sided with the Social-Revolutionary Party. But they had mishandled the situation when determination was necessary, and been confused by circumstances which the Bolshevik revolutionaries had been preparing to provoke and planning to exploit for years.

Britain's Admiralty were also informed by the SIS of Reilly's intention to overthrow Lenin and Trotsky, and were keen for him to return to Russia, too, since he had earned their respect: "Look how he reconstructed the Russian Navy," they said, "and sent us plans of the German Fleet."

The admirals were worried that the Germans might seize Russia's Baltic Fleet. Five battleships, nine cruisers, seventy destroyers and twenty-six submarines had to be prevented from falling into German hands, or the naval situation could become perilous for the Allies. They had already ordered the British Naval Attaché in Moscow, Captain Cromie, to prepare a plan to blow up the battleships, but felt he was too inexperienced on the political side to do it successfully.

The order went out from the Admiralty: "Instruct Reilly to destroy the Russian Fleet instead."

The irony was that Reilly, more perhaps than anyone else, had been instrumental in getting it built and making a fortune from his diplomacy, his business skills, and his labours.

Litvinoff represented the Bolsheviks in London. He gave Reilly a pass for Moscow at the end of April 1918. Reilly was already forty-four years old when he left for Russia on what would be the biggest assignment of his career.

His first hurdle turned out to be not the Bolsheviks but the Royal Navy, who were taking care of British interests in Murmansk. The commanding officer immediately arrested him on seeing his official documents, saying "Reilly? You don't look Irish to me!"

Reilly was locked up in HMS *Glory*, on the grounds that his name had been incorrectly spelt on his pass. Major Stephen Alley was sent for, to interrogate him.

Alley had grown up in Russia and been chief of the British Secret Service there until April of that year. He examined Reilly in his cell on board ship, and Reilly was able to show him a coded message for Bruce Lockhart on a tiny shred of paper he had kept hidden beneath the cork of an Aspirin bottle. As soon as he was released, he hurried to Petrograd.

Petrograd had changed vastly. Its main thoroughfare, the Nevsky Prospekt, was unswept and almost deserted, with endless bread queues, and skeletal-like dead horses and starved human beings lying dead on the streets. Few shops were open. Those that were open were empty of goods. There were no droshkies, since all the horses had been eaten or had starved to death before they could be butchered. A similar air of desolation hung over Moscow.

Captain Francis Cromie had completed his plan to block Kronstadt harbor by blowing up four battleships and fourteen destroyers. But Britain's War Cabinet feared international condemnation and decided that they must consider a policy towards Russia before doing so. They agreed that Cromie and Reilly should only put the plan into action if the Germans were about to seize the ships.

Reilly stayed in Petrograd only long enough to meet Lieutenant Ernest Boyce, who had taken over from Alley as the new head of British Intelligence in Russia, even though Reilly's assignment was completely independent of the Russian section of SIS. Boyce arranged for Reilly to use his cipher staff in Moscow.

Reilly arrived in Moscow on May 7. The ancient city looked beautiful to him in the half-light of early dusk, when he set foot in it again. In the excitement of looking forward to succeeding in his mission, he thought the streets seemed full of life and inviting. Although already late in the day, he went straight to the Kremlin, and banged for entry on the huge red gates. When the surprised sentries appeared, he demanded to speak to Lenin immediately.

Lenin was unavailable, but he met Bonch-Brouevich, who was Lenin's closest friend. Reilly explained to him: "I have been specially sent by the Prime Minister of Britain as a messenger to find out the Bolsheviks' aims."

"What about the British Embassy?"

"The British Government are not satisfied with our diplomat's report."

One of the Soviet Commissars for Foreign Affairs, named Karachan, was suspicious and went to Bruce Lockhart at the embassy to check Reilly out. Lockhart cleared him of suspicion.

Reilly's commanding manner was even more effective in Russia, where he had grown up. Bonch-Brouevich took a liking to him, and thought that Reilly could be useful in representing the Bolsheviks favorably to the British, since they were keen to have the British fighting with them against the Germans, who had angered them by arrogantly imposing what the Bolsheviks considered to be unacceptable

Major Stephen Alley served in Britain's SIS in 1914 and was posted to Petrograd

terms for peace.

Reilly explained that he had returned to Russia because of his interest in the triumph of Bolshevism. After about five meetings between them, Bonch-Brouevich stated that he had now obtained official authorization from Lenin and Trotsky to supply the British with military intelligence.

The War Cabinet in London held a special session on May 11. They decided first to induce Trotsky to blow up the Baltic Fleet, instead of using Cromie's plan. But Trotsky resisted being used by the British, and Britain's War Cabinet hesitated indecisively again. It was, they said, "an unprecedented situation that required considerable thought and planning."

Reilly was now disguised as a Greek from the Levant. He returned to Petrograd to meet with his old friend Sasha Grammatikoff, who was fortunately safe as a result of his friend Vladimir Orloff who had infiltrated the *Cheka*. This was the secret police organization headed by the stern, fanatical and sinister Feliks Dzerzhinsky with his heavy black van Dyke beard and moustache. The *Cheka* was a successor to the Tsarist *Okhrana*.

Orloff was able to provide Reilly with a pass in the name of Mr. Constantine from Moscow, with the *Cheka* imprint stamped on it that enabled him to move around freely. He used a different name at his headquarters at 10 Torgovaya Ulitza in Petrograd, where he was a Turkish merchant from the Far East. Orloff provided him with a franked pass for Mr. Massino. It was Nadine's maiden name.

Reilly lived under three different identities in Russia at first. As well as his own, he was "Massino" in Petrograd and "Constantin" in Moscow. Massino would vanish on arrival in Moscow, and Constantine would disappear before Reilly arrived in Petrograd.

It must have been confusing when he might suddenly have to show his pass, or any other identity documents to the grim gaunt men in the long greatcoats with enormous *Mauser* pistols strapped to their shoulders. They were the dreaded figures of Dzerzhinsky's *Cheka*. Most could neither read nor write and could only recognize the official *Cheka* stamp on identity papers. Travelling was risky, and any behaviour they thought suspicious could result in Reilly's arrest.

Reilly established his main Moscow headquarters in Grammatikoff's niece's flat in the Cheremetoff Pereulok. Her name was Dagmara, and she was a dancer at the Moscow Arts Theater. She shared the flat with two other actresses. Such was Reilly's charm, even in middle age, that it seemed there was nothing that the trio of attractive young girls would not do for him. But, in spite of a number of other mistresses with whom he dallied during his missions in Moscow, Reilly was most often in Dagmara's bed.

When he met in secret with many of the counter-revolutionaries in Moscow, they told him, "There is considerable antagonism against the Bolsheviks, even among the working classes."

It gave him great confidence in the success of his mission. As Robert Bruce Lockhart remarked, "Reilly is cast in the Napoleonic mold. If Napoleon could conquer most of Europe, why shouldn't Reilly take over Moscow?"

Like Lenin, Reilly was convinced that he had to have an alternative government set up in readiness to replace the existing one, before he could plan and direct the overthrow and arrest of the Soviet Government. So, at one of his meetings, he appointed the former Tsarist General Yudenich as the future head of his Russian army.

British Intelligence officer Captain George Hill worked in the SIS with Reilly in Soviet Russia.

Yudenich was very positive, saying "There are thousands of other Tsarist officers in the Moscow area who will join me."

Reilly's Minister of the Interior would be Grammatikoff. He chose Chubersky, another former business friend, to be his Minister of Communications, since it was essential that the telephone and telegraph services, railway tracks, junctions, and roads would be wrestled from the hands of the Bolsheviks to establish sound communications with other counter-revolutionary organizations in other parts of Russia, which was vast. As soon as General Yudenich captured Moscow, he would want to join up with other anti-Bolshevik armies elsewhere. Communications must also be made with other White Russian generals who were resisting the Reds in the south.

Reilly's intention was to orchestrate the entire counter-revolution himself. He told his supporters that, "When victory is assured, our new provisional government will take over. Once we've soundly beaten the Bolsheviks and restored peace, we'll hold democratic elections."

He spent most of June and July identifying and organizing new hideouts for counter-revolutionary cells in both major cities, and making administrative plans for his new government. As part of his mission, he sent reports in cipher to London through Boyce's staff at the British Consulate-General in Moscow. He occasionally met with Boyce and the young British Royal Naval Attaché, Captain Cromie, in Petrograd.

Most of the original Embassy staff had been sent to England for safety in January, when it was downgraded as a consulate. Cromie remained to hold the fort and ensure that the Russian navy would not be lost to the Germans, or the enemy would be more powerful than ever.

Commander Ernest Boyce worked in Soviet Russia as an undercover agent in the British Secret Service under Robert Bruce Lockhart in 1918, and led Reilly into a trap in 1925.

In order not to compromise Bruce Lockhart's cover as a diplomat, Reilly rarely made contact with him at his headquarters at the *Élite Hotel* in Moscow.

At the same time as activities against the Bolsheviks increased, *agents-provocateurs* from the Red side began to appear in greater and greater numbers. Reilly identified each one. Without a legal infrastructure to try them in court or imprison them, his only choice to eliminate them was with a bullet in the back of the head. Since Dzerzhinsky and his *Cheka* randomly rounded up suspected counter-revolutionaries and made arrests or executions instead, Reilly was forced to be as ruthless with his opponents as they were, and was known to be highly dangerous when necessary.

He managed to solve the problem of free movement and communications by having Orloff provide him with identity documents so that his agents could represent themselves as members of the *Cheka*. He now adopted yet another identity as Comrade Relinsky, a plain-clothes *Cheka* agent in Russia, where he could move around in total freedom and even overrule and threaten any *Cheka* police who might stop him for questioning.

Cheka agents almost caught him when he was naked in a girl-friend's flat. She saw him suddenly vanish, wearing only his socks, as they knocked loudly on the door. The agents found only his suit, a shirt, underwear and shoes. Reilly had planned an escape route beforehand, as he always did.

He reappeared calmly and casually and laughing, fully dressed in another suit, an hour after they had searched the premises and left. He grinned at her surprise, and never explained how he had managed to escape, as if it were some kind of a stage magician's trick with a false cabinet.

Another time, when he was travelling by rail to Petrograd, *Cheka* agents halted the train to search for him. As soon as it began to slow down, Reilly surprised a sailor in the lavatory closet, put on his uniform, and pushed his unconscious body out of the window. Then he joined the hunt in the stationery train, wearing the uniform of the Russian sailor.

Reilly was not the only agent spying and working against the Bolsheviks. The French Secret Service Colonel de Vertement was at work in Siberia, where Russia held Czech prisoners of war. He was a small dapper man. But, so far, there was only minimal cooperation between the Allies. Bruce Lockhart was successfully negotiating with Trotsky to release the Czechs to fight against the Germans, while the French colonel was attempting to persuade the Czechs to join French officers and fight the Bolsheviks. French Secret Service headquarters was piled to the ceilings with bombs and dynamite for sabotage operations.

To add to all the confusion, the German Ambassador, Count von Mirback, lived in the same hotel as Bruce Lockhart. Mirback was assassinated on July 6 by a Social-Revolutionary named Blumkin. It was hoped that his murder might provoke the German Government into resuming war with Soviet Russia, which could topple the Reds and enable White Russians to continue fighting against Germany on the side of the Allies.

On the very same day as the assassination, a Congress of eight hundred left-wing Social-Revolutionaries met in Moscow's Opera House. The young Maria Spiridonova was one of its leaders. She had assassinated the Tsar's cruelest governors and was subsequently raped many times over by Cossacks. She made an angry speech against Lenin on the first day of the Congress.

"I accuse you," she cried out, "of betraying the peasants for your own ends and of treating us all like shit."

7
Comrade Relinsky

THE COUNTER-REVOLUTIONARIES HAD MADE THEIR MOVES too soon, before they were ready for a coup. They even managed to arrest Feliks Dzerzhinsky. Although it was one of Reilly's aims, he was not yet ready to hold him. As soon as he heard from his spies that the Bolsheviks were preparing for a *coup d'état*, he hastened to the Opera House in order to warn Lockhart and several agents that the theater was fast becoming surrounded by army transport, armored cars, and Soviet troops barring all exits.

Before reaching Lockhart's box in the theater, he destroyed all his documents in case of arrest, tearing up what paper he could into tiny fragments and hurriedly swallowing them. He tucked others down the side of the seats while the stage and the auditorium were in a state of noisy chaos.

The counter-revolution crumbled. Alexandrovich, who had organized it, was shot by the *Cheka*. Spiridonova was imprisoned in the Kremlin.

Now the fanatical Dzerzhinsky began his revenge in earnest frenzy. Unfortunately for Reilly, he was not only a fanatic who had murdered his own mother, but was also responsible for torturing thousands of innocent people. He once said, "I would order the murder of every bourgeois child in the world if I thought it would further the cause of Communism."

He had organized himself against any counter-revolutionary forces by the day after the Opera House meeting of his opponents. It was the beginning of his frenzy of murders. It would be called the "Red Terror," in which thousands were arrested, many of them hauled out of their beds at night to face a *Cheka* firing squad. Only ten days later, on July 16, the Romanov Tsar and his wife and children were shot dead in the confines of a room where they had been kept imprisoned. It was a message to the world that the tyranny of the Romanov dynasty had finally ended. It also sent a message that it had been replaced by an even more barbaric tyranny of Communism.

Reilly's *Cheka* pass enabled him to escape from Moscow to go underground and reorganize his agents and his forces. He met with Colonel de Vertement, who was now head of the French Secret Service in Russia, and urged him to increase the amount of funds to Boris Savinkov, whom the French were already investing in. Savinkov's anti-Bolshevik forces had advanced on Yaroslavl, whose seizure was intended to coincide with the landing of Allied troops at Archangel.

Savinkov was unaware that the Allied landing had been postponed for two weeks. It resulted in the Reds recapturing the town.

As well as seeking cooperation from the French, Reilly also kept close connections with the United States Secret Service, which was headed by Kalamatiano, a Greek-American who was leading his own anti-Bolshevik activities.

Reilly used his own savings to support his agents and fund his counter-revolutionary units in Moscow and Petrograd, and also obtained more funds from Lockhart in Moscow, as well as from donations by anti-Bolshevik Russian bourgeois families, and from black market activities. In return for individuals funding him, Reilly supplied those who could still afford it with black market food and fuel for the coming winter. He had become a warlord.

Surprisingly, in all the chaos and shortages, the cabarets were still open in Moscow, where there was entertainment to be had in "Yards," at *café-chantant*, in Jan's night-club, and in Petrovsky Park. But Trotsky forbade Allied officers to travel, and warned that Bruce Lockhart might be placed under protective house-arrest.

Ever since the failure of the intended counter-revolutionary coup by Alexandrovich, Reilly had been forced to reorganize and regroup his own forces without its weakest links, and seek out possible collaborators and suspicious *agents-provocateur* he was not sure he could trust. He was still called Comrade Relinsky, and continually active in the heat of a Moscow summer, energetically working day and night to maintain contact with his agents, couriers, and spies.

Meanwhile, the Allied landing in North Russia, which had been delayed, now appeared to be imminent by the middle of July. Lockhart had fallen into line with

Allied policy, but was well aware it was too tragically half-hearted. They could not depict the full picture as he could. He was the man on the spot who knew better about what was happening. But with all the confusion of contradictory information, no one knew what was really going on. Each saw it only from his own different perspective.

Lockhart was now isolated in Moscow, while intervention by allied troops was about to take place in Archangel. On June 4, he told the Foreign Office, "If you do not intervene within the next few days or weeks if possible we shall have lost a golden opportunity."

Captain George Hill was now working with Reilly, of whom he wrote later; "He was a dark, well-groomed, foreign-looking man who spoke English, Russian, French and German perfectly though, curiously enough, with a foreign accent in each case. I found that he had an amazing grasp of the actualities of the situation and that he was a man of action."

Hill had been busy organizing a network of agents and safe houses with couriers, and coding operations, in preparation for the imminent allied military intervention. He also ran a small destruction outfit. He wrote that Reilly "knew the situation better than any other British officer in Russia . . ."

When the Allied Armies finally arrived at Archangel on August 2, in 1918, they were in shamefully small numbers that doomed the expeditionary force from the start: only 1,500 British and French troops. It seemed that, despite their decision to intervene, they were cautious and hesitant about how to go about it. A further 10,000 reinforcements would arrive later on. The final total of 180,000 allied troops included Americans, Italians, Greeks, and Japanese, Serbs, and Czechs.

Only Churchill was firm in his resolve to defeat the Communists. By 26 November he knew enough of what was happening in Soviet Russia to inform his constituents in Dundee that the Bolsheviks were reducing Russia "to an animal form of barbarism," and maintaining themselves by "bloody and wholesale butcheries and murders carried out to a large extent by Chinese executions and armoured cars . . ."

But Winston did not yet have the power to act as he might wish. He was still a young man, and not yet trusted enough to be appointed to the War Cabinet.

As for the others in Britain's Coalition Government, even the Prime Minister was unfamiliar with foreign parts, their culture, their societies, their views or values, or even where specific cities or small nations were on the map. Foreigners and foreign affairs had been disdainfully pushed aside by successive Governments for generations in the complacent British Empire. That was probably why so many British civil servants and army officers often described Reilly as foreign-looking or foreign-sounding, or foreign in his business methods—it was a traditional part of

Feliks Dzerzhinsky, Chairman of the OGPU secret police, was thought to have had Reilly executed on Stalin's orders.

British culture to disdain all foreigners, since they seemed always to be up to some deceit, dishonesty, ineptitude, mendacity, or other form of mischief. How could they be relied upon?

The United States had followed its own isolationist policy towards Europe and took a similar view of foreigners. Both governments were disconnected from reality. And their electorates—who were too uninformed to be able to think clearly about the consequences - wanted a speedy end to the war.

The Bolsheviks quickly requisitioned Lockhart's headquarters, and the *Cheka* invaded the British Consulate-General. Boyce's staff, whom Reilly had used to send his reports to London, desperately burnt their ciphers at the very last moment.

Now that Reilly felt he was almost ready to launch his coup against the Soviet Government, he was limited in the power and range of his activities by a shortage of funds. Bruce Lockhart supported him by providing promissory notes which would be payable in London in pounds sterling. Reilly obtained a great many Russian roubles from willing contributors who were pleased to be able to receive a promise of real money in exchange for the declining value of the rouble. About eight and a half million roubles were obtained in exchange by one small British firm alone, named W. B. Combes Higgs.

Reilly and his agents were now able to distribute hundreds of thousands of roubles to their anti-Bolshevik forces. Other funds were provided to Savinkov, and also to General Alexeyev, who led a small army of former Tsarist officers and Cossacks in fighting against Trotsky's Red Army forces south of the River Don.

8
The Lockhart Plot

Lieutenant Ernest Boyce was Cumming's station chief heading the Russian Section MIIc, and in charge of British Secret Service work in Russia. Captain George Hill headed a separate intelligence bureau which was also responsible to the Director of Military Intelligence at the War Office. His code-name as a British agent was IK8. He was one of the first British officers to land an aeroplane behind German lines, and was considered to be outstandingly brave. He had also masterminded a team of spies who were landed by aircraft behind enemy lines in Bulgaria.

His main job in Moscow was to spy on German troop movements and collect intelligence of Soviet Russian aims. To do so, he had established a personal relationship with Trotsky, and become his air adviser. He also helped Trotsky to organize his own intelligence gathering organization. At the same time, he had to keep track of a German Secret Service headed by Colonel Rudolf Bauer that operated in Russia.

Hill directed bands of mostly former Tsarist officers as guerrilla fighters to harass the German army. As he explained to Reilly, "I've organized my own communications system with a small group of Lett and Estonian couriers, since their own countries were overrun by German troops. So the Letts have been forced to become mercenary soldiers, loyal only to money, to survive. They are a well-trained and disciplined fighting force. But some Letts are already becoming an important part of a loyal guard for Lenin's Soviet Government in Moscow. So it's difficult to know who you can trust."

Lockhart used Swedish couriers from the Swedish Consulate. He informed Reilly that, "The only well-trained and dependable fighting regiments in Soviet Russia are the Letts and the Czechs. Most of the Russian soldiers are fighting only because they are under constant threat of a firing squad from their officers. They stay in the army because the alternative is death from starvation."

But, as soon as the Allies landed in Archangel, Hill was compromised as an enemy, and the Russians ordered his arrest. He swiftly changed his name to Bergmann and escaped underground. Before vanishing, he arranged with Lockhart and Reilly that he would continue to act independently and meet with them daily by arrangement in Tverskoy Park.

All of this information was sent to 'C' in London, and from him to Winston

Latvian rifleman and secret police Checkist, Colonel Eduard Berzin infiltrated British Intelligence in Petrograd to uncover the so-called "Lockhart Plot" for a counter-revolution.

Churchill, who, despite all the complexities and confusion, knew as a consequence what was happening in Soviet Russia better than anyone else.

Reilly's main worry by the middle of August was the inefficient organization of General Yudenich's former Tsarist officers. They were brave but undisciplined, and he was anxious that they might not be able to work according to the precise timetable he had scheduled. He planned to arrest all the Red leaders simultaneously on August 28. The coup was to take place at a meeting of the Soviet Central Executive Committee.

"Instead of hauling them in front of a firing squad and shooting them out of hand, I've decided the best tactic to discredit them is public ridicule - we'll parade them through Moscow's main streets without trousers or under-pants. We can lock them up in cells afterwards."

Reilly's plans did not exclude the influential head of the Russian Orthodox Church, since it detested the godless Bolsheviks who continually repeated Marx and Engels's claim that "religion was the opiate of the people." Reilly and Hill visited Archbishop Tikhon, who was the Grand Metropolitan of Moscow and Patriarch of the Russian Church, and a formidable personality. To make sure of his support, they brought with them two huge suitcases bulging with five million roubles for his offertory box.

Reilly worried about the lack of discipline among anti-Bolshevik troops fighting the Reds. But Hill said "The Red Army are nothing more than an unreliable rabble without leadership at the moment. The Reds depend heavily, instead, on a regiment of Letts as their élite troops."

It was towards the end of August 1918, when the Allied expeditionary force expected to land at Archangel, that Colonel Berzin, who commanded one of the three Lett regiments, and another officer named Schmidhen, visited Bruce Lockhart with a letter of introduction from Captain Cromie.

"We Latvians," they explained to Lockhart, "have no desire to fight for the Bolsheviks against the Allies. We want you to connect us with the Allied forces in Archangel. For that, we need official passes."

Lockhart gave them passes to Archangel and introduced them to Reilly who, as it turned out, already knew them. The Lett officers had previously initiated discussions with Reilly at several meetings at the *Tramble Café* in Yverskoy Boulevard over a period of two days, when they claimed they despised Soviet Russians, and had already begun to make plans to overthrow Lenin's Government.

Berzin commanded one of the Latvian regiments which was scheduled to guard the theater where the Soviet Central Executive Committee planned to hold a meeting. So his visit was fortuitous. It meant that Reilly might even have Lenin and Trotsky arrested by their own paid security guards. To ensure the loyalty of the Latvian regiments, Reilly provided them with a generous supply of roubles and promised them more after the coup.

In the event, the Bolshevik meeting was postponed from August 28 to September 6, giving Reilly and Boyce more time to organize their plans for an uprising in Petrograd to coincide with a coup in Moscow. Reilly also had plenty of time to schedule meetings with Captain Cromie; and with Colonel de Vertement, in order to involve the French Secret Service in the plan.

Unknown to Reilly until several days later, the *Cheka* invaded the French Secret Service

Captain Francis Cromie, heroic Naval Attaché at the British Embassy in Petrograd and undercover agent for the Secret Service under Robert Bruce Lockhart. Murdered by the Cheka while protecting confidential embassy documents.

Headquarters in Moscow after he had left for Petrograd. De Vertement made a sudden and swift dash to escape across the rooftops. But Dzerzhinsky's police found the stockpiled explosives, and arrested six French agents. They were accused of plotting with Lettish agents to overthrow the Soviet Government.

As soon as Hill learned what had happened, he sent a courier to warn Reilly in Petrograd. But his courier never arrived at the destination.

Reilly finalized his plans in Petrograd, but was shocked to discover that two of his hideouts had been raided by the *Cheka*. Evidently Soviet Russia's secret police were intent on hunting him down. Just as Reilly had been satisfied that he was about to achieve his objective, he became overwhelmed by doubt and a devastating anticipation of failure.

Then—on the last day of August, when Lenin was about to leave a meeting at a factory in Moscow—a young woman Social-Revolutionary named Dora Kaplan fired three shots at him at very close range. She did not manage to kill him outright, but his chances of living much longer were considered only slight.

Despite the fact that Lenin's attempted assassination had been carried out by Russian Social-Revolutionaries, it resulted in Bruce Lockhart's arrest by *Cheka* gunmen, who hauled him to their headquarters in the Lubianka Prison.

Once there, he was taken into a temporary room for interrogation, together with Dora Kaplan, while his flat was being searched. They thought she was one of his agents. While there, Lockhart managed to get rid of an incriminating notebook by tearing out pages and throwing them down the lavatory with two armed guards outside. Since there was usually a shortage of toilet paper, the torn scraps raised no suspicion.

Both Dora Kaplan and Lockhart were interrogated by Dzerzhinsky's chief assistant, Peters, who was Vice-President of the *Cheka*. He wore a leather jacket over khaki trousers, and carried a huge *Mauser*. What he wanted to know was their relationship, and where Reilly was. Lockhart insisted on his diplomatic immunity and refused to answer. He was released for the moment.

Dora Kaplan was not so fortunate: she was shot dead by the Commandant of the Kremlin, named Malkoff. It was said that she was in a state of exaltation, believing she had succeeded in ridding the world of Lenin. One of her bullet shots had gone through his coat. Another entered his left shoulder. Her third bullet struck his jaw. Although Lenin survived, he never completely recovered. Her assassination attempt probably resulted in the strokes that affected his health and eventually killed him.

Known by her closest friends as "Fanny," Kaplan was one of seven children born to a middle-class Jewish family. She was twenty-eight years old when Malkoff killed her. She was one of the very few people who had the courage to attempt to assassinate a ruthless tyrant who was prepared to sacrifice the lives of millions for his compulsion to dominate. Fanny belonged to the same revolutionary group as Usov and Kozlov, who had attempted to assassinate Lenin previously but failed. It was headed by Semenov. She had been Semenov's third choice only because she was partly blind.

Reilly was still in Petrograd on the day of Lockhart's and Fanny's arrests. The sudden and unexpected situation forced him to recognize that his plan for a surprise coup had failed. Disguising himself as an unshaven workman, he attempted to make contact with Captain Cromie in what was the former British Embassy. But he was too late. *Cheka* gunmen had already gone there to search for him, and raided the premises.

Naval Officer Cromie had resisted to the end; "with a Browning in each hand," he had managed to kill a commissar and fight off several *Cheka* thugs, before being riddled with bullets. Falling to the foot of the consulate staircase, he was kicked and trampled on, before his body was tossed out of a second floor window.

Cromie's body was recovered by the Netherlands Minister in Russia who looked after British interests. A Swiss Minister stood by Cromie's graveside to express his sympathy and admiration for the courageous British hero who had died fighting the Communists.

9
"The Extraordinary Commission"

ONE AMONG MANY QUESTIONS that confused the British Government was precisely what was happening in Russia. As a parliamentary democracy, they needed to understand, for example, what exactly was Dzerzhinsky's Red Terror?

The "Extraordinary Commission," popularly known as the Red Terror, was unprecedented in that it was not an investigating commission. Nor was it a tribunal. The Bolsheviks had dispensed with such legalities. The Red Terror was an organ of struggle in a civil war, in which they did not even bother to judge their enemies before torturing or killing them. As they described it, their intention was to "exterminate the bourgeoisie as a class."

"We are not looking for evidence or witnesses to reveal deeds or words against the Soviet power. The first question we ask is—to what class does he belong, what are his origins, upbringing, education or profession? Those questions define the fate of the accused. This is the essence of the Red Terror."

Without that knowledge of what Lenin was up to, many of the British public thought that the Communist Revolution was "a good thing." There were already plenty of communists in Britain who were completely ignorant of what was going on or what communism actually meant.

Lenin was keen to *exterminate*—his word—as many people as he could who did not fit into his own ideological theories of what a Marxist society should look like. He condemned specific categories of people whom he considered did not belong. He had his own little list for executions. They included prostitutes, work-shirkers, bagmen, speculators, and hoarders, whom he labeled as criminals.

Lenin was a puritan, and they were only some of the "harmful insects" he listed for extermination. That loose epithet of his was a catch-all to include anyone who might disagree with him. Among them were "former *zemstvo* members, people in the Cooper movements, homeowners, high-school teachers, parish councils and choirs, priests, monks and nuns, Tolstoyan pacifists, and officials of trade unions". All would soon be classified as *former people*.

Zemstvo was a liberal institution in Tsarist Russia dedicated to emancipation and reform. Cooper followers were Black feminists named after Anna Julia Cooper.

The alert and efficient Dzerzhinsky put his firing squads in action again by executing 500 people in Moscow and 700 in Petrograd. It was estimated that more than 8,000 were believed to have been shot to death in similar executions in other parts of Russia. No prominent Social-Revolutionary remained alive by the end of the Red Terror. Even so, the Bolshevik press howled for blood and still more blood. Zinoviev, who was one of Lenin's closest friends, called for the annihilation of ten million so-called anti-Bolshevists.

All of it would have been inconceivable to the law-abiding British Government and people, who wanted to know what was happening in Soviet Russia. And yet, the Soviet Government were not in the least bit reluctant to boast about what they were doing:

"We will make our hearts cruel, hard and immovable," they claimed, "so that no mercy will enter them. Without mercy, without sparing, we will kill our enemies in scores of hundreds; let them drown themselves in their own blood. Let there be floods of blood of the bourgeois—more blood, as much as possible."

10
Blood-Lust

EVERY POSSIBLE CRUDE AND BRUTAL MURDER was committed gleefully by a gloating savagery that undertook revenge against former imperial officers, out of relief and jubilation at no longer being restricted by the authority of the Tsarist regime. The excitement of torture, the screaming of their victims in pain, and the abundance of blood, appeared to have turned them into wild animals. But that would be a generalization, since the bloodbath was perpetrated by those who were already wild animals, criminals, or men made mad beforehand by oppression. Everyone had a score to settle, and now that they were given permission by their new leaders, they could not stop. To call their murders an addiction would be an understatement, since it was an obsessively powerful and unrestrained blood-lust.

Concerned at what was to come, Reilly headed immediately for Moscow. His *Cheka* pass got him onto the train at Petrograd. He left it forty miles before Moscow at Kline, to avoid a thorough inspection at the barrier in Moscow train station, since he knew the *Cheka* were looking for him. Then he hitch-hiked in short stages whenever he saw a horse and cart.

Placards were placed throughout the city featuring a portrait of Reilly with a reward of 100,000 roubles for his capture, dead or alive. His photograph and description were also featured in the press. The *Cheka* had orders to shoot him on sight.

"The Lockhart Plot" to murder Lenin and Trotsky was headlined across all the newspapers. Russian journalists denounced "Anglo-French bandits" who had conspired in a foreign plot to overthrow the Soviet Government. Bruce Lockhart was named as the planner and organizer, and Reilly as his chief spy. The Lettish Colonel Berzin was said to have confessed. Pravda demanded that the scoundrels be handed over to the Revolutionary Tribunal and shot.

When the Cheka arrested a number of young women, according to Hill—who was in the same prison—eight of them admitted under interrogation to being Reilly's wife. Although they came from all levels of society, they had one thing in common; they were all beautiful. Hill said afterwards that there was furious jealousy and fighting between the eight so-called wives. They were placed in a cell with thirty other women. What happened to them afterwards was unknown.

What was known was that Reilly's clear and disciplined plans suddenly collapsed. And, since evidently someone, or several of his agents, had confessed and provided information under torture or threat of a firing squad, he dared not go to any of his usual hideouts. He went instead to a cheap attic in the Malai Brommaia off the Tverskoy Boulevard, where a White Russian was unquestionably loyal to him and they had never made contact at his home before.

He sent a message to Dagmara from there, and found that she was still alive. He heard from her that Bruce Lockhart was now imprisoned in the Lubianka Prison. Hill, still posing under his Bergmann identity, had managed to be released and was working underground again.

The *Cheka* had made a random search of Dagmara's flat on the previous day. Although she had been able to conceal a bundle of roubles in her knickers beneath a spacious skirt, one of Hill's couriers arrived when the gunmen were there. Her name was Vi. She was quick enough to assess the situation and say that she was a seamstress. Hill always used female messengers who carried packaged handmade blouses with them as evidence. But soon after Vi had been allowed to leave, an American secret service agent arrived with a message for Reilly and became hysterical when grilled by the *Cheka*. Although Dagmara had convinced the *Cheka* of her own innocence, they arrested the American agent and Dagmara's flatmates.

Dagmara's father was taken soon afterwards, since it was his residence. He was shot to death by the *Cheka*. They also arrested another mistress of Reilly named Yelizaveta Otten, and a divorced lady he had promised to marry, named Olga Starzheskaya - both of whom insisted he had never discussed politics with them. Olga knew him only by his cover-name of Konstantin Massino, whom, she said, supported the Bolsheviks.

Reilly heard the bad news and sent Dagmara to Hill, to let him know he was safe. She was to ask Hill to visit him. Hill did so

"We need to regroup," Reilly told him eagerly. "We must contact all our couriers, our agents, and our forces again, to reorganize and renew the fight."

Hill could see he was undefeated. "It's no longer safe," he argued. "We can't trust anyone. The timing isn't right. Dzerzhinsky's men are under intense pressure to find you and kill you on sight."

Reilly was hesitant to give up after all he had already organized.

"Your priority is to escape," Hill assured him, "while it's still possible to return to England and make your report to SIS headquarters in London. They'll be expecting you to do that."

Reilly always preferred to do the unexpected, and hesitated again.

"You can't let them down."

Although Reilly hated to give Dzerzhinsky the satisfaction of capturing him, he wavered. When he and Hill considered who might have been the traitor who had given them all away, they could not come to any firm conclusion.

"I can't believe it was Berzin," Reilly said. "I'm absolutely convinced he was loyal to us, He really hated the Bolsheviks."

"Even so, one of the Colonel's own men could have betrayed him".

In what was an inflammatory situation, Reilly finally agreed to escape to London. While Hill made all the arrangements, Reilly slept somewhere else every night in his clothes, with his boots on in readiness, in case of betrayal. They met by arrangement each day at the Paskeller Café.

As soon as Hill provided him with his own passport in the name of Bergmann, Reilly prepared to head for Petrograd for the last time.

Remember *Hillishka*," he reminded Hill on parting, "I promised to give you Feliks Dzerzhinsky's Rolls Royce when our counter-revolution succeeded?"

"There'll be another chance."

Reilly looked doubtful for the first time. "Perhaps. You were going to give me your beautiful matching tortoiseshell hairbrushes in return."

Hill nodded. "I remember."

He brought them to Reilly as a parting gift before Reilly escaped safely on the train to Petrograd.

From Petrograd, Reilly bribed his way aboard a cargo ship on the River Neva. As he made his way back to London, the story of who had betrayed him appeared in the Russian newspapers. It turned out to be the French journalist René Marchand. Marchand proudly boasted to the press of his loyalty to Russia's new government and the newly freed Russian people, by betraying Britain's spy. The French Secret Service had made the mistake of passing confidential information to Marchand when his sentiments were evidently on the side of the Communists.

It was the end of Reilly's monumental dream to free Russia of tyranny and provide justice for everyone by crushing the Communist bandits at birth.

With the failure of Reilly's counter-revolution, British Prime Minister Lloyd George's patience with Winston was almost exhausted. He threw up his hands with impatience.

"You and I have got a problem, Winston. You see yourself as some kind of Saint George on a white horse. You've never forgotten that cavalry charge with your lance at Omdurman. You are obsessed with freeing the Russian people from slavery by charging through Moscow to slay the dragon."

Winston puffed equably at his cigar. "You may be right, David. But keep in mind that what Soviet Russia is implementing is the biggest social engineering experiment ever in history. They are forcing people to fit into their own blueprint. Those who don't fit are cut down to size until they do."

The two politicians had generally seen eye-to-eye in the past. Only a decade earlier the Conservatives had nicknamed them the

Known as the "Terrible Twins" by the Conservative Opposition, Lloyd George was Chancellor of the Exchequer when young Winston was Under-Secretary of State for the Colonies in Prime Minister Campbell-Bannerman's Liberal Government. (1907 Photo).

"Terrible Twins" when they had attempted to redistribute more wealth to the poor by increasing taxes on the rich. Now Lloyd George was caught in a moral dilemma, as well as a political one, in which he knew he'd be damned if he intervened in Russia's revolution, and damned if he recognised the Bolshevik Government.

Lloyd George had learned a great deal about the situation in Soviet Russia from Reilly's confidential reports to Cumming, which had never been equalled before in their searching and common sense observations of situations and their analysis and conclusions and advice to the War Office. As a result, Lloyd George would surprise others with his own newfound knowledge of Russian affairs. But despite what he read, he still thought in parochial British political terms and was convinced that Communism was just a fad, a mere whim that would soon pass away.

11
Sentenced to Death

IN A TIT-FOR-TAT RESPONSE TO BRUCE LOCKHART'S ARREST by the Russian Communists, the British Government arrested their London representative, Litvinoff, and held him in Brixton Prison. A prisoner exchange of Litvinoff and several other Bolsheviks was arranged, with Lockhart, Hill and Boyce being duly released from a common jail where they had been held with Russian criminals, fifty or sixty to a room, and barely survived on starvation rations of cabbage water and tiny pieces of black bread. Fortunately, their menu was supplemented by the American Red Cross.

They left for London on October 2, guarded in a special train by reliable Latvian soldiers. They arrived in Aberdeen on October 18 without Hill. When they had passed through Finland, he had been ordered by the SIS to return to Russia to undertake sabotage, including blowing up bridges. He completed his sabotage operations in Russia and reached London soon afterwards. Major Alley had returned to London much sooner when he and Boyce had been posted to SIS headquarters to work with Cumming in London.

Reilly had to find his own way back to England by boat, through Sweden. He was in London at the beginning of November, where he and Hill were instantly awarded with medals—Reilly with a Military Cross and Hill with a DSO—in recognition of acts of exemplary gallantry during active operations against the enemy.

Due to lack of coordination between civil service departments in Whitehall, at the same time as Cumming was making arrangements to honor Reilly, Britain's Foreign Office was doubting Reilly's good faith. As Robert Bruce Lockhart had been the man-on-the-spot working with Reilly, he confirmed Reilly's loyalty to the Crown.

As soon as he made his official visit to 'C,' Reilly said eagerly, "I want to return to Russia immediately."

"What's the hurry?" Cumming said. "It will still be there for you tomorrow."

"I've been thinking a lot during my trip back home about how to arrange another operation to overthrow the Soviet Government."

Cumming shook his head wisely. "You and Hill are going on leave first. You can return to South Russia in December. Now, sit down—I've got a lot of questions for you and I'm all ears. I want to know the strength of the anti-Bolshevik forces in Russia, particularly General Denikin's White Russian forces. As you know, Mr. Churchill is now Secretary of State for War, and he is one of the biggest users of our intelligence information. Denikin is his man. And the Prime Minister, the

War Office, and the Admiralty all need information to make their own decisions."

Reilly had had few opportunities to wash or shave properly for months while hiding in Russia and travelling by sea and across continents. After being debriefed by 'C,' he said, "Now I think it's time for a bath."

"Somewhat overdue, I'd say!" Cumming remarked jovially.

Reilly went to the *Savoy Hotel*, where he had a bathroom adjoining his suite. He had invited Lockhart and Boyce to a champagne lunch, over which he described how he had escaped.

The war against Germany ended on November 11. Reilly celebrated by inviting Lockhart, Rex Leeper, and their wives, to a party at the *Savoy Hotel* on the following day. Leeper was in the Intelligence Department of the Foreign Office and had been a party to the exchange of Litvinoff for Lockhart.

Reilly greeted his guests in the immaculate Captain's uniform of the Royal Canadian Air Force. They had supper in Reilly's suite, where the women were dazzled by the magnificent claret-colored silk dressing-gown which he changed in to in order to show off. They also admired his tortoiseshell hair brushes which, he told them, he had received as a gift from Hill.

Next day, Lockhart took Reilly to the Russian Ballet at the Coliseum Theater with novelist Hugh Walpole and Don Gregory. Walpole had been involved in propaganda work in Russia. Gregory was the head of the Foreign Office's Northern Department, which included Russia. Hill joined them for supper afterwards in Reilly's suite.

"I must apologize again *Hillishka*," Reilly said on greeting him, "for not being able to give you Dzerzhinsky's Rolls Royce."

Instead, Reilly presented him with a pair of inscribed silver hairbrushes to replace the tortoiseshell ones that Hill had given him. The inscription engraved on the silver read "From S.T.1."

The young woman in Reilly's life for the next month, at least, was a London hooker who apparently plied her trade in the agreeable West End neighborhood of Curzon Street, or some other such oasis in Mayfair, off of Park Lane. She was in her early twenties, fair-haired and always elegantly dressed. She possessed a joyful and exuberant view of life, encapsulated in her nickname, which was "Plugger." She knew nothing about Reilly's previous life since, as a secret agent, he had received no public credit for his mission to overthrow the communist government in Russia. It was Robert Bruce Lockhart who was hailed as the hero for the alleged "Lockhart Plot."

Regardless of their heroism and the secrecy about most of what had happened in Soviet Russia, Reilly's name and his covert operations had been raised on at least eight occasions in the House of Commons during October and November in 1918. Opposition leader Ramsay MacDonald and Joseph King (Liberal M.P. for North Somerset) demanded details from the Government about the situation which had resulted in Lockhart's arrest. They asked for a complete report on his work in Russia. But Secretary of State for Foreign Affairs Arthur Balfour, and his Secretary Lord Robert Cecil, deftly countered all questions – an almost careless skill for which the cool Balfour was known.

Nevertheless, Joseph King launched a firm and angry attack on the Government on November 14 for its policy towards Russia and its misuse of Secret Service funds. He accused the Government of withholding the facts because it might damage its electoral chances:

"We may be sure it [the report] is not going to be communicated to this House before the General Election."

Having referred to the remarkable case of Mr. Lockhart, "whose report on very important events is not yet available," he made an indirect reference to Reilly, by pointing out that the government had immensely increased the amount of Secret Service funds in recent months. Records showed that one officer had been provided with £120,000 in one week in Russia with the purpose of starting a counter-revolution.

"What are all those operations which our Government do not dare for a moment to disclose to us?"

No reply came from the Government, since the "Lockhart Plot," as it was called, had failed, and they were eager to consign it to the past. Nor did Prime Minister Lloyd George wish to draw attention to the failed allied military intervention which had been too weak and in which losses had been too many.

In the meantime, the Communists in Russia staged a trial of Bruce Lockhart in his absence, in which both he and Reilly were sentenced to death. The sentence would be carried out on either of them if they ever returned to Soviet Russia. The *Cheka* held other prisoners who had been involved with them and who were destined to be moved from the court to a firing squad. They included Kalamatiano, who had headed the American Secret Service, a Russian staff officer who had been one of Reilly's most effective agents named Colonel A. V. Friede, his sister and one of Reilly's women, and also the headmistress of the French school in Moscow, Jeanne Morans.

Reilly and Hill were briefed by 'C' before they returned to South Russia. They were surprised to run into the famous Polish pianist Paderewsky on board the cross-channel steamer for the night-time crossing from Southampton to *Le Havre*. He had been a friend of Reilly's mother, and it was said that he had given piano lessons to Reilly's half-sister. He was now on his way back to Poland to become

Prime Minister. He invited Reilly and Hill to share his cabin.

Once arrived on the other side of the Channel, the two British agents took a train to Marseilles, then embarked on several trips in British destroyers to Russia on Christmas Day. Their cover identities from the Department of Overseas Trade described them as two British businessmen investigating trading possibilities with the Russians. What they found was that, despite the chaos all around them and in the White Russian forces, the military position of the White Russian troops appeared to be firm, and they would continue to fight the Red Army.

Hill returned to London after only a few weeks, to report to 'C', while Reilly stayed in Russia for another fortnight. He returned to England in February 1919, when Cumming had another assignment for them both: they were invited to attend the Peace Conference in Paris and observe the White Russian delegation and the Bolsheviks.

Cumming had arranged with the Director of Naval Intelligence, Rear Admiral "Blinker" Hall, that the two agents should pose as Russian experts attached to the British Naval Mission to the conference. They stayed at the *Majestic Hotel* for their first week in Paris. It was there that Reilly was introduced to Winston Churchill for the very first time. Reilly was so deeply impressed with Churchill that he idolized the new British Secretary of State for War.

A frustrated Churchill had written to David Lloyd George at that time to say that he deplored the absence of British policy towards Russia, and that he had none himself.

Reilly introduced Churchill to Boris Savinkov, who had managed to escape from Russia and continued to fight Bolshevism from the West. Churchill respected Savinkov greatly, and proceeded to provide a great deal of encouragement and support to Savinkov and Reilly from then on.

Winston Churchill was by no means a typical aristocrat. Nor could he be categorized as a member of the ruling classes. He had rebelled against his class, like Sidney Reilly had done, partly because of their complacency and injustices. In retaliation, gentleman of the ruling classes did not recognise him as one of them. Churchill felt that was to his advantage, since, as far as he was concerned, what was typical of them was lassitude, complacency, incompetence, and confusion.

He was viewed as a "cad" and a political turncoat for abandoning the Conservative Party for the Liberals. Moreover, his close friends were considered to be raffish because they were individualists. At best, Churchill was considered to be a "delightful rogue who lacked political judgment."

Churchill's image would change sharply later on when he had proved his leadership abilities, so that people forgot his earlier image, or the one with which he had been smeared by the political opposition. Nevertheless, his reputation hung in the balance for some time as "unscrupulous, unreliable, and unattractively ambitious."

Ambition was disapproved of in England as ungentlemanly; a deplorable characteristic of new-rich adventurers and Americans. Despite the findings by the Dardanelles Commission which exonerated him from any blame, his so-called "failure" at Gallipoli was deliberately blamed on him by his opponents at every possible opportunity, hoping that it would smear his reputation for all time.

With all that adversity from the ruling classes, his increasingly successful career as a politician and a Minister of the Crown demonstrated his extraordinary gifts. They were so unusual for a civil servant or a politician at that time that, despite continual disparagement by the Conservatives, he could not be ignored for long.

Churchill had only just been appointed as Minister of War and Air, and had already begun to do what he always did when given the responsibility of heading up a new Ministry: he sought out all the information he could obtain through his personal contacts and relevant literature, and from what were called the "flimsies"—meaning reports from Britain's espionage agents, like Sidney Reilly. He knew that situations changed from day to day, so he was a keen, quick, and enthusiastic learner of new intelligence information.

When Churchill had been Minister in charge of the Home Office, he had taken a personal view of the situation of émigrés from overseas at first-hand. They included Anarchists and Marxists who stirred up trouble with their guns and bombs. He had studied the penal system and improved the conditions of Briton's prisons and its prisoners. As First Lord of the Admiralty before and during the war, he had visited all the naval docks in person to improve their efficiency, and proceeded to modernize the Royal Fleet and improve the conditions of its sailors. He had encouraged and supervised the switch of power for battleships from coal to oil, even to the point of ensuring supplies from oil wells in Persia. As Minister of Munitions during the recent war, he had set up arms factories and improved industrial productivity, travelled to battlefronts to experience the effectiveness of weapons, visited Allied battle-fields, and encouraged the invention of tanks. He was one of the earliest pilots and had initiated the use of aeroplanes by the Navy.

Now that Churchill had been promoted as Minister for War and Air, he had already obtained information about Lenin and Trotsky and their aims, And, as he had said grimly to his Private Secretary, Eddie Marsh, who continued to work for him;

"I am determined that Communism must be crushed before it spreads right across the Continent of Europe and over the Channel to us in Britain."

12
End of an Era

ONE OF THE PROBLEMS OF DEFEATING GERMANY was that Allied soldiers wanted to return home immediately the war was over, and Britain's civilians were war-weary and determined to take up their previous lives again. Since Britain was now virtually bankrupt from the cost of the war, Prime Minister Lloyd George was even more intent on cutting back budgets and gaining more popularity from the electorate than when he had been Chancellor of the Exchequer. He had been applauded as a wartime Prime Minister, but was now faced with a war in Soviet Russia that nobody wanted.

A picture taken by a newspaper photographer several years earlier showed him striding along Downing Street to the House of Commons with the young Winston. Their body language, with Lloyd George's averted eyes, already showed they were at loggerheads with each other. Now the ambitious Lloyd George wished to court popularity in the House, while his young Minister for War blamed him, indirectly, for the weakness of the Allied expeditionary force in Russia that resulted in failure to prevent the rise of communism. They continued to feel much the same way now over Russia's Civil War. The frustrated Prime Minister was heard to exclaim to colleagues in consternation, "I don't know what to do with the boy!"

Reilly was still in France, where he met Major W. Field-Robinson, who was part of the SIS Paris office in the Rue Joubert. They became firm friends. Reilly also became friendly with another of 'C's agents in Paris. She was a singer named Eleanor Toye. Her cover was useful for a member of the intelligence network, since she travelled to most major capital cities. Reilly enjoyed discussing serious subjects with her and elaborated on his own philosophy of life. Her conclusions about him were that although he was unscrupulous in business affairs, his integrity in personal relations was absolute. He was also enormously generous.

Hill left Paris to return to South Russia, while Reilly travelled to New York on leave, to be with his wife, Nadine. It was now two and a half years since they had first met and she had been unhappily married in Russia. The war and his absence had changed her. She had been unfaithful, and their reunion was not harmonious. Perhaps she was retaliating for his many infidelities with attractive young actresses in Hollywood. Evidently Nadine was as nervous, insecure, despondent, anxious, and fickle, as she had been in her previous marriage.

Another marital complication arose for Reilly, this time in London, where his first wife Margaret arrived to take back her husband. She had spent much of the war in Brussels. Now she went straight to the Foreign Office to find out where

Sir Paul Dukes became Chief of British Intelligence in Soviet Russia.

her husband was. 'C' knew little about his agent's private life at that time, and asked Hill, who had not yet left London;

"Just how many wives has that man got?"

Hill asked Reilly when he returned from New York. "I have no wife," Reilly told him abruptly. "There is nothing to discuss."

Margaret hurriedly left England for Brussels, admitting afterwards that Reilly had paid her £100,000 to go away, and threatened her if she refused or mentioned they were still married.

At this time, there was still much confusion in Whitehall about what Britain's attitude should be towards Soviet Russia. Consequently, 'C' left Reilly hovering between London and Paris until Government policy might become more explicit. The Government still hoped there would be a counter-revolution to overthrow the Bolsheviks. But aristocratic Russian émigrés, and the middle-classes and the Social-Revolutionaries who had managed to flee from Russia, were far too disorganized and at loggerheads with each other to react, other than in words, or in providing funds if pressed.

More Russian refugees were fleeing than ever now, most arriving in France and England, and some to the United States. Reilly helped 'C' to analyze the information they brought out, and check its reliability. Cumming made the best use of his special agent by bringing him into discussions whenever the subject arose at SIS headquarters in Whitehall Court, where Cumming's offices sought anonymity in the top three floors of an inconspicuous block of flats. The commissionaires at the entrance were special branch police in disguise.

One of the Secret Service's other most effective agents was Paul Dukes, who was a master of disguises and false identities. He had returned from Russia in 1919 after an epic tour of spying across the country, and became an overnight hero. Reilly met him at Kings Cross Station. The two of them would discuss revolution and counter-revolution with 'C.' When Dukes had first been interviewed for a position in SIS, Reilly had been present and encouraged 'C' to take him on. They had been close friends ever since. Dukes' code-name was S.T.25.

In a preface to his own memoirs of espionage during the Russian Revolution and civil war, Dukes summed up the falseness of the October Revolution even as it erupted. It was an explanation that would have informed Lloyd George's Government and the British public exactly what had happened in Russia—it had been a triumph of propaganda.

"If ever there was a period when people blindly hitched their wagons to a myth, a delusion, and a lie, it is the present."

They were blinded by communism because they followed slogans instead of facts.

"In the helter-skelter of events which constantly outrun mankind, the essential meaning of commonly used words is becoming increasingly confused. Not only the abstract ideas of liberty, equality, and fraternity, but more concrete and more recently popularized ones such as proletariat, bourgeois, soviet, are already surrounded with a sort of fungous growth concealing their real meaning . . . The phenomenon of Red Russia is a supreme example of the triumph of the slogan over reason, and of the political catchword.

"War-weary and politics-weary, the Russian people easily succumbed to those who promised wildly what nobody could give, the promisers least of all. Catchwords such as "All power to the Soviets," which possessed the power to overthrow the Tsarist government, were afterward discovered to have no meaning whatsoever."

"Our intervention in Russia has entered a dangerous phase," Bruce Lockhart pointed out on the day the armistice was signed between Germany and the Allies. "Our victory over Germany has removed our reason for being there. At the same time, the Bolsheviks will be stronger by no longer being involved in war with Germany."

And he was no longer there to report back to England what was happening,

Paul Dukes was summoned to London by 'C' in the summer of 1918. Like Hill and Lockhart, he had spent part of his childhood in Tsarist Russia, and begun a musical career at the *Marinsky Theater*.

After briefly attending a course in ciphers and invisible ink, he was instructed to return to Soviet Russia, finding his way back on his own. He was passed through the frontier by Finnish smugglers and then pressed on alone to Petrograd.

Meanwhile, the Russian patriot Admiral Kolchak advanced with his troops from the east, while General Denikin pressed forward from the south, and General Yudenich marched his volunteer forces from the north-west; all intent on saving Mother Russia from the Reds.

While Reilly was observing the patriotic generals and their volunteer forces at first-hand in South Russia, Dukes had been able to finance the National Center's organization of a rebellion in Moscow and Petrograd. Unlike the other spies, he was a civilian amateur at first. He was adept at improvising disguises and dressing up as different characters. He passed himself off as at least twenty different people over ten months, with twelve different forged identity documents. He even used the papers of a Cheka officer, joined the Communist Party, and enlisted in the Red Army. Much of his time was spent smuggling fleeing White Russian refugees over the Finnish border and escaping from the Soviet secret police.

Evidently Dukes possessed a romantic view of intelligence work, despite the very real dangers of undertaking espionage in Soviet Russia and the gruesome death it could lead to if discovered. Restless young men of that generation were influenced by the best-selling adventure novels of John Buchan and Jack London, with the venturesome spirits of Edgar Rice Burroughs and H. Rider Haggard thrown in.

But, by the autumn of 1919, the Soviet secret police, the *Cheka*, had outwitted Dukes and the National Center, and rounded up a thousand anti-Bolshevik conspirators in Moscow in one night alone. They executed sixty-seven of its leaders. Dukes escaped into Latvia, and 'C' sent Lieutenant Agar to rescue him.

Relieved and excited to be out of Russia, Dukes talked carelessly to a White Russian about his escape, and his confidant repeated it to the Finnish and Swedish newspapers. It may have harmed his future spying in Russia, but both he and Lieutenant Agar were summoned to Buckingham Palace, where King George the Fifth knighted Dukes and decorated Agar with the Victoria Cross for valor.

It was still an era in Britain in which it was considered heroic to lose after risking everything on success, whereas Reilly was influencing the Secret Service to be more professional by winning after risking everything on the possibility of defeat.

13
The Life of Reilly

SIDNEY REILLY NOW LIVED LIKE A GENTLEMANLY BACHELOR in serviced rooms at the Albany, off of Piccadilly, where he entertained his friends in luxury. They included Sir Archibald Sinclair, who was the personal military secretary to Winston Churchill. There was Admiral "Blinker" Hall who was still Director of Naval Intelligence, and Sir Basil Thompson, who was Commissioner of Police and Head of the Special Branch. It was Thompson's task to choose which Russian émigrés could remain in England and which suspected Bolsheviks should be deported.

Reilly was considered to be an excellent host and an amusing and witty conversationalist who could speak authoritatively on most subjects, including history, art, business and religion. He was no longer a Buddhist, but a convert to the

Greek Orthodox Church after marrying Nadine. His dominant topic was Russia and his hatred of the Bolsheviks.

Reilly displayed his valuable collection of Napoleana all around his apartment, with rows of expensive books lining its shelves, which he ordered in huge quantities from Hatchard's book shop, just across Piccadilly from his suite of rooms in Berkeley Square. It was founded in London in 1797 and situated between Fortnum & Mason and the Ritz Hotel. As the capital city's oldest bookseller, it supplied books to the King and royal family at Buckingham Palace.

When Reilly hired a personal valet named Frank Dougherty to be his bodyguard, Dougherty was described as being as sinister as he was.

Reilly now had his suits made by a leading West End tailor named J. Daniel & Co at the corner of Pall Mall and St. James's Street. He lived right in the center of Mayfair, where fashionable hand-made shirts, hand-made shoes and boots from John Lobb, and hats from James Lock (founded in 1676) were available, as well as uniforms; hand-made guns from William Evans (gun-makers since 1883), fishing tackle; and tobacco and cigarettes from Alfred Dunhill in Jermyn Street (since 1893).

Trumper, the King's barber and hairdresser was situated around the corner at 9 Curzon Street. Expensive silverware, china, and jewellery could be bought within walking distance of Burlington Arcade, the Royal Academy, Green Park, and the tea lounge and dining rooms, and downstairs cocktail bar of the *Ritz Hotel*. Reilly also dined with friends at the *Café Royal*, and enjoyed all sorts of other luxuries and necessities available for the elegant man-about-town in London's West End.

Sidney Reilly's luxurious lifestyle was very different from that of a poor eighteen-year-old art student named Caryll Houselander at St. John's Wood Art School. One of the art students who knew Reilly from mixing with several Russian émigrés, introduced him to her because Caryll had expressed interest in Russia. Houselander assisted her mother in managing a boarding house for social misfits. Her bizarre religious and spiritual life could not have been more different from the sybaritic lifestyle that Reilly was now accustomed to in his elegant serviced rooms in Mayfair. She was an introvert and a mystic who had been baptized as a Roman Catholic.

Caryll believed she saw visions through special powers she had inherited of extra-sensory perception. In 1918 she had experienced a vision of the death of the Russian Tsar, before he was murdered by the Reds. She wrote it down.

"I was on my way to buy potatoes. Suddenly, I was held still, as if a magnet held my feet in a particular spot in the middle of the road. In front of me, above me, literally wiping out not only the grey street and sky but the whole world, was something which I can only call a gigantic and living Russian icon . . . It was an icon of Christ the King crucified."

When she read the news in the papers of the murder of the Tsar, she was shocked to see that press photos of the Tsar were the same as the icon she had seen in her vision. This and other of her mystical experiences would draw her like a magnet into "an ecstatic love affair" with Sidney Reilly.

Reilly's compassion was aroused at the mention of her poverty and he was curious to see some of her drawings. Caryll was too shy to display her work to him at first. But after Reilly had bought several of her drawings anonymously through her girl-friend, she was encouraged to meet him.

Caryll was thrilled by Reilly as soon as they met. While others might explain her passion as love at first sight, the shy and introverted young girl thought that he was "little less than God himself." He had come "straight from heaven." It appeared to be a spiritual attraction for both of them, but was, in any case, more or less, the effect that Reilly had on most women he met. He simply took charge of them and they were overwhelmed by his self-confidence and boldness.

Despite Reilly's longstanding idolization of Napoleon, with whom he identified, and his admiration for Winston Churchill, his Catholic upbringing had triumphed and those role models now came only a close second to his admiration for the legendary figure of Jesus Christ the compassionate. Much of what he had tried to achieve in Russia had stemmed not only from hatred of the Bolsheviks, but from compassion for their victims. It was a strangely religious feeling of self-sacrifice, and a hidden facet of Reilly's overdeveloped sense of responsibility that contributed to his ambivalent attitude towards nihilistic Russia.

Reilly helped Caryll with money, so that she could continue with her art studies. Sensitive of her pride, he did so by claiming that the money came from selling some of her pictures for her as an agent.

Comparative religion was one of the subjects he enjoyed discussing, and he explained the doctrines of Buddhism, Judaism, and the Byzantine Russian Church which she wished to join.

Her hair was long and bright red, like Margaret's, but cut in a fringe in front. To Reilly, she had the appearance of a medieval saint, or perhaps a figure from a pre-Raphaelite painting. She was young and eager for love, and he always found beautiful women irresistible, so it was easy for both of them to give in to temptation. She became an integral part of his life in London from then on.

But Reilly had not abandoned his dream of overthrowing the Soviet Government; he was still largely driven by a compulsion to organize a counter-revolution in Russia. He was so self-confident that, even though he had failed in 1918, he was convinced he could oust Lenin and Trotsky if he had another chance. Or perhaps he would help his friend Boris Savinkov to achieve success in leading his own forces this time.

The British Government, and others, also hoped for and expected the overthrow of the Bolsheviks, since nothing like this kind of irrational tyranny, led by an unproven and delusional economic theory, had ever happened before. And surely it could not possibly last. Nevertheless, despatches that reached Britain's Foreign Office described the terrorism of the *Cheka* as "making the history of the French Revolution and the Spanish Inquisition mild by comparison."

Hundreds of thousands of innocent people were still being murdered with almost unbelievable cruelty. Photographs taken of the atrocities were unprintable in the press. According to one report, "The Communists would first strip their victims of their clothes, break their arms and legs, gouge out their eyes and cut off some fingers or a hand before stabbing them all over with a bayonet and smashing in their skulls with hatchets. Men would have their testicles cut off and many women and even schoolgirls under the age of ten had first to submit to rape. Other despatches to the Foreign Office told of people having their mouths slit by bayonets and their tongues cut out. Ex-Tsarist officers by the hundred had their shoulder straps nailed to their bodies then, bound naked in barbed wire they would be lowered into holes made in the ice until they froze to death. Countless others were burned alive, buried alive, thrown into wells to drown or placed in slag gas-pits to die of suffocation. Luckier victims were shot or decapitated with a sword. Beards were torn from faces with the flesh on them, hot needles thrust under finger-nails. Noses were cut off. Some victims were literally sawn in pieces and given to the dogs in the streets to eat.

Sick and wounded patients were taken from hospitals and hacked to death. The canals in Petrograd were filled with mutilated and decomposed bodies. The population of the city declined by 100,000. People who complained about it were shot. No one was allowed to oppose any injustices. Since the Red Guards left their victims to rot where they lay, diseases soon spread and diminished the population still further.

Lenin's policy was not only to break the spirit of the masses by terrorism aimed at forcing them to submit, but also to break their bodies by starvation, so that they were physically incapable of resisting.

Despite Reilly's determination to free his country of the Bolshevik tyranny, the politicians and civil servants in Whitehall resisted the idea of retaliation or any kind of aggression. Bruce Lockhart dismissed them as Old Etonians in the Foreign Office who had not visited Russia to see the tyranny and barbarism for themselves, and did not even speak Russian.

The Foreign Office viewed Reilly as an ambitious adventurer, an upstart who had no place in international politics, a mercenary soldier motivated only by opportunities to obtain money. Even 'C,' who admired Reilly's courage and his service to the country, was puzzled like everyone else because of the secrecy behind which Reilly hid himself. He was full of contradictions. His delusions of grandeur were worrisome. And his reliability was now in doubt.

He was not the only individual to mistrust Soviet Russia. Churchill had a similar problem making his own views felt by Lloyd George and his Coalition Government, since they had no wish to send more troops to Russia. What to Churchill and Reilly was a moral issue was only a political one to them. The more that Winston discovered what the Bolsheviks were up to, the more he argued with the Prime Minister, and the more Lloyd George described Winston as a dangerous man with an obsession to free the Russian people.

Most of the educated people whom Churchill attempted to persuade to support White Russian generals by funding them to continue fighting Trotsky's Red Army, like Denikin, Yudenich, and Admiral Kolchak, had no idea of the difference between Whites and Reds, Bolsheviks, Mensheviks, Communists, Marxists, Socialists, or Social-Revolutionaries. They were all foreigners and probably barbarians with whom they wanted no contact.

Now that the Great War was over, officialdom and its civil servants did not know nor care. Attempts by either Churchill or Reilly to enter into serious discussion on the subject were met by glazed eyes. All that people wanted was to turn their backs with relief on the ghastly experience of having been involved in a European war once again.

14

Savinkov's Champion

UNTIL NOW, REILLY had always been happy with a loose arrangement with the Secret Intelligence Service, so that he could work independently and choose when and where to operate as he saw fit. But now he approached Cumming and told him that he wanted a more formal arrangement to be enrolled as a member of their permanent staff.

'C' found it out of character. But it was possible that Reilly's failure at working on his own in Moscow had weakened his self-confidence and he preferred to be part of a solid organization until it was restored. His timing was unfortunate, as 'C' was having doubts about Reilly's usefulness now that the war with Germany was over.

So Cumming told him tactfully that since Reilly was a marked man in Russia, he was of little more use there to the SIS. Cumming preferred to continue with the loose arrangement he had become accustomed to. He found Reilly's personal sensitivity astonishing in such an egoist, but there was no doubt that Reilly was hurt and viewed 'C's disinterest as rejection.

Reilly wrote to Lockhart for help:

"I told 'C' (and I am anxious that you should know it too) that I consider that there is a very earnest obligation upon me to continue to serve—if my services can be made use of in the question of Russia and Bolshevism. I feel that I have no right to go back to the making of dollars until I have discharged my obligations. I also venture to think that the state should not lose my services. I would devote the rest of my wicked life to this kind of work. 'C' promised to see the F.O. about all this.

"I need not enlarge on my motives to you; I am sure you will understand them and if you can do something I should feel grateful. I should like nothing better than to serve under you.

"I don't believe that the Russians can do anything against the Bolsheviks without our most active support. The salvation of Russia has become a most sacred duty which we owe to the untold thousands of Russian men and women who have sacrificed their lives because they trusted in the promise of our support."

Reilly seemed to be suffering from remorse and feeling helpless on his own. Apparently he needed the status of being a permanent SIS operative to restore his courage. Or perhaps, with his luxurious lifestyle, he needed the money. Either way, his hatred of what the Bolsheviks were doing to his countrymen still smouldered in his heart. From then on, he was driven—as he told Lockhart—by a single desire to "give up my life to Russia to help rid her from this slavery, that she may be a free nation."

His affair with Caryll Houselander and his identification with "Christ the Compassionate" seemed to have given him notions of self-sacrifice. Or perhaps it was self-aggrandizement. Either way, he was determined to reorganize the ill-disciplined counter-revolutionary forces in Europe and embark on an anti-Communist crusade.

The British Government had not given up completely either. They sent a mission to South Russia and provided arms and ammunition and other supplies to the White Russian troops and the Social-Revolutionaries fighting a violent war against the Red Army.

Reilly felt it was a good time to tell 'C,' "It's laudable to support General Denikin and General Wrangel with arms and money to help them continue to fight the Bolsheviks - but their efforts are being weakened by a lack of coordination. Denikin is not being well-advised by his extreme right-wing political supporters."

"What would *you* do?"

"Send Hill to South Russia to coordinate the White Russian intelligence services."

Instead, about 250,000 Whites had to be evacuated from Soviet Russia and resettled in Western Europe.

Hill was now reporting directly to Reilly, while Reilly maintained his contacts with the most important anti-Bolshevik movements.

He told Hill, "What they need is a powerful leader to use their strengths more effectively."

"Who do you suggest?"

"The best man for the job."

"And that is?"

"Boris Savinkov."

Reilly was frequently in touch with Churchill, who readily agreed with him. He thought Savinkov's stature as a leader was far ahead of any of the Russian émigrés, and had been impressed by him. He made a point of impressing on Prime Minister Lloyd George, the Foreign Office, and the SIS, that Savinkov was the *only* individual who might organize and lead a victorious counter-revolution in Soviet Russia.

Savinkov was now in his forties and going bald.

"I suppose you know he smokes morphine," Winston's Private Secretary said.

"A lot of people do in these harsh and gloomy days. Who are we to judge? I think he is a brave man and filled with resolution."

Savinkov had many admirers who funded him. As a young revolutionary, he had organized thirty-three assassinations, including the murder of the Tsar's uncle. Now he led armies of hundreds of thousands of troops, provided by, among others, the invincible Polish nationalist, Marshal Pilsudski.

Despite all the bickering and hard criticism, Savinkov still appeared to be the right man to lead the opposition, and both Churchill and Reilly backed him. Reilly became Savinkov's champion in France and Poland, to where many of the White Russians had escaped. The French Government was eager to supply the necessary funds for a counter-revolution supported by Mr. Churchill. They feared the spread of communism, just like he did.

15
The Next Attempt

RUSSIA AND POLAND WERE AT WAR with each other for Poland's independence in 1920, when Poles fought aggressive guerrilla warfare against the Bolsheviks behind the Russian lines. It was not the only frontier war that took place after the collapse of four huge empires by the end of the Great War. The disappearance of empires had caused changes in national frontiers from the increasing number of smaller nations now seeking self-determination. Geographical and political border changes would keep Winston Churchill busy in several capacities as a Minister of the Crown for years to come.

The conflicts also kept Sidney Reilly occupied in the SIS for a while longer. 'C' called him in to brief him on his next assignment which involved the Russo-Polish war that began in April.

"It's the disputed frontiers between Poland and Russia," he began.

Reilly was in Warsaw in 1921, where he and Savinkov organized a three-day anti-Bolshevik Congress in the summer. Delegates with all kinds of political opinions were invited as long as they were fighting against the Bolsheviks. Most were Social-Revolutionaries. Boris Savinkov was the President and main speaker at the meeting, where they attempted, without success, to establish working arrangements with the White Russians loyal to General Wrangel. Reilly saw from the meeting that they would need more funds, and hurried to Prague to convince more subscribers.

It was a significant year for Lenin's Soviet Government, because his cold-blooded and ruthless inhumanity had made him and the so-called Soviets unpopular. It was clearly obvious that he did not care for people, only about the ideological theories he used as policy to give him power. The last serious internal struggle against Lenin's police state came with the Kronstadt mutiny of 28 February, which erupted on the battleship *Petropavlovsk*. The hotheaded revolutionary sailors mistakenly thought that Lenin believed in freedom and equality, like they did. They were wrong.

"Hundreds, perhaps thousands, were murdered after the mutiny was crushed," Reilly was told. "Though the details will probably never be known."

It was the last opportunity for freedom from communist rule. Lenin's next step was to crush all overt opposition within the Party. Then he strengthened his power base by eliminating any remaining democrats within it. He viewed Democracy as a dirty name for sloppy liberal ideas that resulted in chaos. Lenin believed only in autocratic rule by one dictator—himself. He had systematically built the most carefully designed machine of state tyranny the world had ever seen. His establishment of Communism was a license for terror.

To some extent, Lenin's mistakes acted as a warning to some central European nations, since his social reengineering amounted to "economic breakdown, starvation, civil war and mass terror."

Filosoff was Savinkov's main man in Poland. He was requested by the Congress to report the results of their discussions to Reilly. Filosoff wrote to him candidly as follows;

"I will tell you frankly that I felt ashamed to associate with people who had come to attend and would return to Russia full of hope and would risk their lives in their work—whereas we are unable to give them help to continue their struggle." The possibility of a counter-revolution depended on obtaining more funds. "The press is ready, the peasants await liberation but without a fully planned organization, it is hopeless."

Even so, Filosoff was encouraged to tell him. "We can count on twenty-eight districts including Petrograd, Smolensk and Gomel, and the Ukrainians, with around ten other governments in the outlying districts."

But neither optimism nor political support was a substitute for money.

Reilly travelled to Poland on October 21, and met up with Paul Dukes on the 29th. One result of that episode was that, when Reilly, typically, went over official heads with his report, he was rebuked by 'C.' And the time he spent on Savinkov's interests in a drive by his military forces in Byelorussia, did not go unnoticed by the SIS. 'C' ordered him to return to London.

"I'll bring Savinkov with me," Reilly said. "I think the Prime Minister should meet him. It could drum up support for the anti-Bolshevik armed forces."

"I don't think so," 'C' said.

"Why should anyone object?"

"The Foreign Office does. As far as they are concerned, the Great War ended in 1918. Russia's Civil War is a different matter altogether, about which the Prime Minister continues to drag his feet."

"Surely that's exactly why he needs to meet him?"

But allowances previously made for Reilly's independent efforts and bravery in wartime no longer applied.

Churchill tried to make up for Lloyd George's indecision by his own obsessive drive to defeat the Bolsheviks. But when Reilly attempted to obtain help from 'C,' Cumming could not and would not argue with government policy. When Reilly appealed to Churchill, he was told that, as usual at war-end, the Intelligence budget had been cut.

Consequently, 'C' had already made personnel changes and altered the structure of the SIS since the end of the war, which he ensured Reilly knew nothing about. Cumming's instructions dated 1 February 1922 clearly stated;

"You should give him no more information than is absolutely necessary. He knows far too much about our organization."

'C' also wrote another letter regarding Reilly to the New York Passport Control Office:

"He knows a certain amount about our organization as it was then constituted." This was the same year when George Hill and William Field Robinson left the SIS. Reilly attempted to hang on in peacetime, but 'C' had already rejected his overtures to serve on the permanent staff.

Cumming was still involved with the SIS when Reilly, Savinkov and Paul Dukes traveled across Poland to obtain feedback from the Polish Colonel Bahalovich, who had earned a reputation for his motley collection of guerrilla fighters, which very largely included White Russian escapees. Bahalovich stole food, arms and money wherever he could to continue fighting the Bolsheviks. Reilly managed to arrange to supply more arms and funds for him.

While the SIS duo from London toured and mingled with the White Russian units and encouraged them to continue the struggle, Savinkov's friend, the stubbornly determined Polish Marshal Pilsudsky, encouraged the peasants to rebel in South Russia. Another enthusiastic fighter against the Bolsheviks was Maclaren, a swashbuckling British SIS agent and one of Reilly's major contacts in Warsaw. He was a former merchant navy seaman, who wore gold earrings, which made him appear piratical.

Soon after the secret Congress, Reilly received another letter from Filosoff, warning that the Bolsheviks had taken it as a provocation to act against them:

"I am very much afraid that the provoked Bolsheviks will now go to extremes and demand the liquidation of all of us."

Behind whichever persona Reilly displayed at the moment, there was always another different one. This time it was hard to know if he intended acquiring counter-revolutionary funds from a new business venture he was planning, or attempting to obtain funding to set up a business enterprise by obtaining political power. His behaviour seemed to display a whole range of contradictions. But that may have simply meant that he was thinking ahead of everyone else. It required a different personality to think in terms of immediate action than to plan for the future. One thing was certain, he was always looking for money to support Savinkov, and often obtaining it from wealthy White Russian families he knew.

Now he began another business career, this time with Brigadier Edward Spears putting up some of his money for a partnership. Spears—later Major General Sir Edward Spears—resigned as head of the Military Mission in Paris at the beginning of 1920 to go into business with Reilly.

Winston never forgot friends who had been loyal to him at the beginning of his career, and was always loyal to them. Young Captain Spears spoke fluent French—an unusual gift for most English, who couldn't be bothered to learn foreign languages and left it to foreigners to learn English instead. He had been liaison officer to the French High Command before heading up the Mission in Paris. Now Spears told his friend Winston that he had received an attractive offer from "a big financial group interested in opening up Poland, the Ukraine and Rumania, and in securing trade privileges in those countries for Great Britain."

It is likely that he mentioned Sidney Reilly's name to Churchill, since he knew Winston admired him. Spears and Winston were very close. But Winston always kept his own cards concealed against his chest.

Spears was keen to make his fortune. At the same time, like Winston and Sidney, he was a supporter of Savinkov, and of Allied intervention against the Bolsheviks.

"It is suggested," Spears informed Churchill in a note, "I'd go on working with Savinkov and Pilsudski, and I w'd hope to continue giving you useful information."

Boris Savinkov held out extravagant prospects of the vast economic resources waiting to be developed in areas of Russia when liberated from Bolshevik control. So, clearly, Savinkov, Reilly, and Mr. Churchill still viewed with optimism the possibility of overthrowing the Soviet Government. Spears told Churchill that Savinkov had praised him [Spears] for his "exceptional understanding of Russian affairs," and suggested him as a possible Allied High Commissioner in South Russia." So Spears too was evidently feeling optimistic.

Spears was provided with an opportunity to set up a radium company to handle Czech radium exports, while Reilly, with his intimate experience of Eastern Europe, would help Spears to exploit his connections with the Czechs. As Spears candidly explained later on, "Reilly accompanied me in the capacity of an able businessman, which I certainly was not myself at the time."

Spears found Reilly "rather seedy but really quite nice" at first. And "quite interesting." But Reilly's informal and extroverted business style was something that the army officer was unaccustomed to. He made brief notes in his diary in 1921 of Reilly "playing the goat over phosphates." Reilly took Spears out for a night in Prague which finished off with Russian émigrés singing Gypsy songs. There was no doubt that some of Spears's more formal English associates were "not at all keen on Reilly." The straight-laced Spears himself sometimes found Reilly exasperating. On one occasion he confided in his dairy; "I won't stand cheek."

On the other hand, and more to the point in their collegial relationship, Spears found Reilly's cosmopolitan business experience indispensable, and admired his endless ability to concoct new, if sometimes fantastic, business schemes, and tried to 'calm him' when he threatened to resign. The staid military temperament of the British Army Officer and the volatile moods of the Russian could not be more different.

What was more, Spears was uneasy that Reilly spent too much time plotting with Savinkov, who had organized an intelligence network based in Poland to undertake a number of covert operations in Russia. Spears rebuked him for dealing with shady people and mixing politics with business.

Savinkov also had the cooperation of 'C's station chief in Warsaw, Commander Andrew Maclaren - Reilly's piratical friend with the gold earrings—whom Spears felt was a "shady" individual. One day Spears arrived at his office to find the telephone cut off because the bill had not been paid. Reilly was still contributing funds to Savinkov from his various business ventures, and was always short of ready cash. Invitations to foreign investors to apply for oil concessions, mining concessions, timber and other industries, never came to fruition.

Meanwhile, famine spread across Russia during the summer and the Bolshevik regime was desperate to obtain foreign aid.

On August 2, Spears noted in his diary, "Important day. Bm and I broke our connection with Reilly at lunch—v. pleasantly."

Brunström was Spears's business associate.

Three days later, on August 5, Reilly tried to convince Mr. Churchill to exploit the opportunity provided by famine to remove the Soviet regime. Churchill encouraged him to present his views to Lloyd George. But the Prime Minister was unimpressed with Reilly's arguments—he was fed up with the whole Russian affair, and Reilly and Savinkov with it.

Since Savinkov established his headquarters in Paris, Reilly was often drawn there. So were his other friends who were involved, like Grammatikoff, and Major Field-Robinson who was in charge of the Paris office of the SIS, with Commander Ernest Boyce.

Meanwhile, Reilly's marriage to Nadine was, to all effects, ended. Now he launched himself on another affair with a twenty-three-year-old French actress who was intelligent and well-educated. But she wanted to marry him. Since he was already at least twice married and a bigamist, he refused. Then, when she became pregnant, he found himself trapped into making a decision, which was resolved when he paid for an abortion. But the actress was not satisfied with being merely his mistress, and broke off their affair.

Reilly lunched in Paris with Sasha Grammatikoff, who was a close and sympathetic friend, at *La Rue's*, near the *Madeleine*. "Do you know," he said, "It's now managed by the former maître d' of *Kuba's*? He had to flee from Petrograd."

Paris flowed with Russian escapees who now worked as waiters, cab drivers and hotel commissionaires, or as musicians in fashionable Paris restaurants and cabarets, or as gigolos.

Grammatikoff had organized Nadine's divorce so that Reilly could marry her. Now that Nadine wanted a divorce from Reilly, his friend remarked, "I keep telling you that a divorce is unnecessary in a bigamous marriage." But when Reilly insisted, he put him in touch with a French lawyer so that they could divorce. Reilly was prepared to go through with it to avoid Nadine knowing about Margaret. She never would know, and married Gustav Nobel, of the family who awarded the Nobel Peace Prize.

Reilly's main duty now was to continue to obtain funds for the anti-Bolshevik counter-revolution, since money was the prime ingredient for its success. He was constantly on the move, visiting one capital city after another. Sometimes Savinkov joined him as the star turn in order to encourage funding. They visited Prague several times for money to organize a peasants' revolt in Russia. Bruce Lockhart was in Prague on one of those occasions and gave his opinion that Reilly was the star turn, not Savinkov, who played a secondary role.

Reilly met up again with Eleanor Toye when he stayed at the *Passage Hotel* in Prague. She was working for 'C' in Central Europe, using her job as a singer for cover. He entertained her to a champagne dinner at the "Chapeau Rouge" which was a night-club in a hotel. But for all his extravagant living and his generosity to others, in fact Reilly was running out of money. He had spent much of it on legal fees and hand-outs to Margaret and Nadine. And he had always used his own money when funds were short for the anti-Bolshevik fight.

A typical example of the money shortage that occurred intermittently was in a letter he received from Maclaren in Warsaw:

"The position is becoming desperate. The balance in hand today amounts to 700,000 Polish marks, not even sufficient to pay the staff their salaries for the month of July. Savinkov, who is wanted in Finland urgently in order to bring the Petrograd organization into line and keep them from starting the revolution prematurely, cannot go there, not having the wherewithal to pay for his journey."

HARD-UP IN LONDON

1
Hard-Up in London

BACK AGAIN IN LONDON, REILLY moved out of his luxurious serviced suite of rooms at the Albany into a more modest flat at 5 Adelphi Terrace in WC2, where he mixed his fund-raising activities for Savinkov with a new business enterprise. He was back again in chemicals, pharmaceuticals and patent medicines.

He also openly contacted the Soviet representative to the British Government—a man named Krassin—and told him that he was only interested in making money now. Krassin, like many other people in war-torn countries, was very keen to make money for himself, and was skimming off some of the funds that the Soviet leaders were accumulating in London's banks in case their game was up and they might have to flee from Moscow. Krassin was recalled when the Kremlin discovered his frauds, and disappeared.

But before Krassin left London, Reilly managed to skim off some of his Soviet funds, which he passed over to Savinkov for his counter-revolutionaries. Reilly's opinion of Krassin was similar to that of Mr. Churchill, who referred to him as "the hairy baboon," and had refused to shake hands with him.

An important anti-Bolshevik émigré from Russia was its former Prime Minister of the Provisional Liberal government, Alexander Feodorovich Kerensky. He had escaped from the Bolsheviks on a Serbian passport that Lockhart had provided for him. But Kerensky rarely, if ever, took part in counter-revolutionary activities and was not an admirer of Savinkov. Reilly joined him several times in the hope of moving them closer to each other, but without success.

Finland's capital city of Helsinki was a counter-revolutionary center at this time. It bubbled with spies, counter-revolutionaries and counter-espionage agents. The Finnish Government and General Staff were very largely against the Soviets. It became the main route from which anti-Bolshevik Russians managed to escape across the Russo-Finnish border. This escape route was known as "The Window."

The anti-Reds were still incapable of organizing themselves and preferred to quarrel with each other instead of cooperating. Despite that, Reilly had been invited to an anti-Bolshevik Congress there.

As he'd expected, there was a great deal of talking, but they could not put words into action. To avoid chaos, he insisted on order. But it was impossible. On the other hand, the successors of the *Cheka* Secret Police—renamed the GPU in

1922—were most efficient. And Reilly had to take care against Bolshevik agents attempting to infiltrate any of his or Savinkov's counter-revolutionary groups. Soviet Russia's secret police were skilled in deceptions.

One of Reilly's many novel ideas was to get his own spokesman into the British House of Commons to initiate and lead an anti-Bolshevik lobby.

"Why not stand for Parliament?" he suggested to Paul Dukes.

Dukes gave him a quizzical look.

"No, seriously, the Russian Question is one of the most important issues in politics. Whether or not to recognize the Soviets, British trade with Russia, and so forth. It could become one of the most vital topics in international politics, and you are recognized as an expert on Russia."

"You mean, my knighthood," he murmured sardonically.

"Use it! Use whatever helps our cause. You know the country far better than most British politicians, and the voting public know nothing. It's an opportunity to sway public and government opinion towards intervention."

Dukes barely gave the idea any thought, and made no comment, while Reilly continued to try to persuade him. "I can even tell you the most likely party to stand for at the next election, because I'm sure it would be elected."

Still Dukes made no answer.

A year after raising the idea, Reilly wrote him a long letter to which he added a paragraph by informing him that Boris Savinkov was now living at 32 Rue de Lubeck in Paris, and gave him his phone number. He insisted that Savinkov "was and is and always will be the only man outside of Russia worth talking to and worth supporting."

Savinkov had kept his organization alive and was the only active individual in it. But Dukes had no ambition to become a politician.

Meanwhile, since Reilly kept the SIS chiefs and the British Government informed of all the plots and counter plots relating to the Bolsheviks, Mr. Churchill was kept up-to-date as to what was happening in Russia almost on a day to day basis. The SIS gained a great deal of useful intelligence information from both Reilly and Dukes, and Churchill encouraged them to continue. But Britain's War Cabinet were skeptical about the chances of a counter-revolution succeeding, and unwilling to commit more funds to counter-revolutionary organizations.

As usual in his travels, Reilly met a great many interesting people and a number of beautiful women. In 1922, at the *Hotel Adlon* in Berlin, he met a delightful young blond actress who said she was from South America. Her stage name was Pepita Bobadilla. She was the widow of a well-known playwright, and had begun her own stage career as a chorus girl; one of Cochran's so-called "young ladies." She had also played several parts in London theaters.

Her first awareness of Reilly at the *Adlon* in December, took place when the Reparations Committee of the Paris Peace Conference was still attempting to sort out where the money should come from to pay for the 1914-1918 war. It had been started by Germany. But now their armies had been resisted and conquered by the Allies, they were bankrupt. Reilly was one of the advisers to the British Mission.

A British delegate was holding forth over the teacups and saucers in the hotel and painting a heroic description of a British officer named Sidney Reilly. Pepita's attention was caught by the gossip, and held by the story's depiction of an officer of great courage who was about to return to Russia, where he had been condemned to death by the Communist Government for attempting to overthrow them in a counter-revolution which had ended in failure.

Later that evening, while having coffee in the hotel, she caught a glimpse of a well-groomed and well-tailored man eyeing her from the other side of the lounge. She recalled later that he had a lean and sombre face which conveyed an impression of strength of character. His eyes were kindly but rather sad. Here was a man, she thought, in her usual theatrical terms, who "had laughed in the face of death." Despite her typical use of clichés, Pepita was not far wrong.

Involved in the theatre as she was, she also saw herself as central to a romantic scene, as in a talking picture on a huge silver screen; since Hollywood movies had just arrived and taken over the sensibilities of huge audiences. She visualized herself in close-up, in a silent movie, smoking a cigarette and gazing speculatively through the rising blue-tinged haze at the object of her desire.

As it happened, Sidney Reilly's roving eye had very soon caught sight of her, and he was attracted by her as she was to him. He immediately found a way to be introduced to her. After they had engaged in polite conversation about foreign affairs for a while, she realised that he was the mysterious British secret agent whom she had only just heard about. It was love at first sight for both of them.

Pepita was not the only lonely widow looking for a husband. It was a competitive market inundated with single young women and middle-aged widows during and after the war, so a charming RAF officer like Reilly was in great demand, and she lost no time.

Sidney Reilly and Pepita became engaged only a week after they met. First he had to rush off instantly to Paris and Prague for business on behalf of Savinkov. Then Reilly married Pepita on May 18, 1923 at the Registry Office in Henrietta Street, Covent Garden. Their witnesses were Captain Hill and Major Alley.

Pepita—like Nadine—was totally unaware of his previous marriage to Margaret. 'C,' who was well aware of it and knew all about Margaret, never-

"Playwright's Widow Weds." Mrs Haddon Chambers with bouquet, and Captain Sidney G. Reilly. At Henrietta Street Register office in London after their marriage. *Daily Mail.*

theless, met and congratulated Pepita when he attended their wedding reception at the *Savoy Hotel*. He had decided that Reilly knew too much about the SIS to be on bad terms with him.

Reilly's affair with Caryll had run its course after three years. Although she was heartbroken, she returned to the Catholic Church and became one of the most widely read Catholic writers of her generation. She also developed a talent for healing mentally ill people. The President of the Psychiatry Section of the Royal Society of Medicine, Dr. Eric Strauss, a practicing clinical psychiatrist, would send her his hopeless cases and, as he said, she would "love them back to life."

Reilly's pharmaceutical business was not a financial success, and both his own personal finances and Boris Savinkov's were in even poorer shape. The French Government and others had ceased to support his activities, since the opportunities expected for a counter-revolution had not materialized. Nevertheless their agents were still moving in and out and around Russia to obtain information, but they needed funds to cover their costs. They relied now mainly on private donations.

Even so, Reilly was still optimistic about what they could do for the Russian people. To continue to fund the operation, he sold his collection of valuable Napoleana which he had spent many years collecting.

Churchill had been impressed by Reilly's friend, Savinkov, and continued to encourage him. He wrote praising him because his life was devoted to a worthy cause.

"That cause was the freedom of the Russian people. In the cause, there was nothing he would not dare or endure". He went on; "he displayed the wisdom of a statesman, the qualities of a commander, the courage of a hero, and the endurance of a martyr."

Savinkov, still largely financed by Reilly, continued fighting in Poland against the Red Army.

"This last feat was little short of miraculous," Churchill wrote. He sent several documents about Savinkov to Prime Minister Lloyd George with a note hand-written in red ink; "He is the only man who counts."

Savinkov had displayed the courage of a hero, supported by one of his few old friends, the Head of State in Poland, Marshal Pilsudski. But endurance was no longer enough, particularly since there were no more funds to continue, few staff and little equipment. Lloyd George was not about to fund him anymore, and insisted that Churchill's moral support of Savinkov and all the other anti-Bolsheviks amounted to an obsession. The game in Russia was over.

Even so, Lloyd George spent some time with Savinkov, and invited him home to dine with his own family. Savinkov was surprised at the Prime Minister's knowledge of what was happening in Russia, without realizing that much of it came from Reilly's intelligence reports and recommendations. But Lloyd George still felt that Bolshevism was just a phase, a whim, a notion that would run its course and then fade away.

Churchill accompanied Savinkov to the dinner as a guest, and told him pointedly on the way out, "Do not put too much trust in Lloyd George, he is first a nationalist, but one also meets in him a desire for personal gain, and the elections play a part in this."

It was about this time that Boris Savinkov's mother wrote a confidential letter to Reilly, begging him to use his influence to stop Savinkov stirring up riots in Russia, since he did not possess sufficient money to do it successfully. She felt it would be more economically effective for him to concentrate on propaganda. She insisted that it was impossible for him to plan armed resistance in Russia while living in Paris. She had written to Reilly because Boris had told his mother, "I listen to many but put my faith only in Reilly: he is a tower of moral strength."

She cautioned Reilly with a remark that Lloyd George had made to a friend of hers that "Savinkov is no doubt a man of the future but I need Russia at the present moment, even if it must be the Bolsheviks."

She knew her son's days as a hero were over and expected he would be betrayed.

Reilly was so desperate for cash by July 1923 that he planned to leave for New York with Pepita, where his lawyers had made little progress in attempting to obtain a great deal of money from the Baldwin Locomotive Company, which was still owed to him. He had to borrow money for their passage on the Holland-Amerika steamship line from his SIS friend, Major Field-Robinson.

"Robbie," Reilly told him, "I am broke. My credit in London is finished. I must get over to New York to fight my case. It is my last chance. Will you help?"

Robbie gave him £200 for the fare.

Reilly faced a complicated legal case resulting from his business deals with a British company which had subsequently been taken over by an American one. In the meantime, he had to watch out for an increasing number of Bolshevik agents coming to the United States. Agents of the Soviet GPU were watching him, too.

But he had to stay in New York to wait for his case to come up in court. To fill in time, he helped Dukes, who was lecturing in the United States.

Paul Dukes would recount later on a strange remark that Reilly made that had not seemed particularly significant at the time:

"I am going to tell you something very, very private. I am not telling anyone else and no-one must know. Savinkov is going back to Russia to give himself up. I too am going back but I shall continue to fight."

Reilly was still supporting Savinkov financially, and running out of funds, while Savinkov pressed him for more. He answered Savinkov in writing on 19 February and 15 March, 1924, that the situation with his creditors in London was dire: he might be declared insolvent at any moment.

Reilly's case against the Locomotive Company had still not come to court by the summer of 1924, when he received an urgent appeal from Savinkov to meet him in Paris. Before traveling to Paris with Pepita, Reilly made financial arrangements in New York to look after her in case of his death.

Savinkov was in Rome when they arrived in Paris, seeking financial support from Italy's Fascist leader, Benito Mussolini. So Boris's secretary filled him in.

"What is most significant is that Boris's agents have been free to travel in and out of Russia with ease. The information they brought back was of strong anti-Bolshevik sentiment building up inside Russia. It involves men in high places—some even in the GPU! Their resistance movement is called the Moscow Municipal Credit Association. But it's generally known as "The Trust." Its leaders include someone named Yakushev, and another man named Opperput. Apparently the White Russian General Kutyepoff, who formerly commanded an anti-Soviet combat group, has complete faith in this mysterious organization."

It was through the help of this shadowy organization that Savinkov and Kutyepoff had managed to travel around Russia with ease and in freedom. They had crossed the Russo-Finnish border so seamlessly back and forth through "The Window," that Savinkov and his agents had been impressed by the efficiency of the organization and its messengers.

"What's more," Boris's secretary reported, "they say "The Trust" is ready to stage a counter-revolution. All it lacks is a suitable leader, like Savinkov or you."

"Is that what they said?"

"Apparently. But they want to be assured of the support of the anti-Bolshevik movement outside Russia."

"It sounds too good to be true."

"That's what I thought. But Boris seems hooked on it."

"He must be desperate."

"He is."

2
"The Trust"

THE POSSIBILITY THAT THE SO-CALLED "TRUST" might be a GPU plot to lure the counter-revolutionary leaders into exposing themselves and their organization, which could then be easily crushed, had been seriously considered. Reilly was well aware of such deceptions by secret police organizations.

He had already learned much of the situation while in New York from Savinkov's letters and messengers. Now that Boris's secretary filled in the details in Paris, Reilly was encouraged at this turn of events and impressed by what he now learned at first-hand from two of "The Trust's" agents who had worked for Reilly before in 1918. He saw it as an opportunity to turn failure into success.

Boris Savinkov returned to Paris after being turned down for funding by Mussolini. The most that the Italian leader would do was provide him with an Italian passport and promises of assistance from the Italian Legation in Russia. Nevertheless, Savinkov's disappointment appeared to make him more optimistic about the possibilities that "The Trust" might represent.

"I hope you're not serious about returning to Moscow?" Reilly said.

"The Bolsheviks need a loan of money from America. So they want favourable propaganda to help them. They say I'll be freed if I agree to be the central figure in a fake trial."

"And you believe them?"

"It's a risk I must take."

"You'll be in all the international newspapers."

"That's the idea."

Reilly took a hard look at Boris Savinkov and saw a broken man after all his failures and the effects of his morphine addiction. He was clutching at the only straw available to him: otherwise he had visions of being a loser and a forgotten man, while his funds ceased and he died alone in poverty.

"They won't let you go without some kind of a confession—to an anti-Soviet crime."

Reilly had been so close to Boris for so long that he had failed to see him in the fresh light that Pepita did. She was unimpressed by Savinkov when she saw him for the first time at the *Chatham Hotel*. What she saw was a vain and plump little man who strutted in with what she thought was a ridiculous air of self-assurance and self-esteem. As she described him, he had a high forehead, beady little eyes and not much chin.

"Now he gave us a view of one side of his profile, now of the other. Now he thrust his hand into his breast in the approved Napoleonic manner, now he flourished it in the air with a theatrical gesture. Every pose was carefully studied, and had been studied so long that he had passed beyond the stage of taking even a glance at his audience to gauge the measure of its appreciation."

Savinkov was followed everywhere by two bodyguards who posed for effect instead of being unobtrusive, as if he were an influential and self-conscious warlord canvassing for donations.

As an actress accustomed to posing on the stage for audiences, Pepita thought she recognized what was spontaneous and what was false. Her observations were unclouded by Sidney Reilly's emotional fixation on him as a possible leader of a counter-revolution. In her opinion, Savinkov was no longer a real hero, but only the shadow of what he might once have been when he was a young revolutionary and prepared to risk his life for a patriotic cause. Now he was only a showpiece, expected to put on a performance as a fund-raiser. Instead of still being financed by Polish, Czech and French governments, as he had previously been, he now depended on funds from individual donors, anti-communist corporations, Russian groups of émigrés, and handouts from Sidney Reilly.

On the other hand, her view of Savinkov may have been biased because she felt angry at Sidney's money going to Boris instead of to her. Or she may have felt jealous at her husband's attention being devoted so much to this vain little man whom she felt had nothing to be proud of. Or she may have found him ridiculous and tragic, as she remarked, when he pranced and simpered like a prima donna accustomed to adulation from a thrilled and eager audience watching a grand opera.

Reilly might even have suspected the truth at that moment, but still refused to admit it to himself, while wondering in awe at the tragedy of Boris's martyrdom, because Savinkov was still his hero.

Boris—somewhat diminished in Reilly's eyes—gave his friend an ingratiating small shrug.

"I'll simply return to Russia, confess, and turn Bolshevik. To the outside world I might appear a traitor to my cause, but in reality I would move in to the Red camp and be ready to assume leadership when the counter-revolution takes place. Meanwhile, you and General Kutyepoff will continue the fight outside Russia."

"It's a trap."

Savinkov seemed to be convinced he was doing the right thing, the only thing left for him to do. Since Boyce now worked in the Russian section of SIS, Reilly asked his advice.

Boyce said thoughtfully, "The so-called Trust is considered to be a powerful movement in Russia." He paused and shrugged. "Or so some people say. All I know is their agents have supplied useful intelligence to the Secret Services of several nations in Western Europe."

"Was it kosher?"

"Some of it was suspect. It might have been deliberately planted by the GPU. Who knows?"

"How come you never mentioned it to me?"

"Because we don't have an accurate assessment of "The Trust," We need someone who can penetrate it."

Reilly gave him a hard look to see if he was serious. Even though he suspected that "The Trust" might be duplicitous, he was tempted by the possibility of such a powerful organization, so huge that it might topple the Bolsheviks. But he, like Boris Savinkov, had also suffered from defeat and was in an unsettled condition from his financial setbacks.

Even in his unusually defeatist frame of mind, he told Boris, "It would be lunacy for you to return to Russia as a martyr to the cause."

But martyrdom was all that was left for Savinkov. Reilly now agreed to Savinkov's secret journey to Russia with two messengers who arrived as escorts from "The Trust." Savinkov left via Berlin and Warsaw on August 10, 1924, with a Finnish passport in the name of Stepanoff.

The first news that came out of Russia of Savinkov's arrival was when he was arrested in Minsk by Pilar, and taken to Moscow on August 29. Instead of immediately facing a firing squad in a courtyard of GPU headquarters, Savinkov paid lip-service to Stalin in muted tones by declaring, "I honor the power and wisdom of the GPU."

Further announcements followed: He had been condemned to death. His sentence had been commuted to imprisonment for ten years. He had been completely acquitted. He was a free man.

Reilly marvelled at the apparent power of "The Trust," and was glad to hear that his friend had not been executed in a cell in the Lubianka Prison. But he was sad to read the conclusions of the news media that Savinkov had turned traitor by joining the Bolsheviks. It was bound to discourage all his former supporters.

In an attempt to counter their disappointment, Reilly wrote a clumsy letter to the *Morning Post*. It was published on September 8, 1924.

Reilly referred to their claim that Savinkov's trial was only a stunt which he had arranged himself with the Kremlin "and that Savinkov had already for some time contemplated a reconciliation with the Bolsheviks." He accused the *Morning Post* of carelessness in making their allegations without producing any evidence to back it up. He expected to inject some hope into the hearts of his and Savinkov's supporters by casting doubts on the newspaper reports of Savinkov's supposed treachery to the anti-Bolshevik cause. Reilly claimed the allegation was nothing more than a copy of a report by the Soviet news agency *Rosta*; a libel intended to disgrace Savinkov's reputation.

"Where is the proof," he asked, "since *Rosta* stated that he was tried behind closed doors?"

Mr. Churchill's opinion of Boris Savinkov was of particular concern to Reilly, since Churchill had always admired and championed him. Reilly had been convinced that Churchill would eventually persuade the British Government to support a counter-revolution in Russia, if it could be shown to succeed. So he anxiously wrote him a letter.

> Dear Mr. Churchill,
> The disaster that has overtaken Boris Savinkov has undoubtedly produced the most painful impression on you. Neither I nor any of his intimate friends and co-workers have so far been able to obtain any reliable news about his fate. Our conviction is that he has fallen victim to the vilest and most daring intrigue the *Cheka* has ever attempted. Our opinion is expressed in the letter which I am today sending to the *Morning Post*. Knowing your invariably kind interest I take the liberty of enclosing a copy for your information.
>
> > I am, dear Mr. Churchill,
> > Yours very faithfully,
> > Sidney Reilly.

Winston Churchill immediately pointed out that in neither letter from Reilly had he explained why Savinkov had gone to Russia. He courteously replied to Reilly's letter:

> > Chartwell Manor,
> > Westerham, Kent.
>
> September 5, 1924.
>
> Dear Mr. Reilly,
> I was deeply grieved to read the news about Savinkov. I do not, however think that the explanation in your letter in the *Morning Post* is borne out by the facts. The *Morning Post* today gives a fuller account of the *procès verbal*, and I clearly recognise the points we discussed at Chequers about free Soviet elections, etc. You do not say in your letter what was the reason and purpose

with which he entered Soviet Russia. If it is true that he had been pardoned and liberated I should be very glad. I am sure that any influence he could acquire among those men would be powerfully exerted towards bringing about a better state of affairs. In fact their treatment of him, if it is true, seems to me to be the first decent and sensible thing I have ever heard about them.

I shall be glad to hear anything further you may know on the subject, as I always thought Savinkov was a great man and a great Russian patriot, in spite of the terrible methods with which he has been associated. However it is very difficult to judge the politics in any other country.

Yours very truly,
Winston S. Churchill

Reports later in the month in *Izvestia* seemed to clarify that Savinkov had in fact betrayed his cause. Although it appeared to follow the deception plan that Savinkov had described to him before his departure, Reilly now feared that Boris was in fact the traitor that the newspapers made him out to be.

When the Soviet Government permitted Savinkov to write to Reilly—which was suspicious in itself—Boris wrote:

> "Never have I fought for the interests and dubious welfare of Europe, but always for Russia and the Russian people. How many illusions and fairy tales have I buried here in the Lubianka! I have met men in the G.P.U. whom I have known and trusted from my youth up and who are nearer to me than the chatter-boxes of the foreign delegation of the Social-Revolutionaries . . . What does prison mean here? No-one is kept longer than three years and is given leave to visit the town during this time . . . I cannot deny that Russia is reborn."

It was all lying propaganda of course. Reilly was sure the letter was forged and that Trillisser, the head of the Foreign Section of the GPU, was responsible. To clarify his own position and rally the depressed anti-Bolshevists, Reilly wrote again to the *Morning Post*:

Sir,
I once more take the liberty of claiming your indulgence and your space. This time for a two-fold purpose, first of all to express my deep appreciation of your

fairness in inserting (in your issue of the 8th inst.) my letter in defense of Boris Savinkov when all the information at your disposal tended to show that I am in error; secondly, to perform a duty, in this case a most painful duty, and to acknowledge the error into which my loyalty to Savinkov induced me.

He went on to admit that detailed press reports by stenographers, in many instances, were supported by reliable and impartial eyewitnesses, and established Savinkov's treachery.

"He not only betrayed his friends, his organization, and his cause, but he has also deliberately and completely gone over to his former enemies. He has connived with his captors to deal the heaviest possible blow at the anti-Bolshevik movement, and to provide them with an outstanding political triumph both for internal and external use. By this act Savinkov has erased for ever his name from the scroll of honor of the anti-Communist movement."

However, he added "The moral suicide of their former leader is for them an added incentive to close their ranks and to carry on."

Winston Churchill did not agree with Reilly's verdict on his old friend and wrote telling him why:

September 15, 1924.

Dear Mr. Reilly,
I am very interested in your letter. The event has turned out as I myself expected at the very first. I do not think you should judge Savinkov too harshly. He was placed in a terrible position: and only those who have sustained successfully such an ordeal have a full right to pronounce censure.
At any rate I shall wait to hear the end of the story before changing my view about Savinkov.
Yours very truly,
W. S. Churchill

Reilly believed, however, that Savinkov *had* gone over to the Bolsheviks. He had convinced them that he was a genuine turncoat, and "The Trust" had saved his life. He was confined in a room in the Lubianka Prison in the Kremlin, where he was treated humanely. But he was considered too dangerous as a popular leader to be freed. Russian propagandists made the most of his humiliating surrender.

What apparently never occurred to Reilly was that Savinkov may have secretly been working for Britain's Secret Service on Churchill's behalf and—unbeknown to his friend—been sent to Soviet Russia to "spy out the land."

Savinkov appeared depressed at his fate, and successfully managed to smuggle out a letter for Reilly to pass on to General Edward Spears, which asked him to approach Winston Churchill in the hope that he could obtain his release. Or was he simply making contact with his SIS controller? He also smuggled out another letter to Filosoff, who was in Paris and could not believe that Savinkov was a traitor. After reading it, Filosoff wrote to Reilly;

"From these I find (and it is confirmed from other sources) that Savinkov did not name any of his former associates. On the whole I have the impression that I was right in my first opinion regarding Savinkov's behaviour."

Savinkov could even have been a double-agent. But no one voiced any of those suppositions out loud. Now Filosoff invested all his hopes for the future on Reilly being able to obtain financial support from the United States to finance their counter-revolution.

3
Guilty Men

ONE DAY IN MAY 1925, Savinkov committed suicide by throwing himself out of a high window. Many people believed that the story was a ruse to conceal his official execution. For, although the GPU was entirely without scruples, the Soviet Government would surely have preferred Savinkov to have remained as live bait to convince other anti-Bolshevik leaders of the genuineness of "The Trust," and catch other naïve and gullible fish. So a question mark was left hovering over the Savinkov affair: had he committed suicide, or was he pushed?

Or was it possible that Boris Savinkov was really now working secretly for the Soviets? Anything was possible with the deceptions, the subterfuge, and the obfuscations of the Soviet regime.

Stalin's task as leader was to restore Russia's economy to what it had previously been under the Tsar. That was likely to take at least ten years. His main problem at that moment in 1925 was to solve the anomaly of a capitalist system in the vast countryside—which was against their Marxist beliefs—and a communist economy in the cities.

The whole burden of imposing collectivization on millions of peasants fell on Stalin's shoulders, since his communist supporters feared either rebellion by the masses or the collapse of the national economy, or both. Only Stalin was ruthless enough to risk the death by starvation of millions, which was already taking place. A hundred million would die in the end. But the communists considered it was more important to prove that Marx's economic theory worked than being concerned over the millions of Russian people who were being starved to death for the sake of an unproven theory. Justifying the revolution had become an obsession.

Evidently they believed it would exonerate them from their criminality. They knew they were guilty men.

4
The Loner

CUMMING HAD DIED IN 1923. A new Labour Government had been elected in Britain since then, and Mr. Churchill was now out of office. Without the support or influence of either them or Savinkov, Sidney Reilly now found himself on his own.

Reilly had no fear of being alone: he was an independent force of nature. But he could not topple the Soviet Government by himself, and he was without funds. Nevertheless—like Churchill who was always saying "Never, never give in!" Reilly did not believe in giving up, either. Since the news about Savinkov had discouraged the counter-revolutionaries, he decided he needed a significant event to discredit the Bolsheviks and rally his former supporters until he was ready to act again. But Boyce and Britain's Secret Service were still cautious in deciding whether it was safe to befriend "The Trust" or not.

Nevertheless, they wanted the Russian Civil War ended, not least because it was considered that there would be immense business opportunities for the West.

In the meantime, there were only illegal grey or black market activities. For example, there was considerable business in forged Soviet documents for individuals and governments, and criminal gangs, who needed an appearance of legitimacy. The forgers worked independently for anyone who paid them, like in any other trade. It was not all that different in principle from forgery of the paintings of famous painters that could be sold to collectors who had no way of knowing if they were genuine or not.

Similarly, foreign governments still felt unsure whether the Soviet Government was genuine or fraudulent. They were bemused by the overthrow of a centuries-old regime by a handful of malcontents and mutinous revolutionaries who behaved like criminals.

Prime Minister Lloyd George was still uncertain whether to grant formal diplomatic recognition to the Soviet Government, or not. Other governments too were unsure of what attitude to adopt towards the Bolshevik leaders in the Kremlin. Since few shreds of information came through the usual diplomatic channels, foreign secret services in every country sought intelligence wherever and however they could. Information from Russia came at a high price, and business with dealers in forged documents was booming.

Since the INO—which was the foreign department of the GPU—was limited in the amount of foreign currency for the funding of its agents abroad, it began to forge and sell Soviet documents itself. It even sold genuine ones if it created revenues and did no harm. Berlin became the center of a black market in forged Soviet documents for agents of any country who could buy and sell them. They were as effective to use as the authorized official ones, since most people were deceived by the skillful forgeries.

Reilly was quick to exploit the jungle of forgeries in which illicit documents were so well copied that only their forgers could determine which ones were the real thing. That was how it came about that he decided to initiate a deliberate fraud of his own in England by engineering what would become known as the "Zinoviev Letter" scandal in October 1924. It succeeded in triggering the collapse of Ramsay MacDonald's Labour Government.

Reilly had become aware from friends and colleagues that a massive flow of subversive propaganda from the Comintern in Moscow was reaching Britain's socialists to rally their support for the Bolsheviks in Russia. Reilly talked confidentially with several secret agents and his friend Grammatikoff, to sound them out. Stewart Menzies was one of the future chiefs of MI6, and Desmond Morton was a military officer who would become Churchill's personal assistant.

"If a subversive letter from Zinoviev could be exposed, British public opinion might be encouraged to back the anti-Bolshevik movement instead of allowing naive students and other sympathisers to view Russia's communists through the rosy-tinted lenses of romance. And it could boost the morale of anti-communists everywhere who were discouraged by Savinkov's treachery to their cause."

Zinoviev had been one of Lenin's closest friends when they were exiles in Switzerland before the Revolution. He was as cold and calculating and ruthless as Lenin, and a bitter enemy of England. Any letter from him would be believed, since he was the President of the Comintern, set up to spread communism all over the world.

Sasha Grammatikoff's friend, Vladimir Orloff, who had once been the Public Prosecutor for the Tsar, had successfully provided Reilly with false names and even documents stamped with the imprint of the *Cheka* while in Soviet Russia. After Orloff had been forced to flee Russia in the revolution, he had made for Berlin where all the other forgers were carrying on their businesses. He was now in business as a free-lance spy, working simultaneously for the White Russians and the Germans.

One of Orloff's many associates was Pavlonovsky, a Pole with a long list of different identities who had fled from Russia in 1922. Allegedly, he had brought with him "a trunkful of stolen *Cheka* papers which served not only as good currency in the espionage market but also as excellent 'specimens' to copy for subsequent forgeries." He also worked for the German political police, like Orloff did.

Reilly met with them and said candidly, "I want a letter forged to look like it came from Zinoviev. Date it September 15, 1924." He added, "The British Government has to believe that Zinoviev's letter is official and genuine."

The two forgers went to work according to his directions. Reilly was easily able to conceal his connection with the forgery, since he was on his own and the three Russians trusted each other.

In Reilly's mind, at least, the forgery was made in a good cause, since it was intended as a weapon to destroy the possibility of a socialist Labour Government, which his experience demonstrated would become communist. The forged letter commanded Britain's Communists and Socialists to organize armed rebellion and subversion in Britain's armed forces. It also mentioned the recruitment of leaders for a future British Red Army.

Reilly had the fraudulent letter delivered to the Foreign Office in London like a time-bomb calculated to explode when the situation was ripe. Meanwhile, he made sure the press knew about it.

Labour Prime Minister Ramsay MacDonald was made aware of the letter, but it was kept from the British public for a while. MacDonald was naïve enough, or proud enough, to continue boasting in his election campaign of the Government's success in achieving understanding and obtaining cooperation with the Russians. So that, when the *Daily Mail* revealed the contents of "Zinoviev's" letter, Ramsay MacDonald was embarrassed, and the Labour Party was discredited and lost the election.

Arguments about conspiracy theories and the genuineness of the letter would continue with similar allegations that Britain's Labour Party took their instructions directly from the Kremlin, and that Labour Prime Ministers were bribed by Soviet Russia. Even so, some British working classes continued to vote for Labour because they had no idea what was going on in Soviet Russia, which they erroneously fantasized as an ideal classless society aimed at high moral and ethical ideals, and a role model for Britain's socialists to follow.

Since the Zinoviev Letter scandal had proved effective in replacing a Labour Government in Britain with the Conservative Party, Reilly revealed his connection to the plot to his closest friends, like Major Alley, who remarked afterwards on how pleased Reilly was with having stirred up the scandal.

The Russian Revolution and Civil War had sent shock waves throughout the United States. One enthusiastic journalist who sent back reports praising Soviet Russia scared Americans even more. The pro-communist journalist was John Reed, who wrote a book entitled *Ten Days That Shook the World*. It was published by the Communist Party of the USA. Like Paul Dukes, he'd had a front seat at the October Revolution. But each of them saw something entirely different from the other, apparently because Dukes valued law and order whereas Reed apparently loved violence and chaos. It seems that his own emotional baggage with its political delusions blinded him to the truth about communism.

The first Red Scare in the United States began immediately following the eruption of the Russian Revolution and created political and social unrest. There was fear to a point of hysteria that a nationwide revolution was imminent in America as well. American communists would seize private property, banish religion, change the family, have a detrimental influence on marriage, trash civility, and altogether alter the American way of life.

News media hysteria transformed the political event into anti-foreign rumors and sentiments. Labor movements were associated automatically with Communism and strikes were viewed as threats to American society. A plot that was discovered in 1919 to mail bombs to prominent members of the establishment fanned the flames of unrest and anxiety. Those who had worked hard all their lives to make and save capital were terrified of losing it. Those who owned homes feared having them confiscated or being forced to share them with several other families, as had happened in Soviet Russia. They were afraid of all infringements of liberty. Just as in England, law and order was undermined by anarchist and communist revolutionaries.

Reilly returned again to New York to continue his legal fight with Baldwin's Locomotive Company. When the case finally came up in court, his creditors admitted the existence of the agreement but claimed they had a legal right to refuse payment to Reilly.

Deflated in his resolve once again, Reilly felt that nothing had gone right for him since the failure of his intended counter-revolution in Russia. He had been extraordinarily successful until then. Paul Dukes attended the court with him and remarked afterwards on how Reilly completely lost his temper and looked ugly. Reilly knew he was in the right and had been tricked. But his claim was dismissed with no case to prove.

His anger gave way to depression. But it did not last long. Like Churchill, he was a fighter who never lost hope in victory. He wrote one article after another for the newspapers and gave lectures denouncing the injustices and horrors of the communist regime.

Surging into the United States were not only White Russian refugees fleeing from communist Russia, but also numbers of Soviet secret agents of the GPU who spied on their activities, like many others who had fled to Paris and London. Since the finances of the Soviet Government were in poor shape, other Soviet agents were also in the United States to obtain a loan.

Perhaps it was the blow from the forged Zinoviev Letter that inspired the GPU to target Reilly and plan his downfall by operating a bogus anti-Bolshevik Front named the "Monarchist Union of Central Russia" (MUCR). This was the organization more generally known as "The Trust." It was specially designed to ensnare any remaining plotters against Bolshevik rule.

Reilly worked in New York for two and a half years. When the GPU planted a female agent in Reilly's office as his secretary, he spotted her immediately and fed her false information for almost a year, providing her with fake documents and letters which she sent on to her Kremlin masters in Moscow. Reilly pursued his work at night after she had left for the day. He followed her contacts, and those of another GPU agent, and uncovered many of the Bolshevik agents working in New York. His anti-Bolshevik propaganda may well have been the main reason why the Soviet Government could not obtain an American loan.

A consulting engineer named Colonel Proskey claimed he believed that Reilly was "one of the most astute and dangerous international spies now at large."

It was also said by those who wished to smear him that "he would do anything for the almighty dollar." No wonder—Reilly's financial position was precarious and he was always battling with impatient creditors! But he managed to do enough business to pay his way, living mostly on credit.

Even so, a personal and business testimonial from Vickers, on their official letterhead, indicated that the crude sneer about Reilly's integrity was unjust and his record was clean. It stated;

"I can only testify to his ability as a diplomatic businessman, whether the matter in hand is great or small, and during the thirteen years I have known Mr. Reilly I have never heard anything disparaging to his character."

And a standard enquiry form sent from Britain's Secret Service on January 30, to MI5, received the following response on February 2:

"We have nothing recorded against the above" [Sidney G. Reilly, RFC Club, Bruton Street and 22 Ryder Street, St James] "Nothing is known to the prejudice of any of the above by the police."

As usual, the truth about Reilly was very different from the derogatory rumors spread by his envious opponents.

At the same time as he coped with financial pressures, Reilly faced shocks from Moscow which upset him, like the disappearance of Maria Schovalovsky whom he had helped escape when she had defected from the Soviet Embassy in Paris, her hair cut short and dressed as a man. She was lured back later to Russia by a forged letter purporting to be from her father who had been arrested. Then she had vanished.

And there was Savinkov's aide, L. D. Sheshenya, a former Tsarist officer, captured by Soviet border guards when leaving Poland for Russia. The GPU then turned him and one of his Russian agents round and used them for an elaborate deception program.

An individual who was often present in Reilly's mind was the Latvian secret police's torturer and executioner named Adamson, who exemplified the essence of all that was evil in human nature. His custom was to take female prisoners from the solitary confinement wing for women and rape them before killing them. There was also "Mad Dora" who went on a killing spree and shot 700 prisoners over several nights, and then hanged herself in a murderous fit. It was said that the cells in the basement were filled with corpses, torn-off fingers and other parts of the human body, which were scattered on the stone floors as evidence of horrendous tortures.

The most common method of execution then and for many years afterwards was for condemned victims to be hauled from their cells with their hands tied, nose sealed and mouth gagged. Their hands were untied on arrival at the scene of execution. They were ordered through a door and shot in the back of the head. The stone floor at the scene of execution in the Lubianka's basement, where thousands of such executions took place in the GPU's inner prison, was stained with the blood of their victims.

5
Commander Boyce's Story

REILLY HAD BEEN IMPRESSED BY ALL THAT HE had now seen and heard about the revolutionary organization known as "The Trust." He felt that much would depend on their cooperation to raise a counter-revolution that he intended to lead now that Savinkov was dead. What he did not know was the names and the status of its leaders, and whether or not it had already been infiltrated by Dzerzhinsky's agents. What he did know was that the SIS had their own doubts about the organization. And it was clear that Boyce was keen to learn more about it from Reilly's infiltration in Moscow and Petrograd.

Boyce was generally available to confirm or deny Reilly's own suspicions. Boyce led his own team of agents at Reval, and watched the daily activities of the communists for the SIS.

"As you know," he said, "most spies travel in and out of Russia through the Baltic countries. As in Finland, anti-Bolsheviks pass themselves off as Bolsheviks and spend their lives on the edge of conspiracy, planning escapes and forging documents. On the other side, Dzerzhinsky's agents come from Russia and pass themselves off as White Russians in Finland. No one can be trusted."

At the same time, one of Dzerzhinsky's section chiefs named Mikhail Vladimiroff was kept similarly busy watching their prey on the Russian side of the frontier. Mysterious refugees arriving in neutral territory from Russia vanished as mysteriously in the Baltic States as others did who crossed into Russia. They were all pawns of no consequence in a serious political game, some killed as possible counter-revolutionaries, some in revenge, and many others in error.

Reilly kept in continuous contact with counter-revolutionary groups outside of Russia who continued to quarrel among themselves after Savinkov's defection, while also keeping in continuous contact with Boyce in the Baltic. Boyce passed him information from his spies:

"The power of "The Trust" seems to be growing stronger. I'm told that it apparently even includes members of the Soviet Government."

The situation looked more and more promising to both of them.

Boyce told Reilly, "Two anti-Bolshevik agents I trust completely are both acting as couriers between "The Trust" and Colonel Kutyepoff. They are Maria Vladimirovna Schultz and her husband George Nicolaievich Radkevich. She is the dominant partner, motivated by hatred of the Communists. She has enormous courage."

When Reilly showed interest, he added;

"Maria spent four years as a private in the Russian army. Her father had been a general. His family had all been murdered by the Bolsheviks. She joined the White Russian resistance movement, and moves in and out of an escape trail known as "The Window." She is one of Kutyepoff's most trusted couriers, and the second in command."

She and other agents in contact with "The Trust" expressed an urgent need for funds from outside. Boyce assured Reilly, "It's a good sign. It may mean that the counter-revolutionary movement is bigger and stronger, and the moment to strike is closer than we thought."

"What's the significance?"

"I see it as a reaction to the increasing struggle for leadership between Trotsky and Stalin now that Lenin's gone."

Boyce wrote to Reilly in invisible ink and code, elaborating on the importance of "The Trust" and recommending him to meet the Schultzes in Paris. The "scheme" that he wrote about, was intended to replace the other "big scheme"

Reilly was working on, but fell through. Boyce pressed Reilly by saying his involvement would "help me considerably."

Reilly took it that Boyce wanted him to penetrate "The Trust" on his behalf.

"The only thing I ask," Boyce wrote, "is that you keep our connection with this business from the knowledge of my department as, being a Government official, I am not supposed to be connected with any such enterprise." He added that he admired Reilly's patience and perseverance against all sorts of intrigues and opposition. "I know also you will look after my interests without my having to make some special agreement with you."

In other words, he was appealing to their special close friendship.

It was the first of several letters written in code with invisible ink between Boyce and Reilly in the first months in 1925. They ended with Reilly meeting Boyce in Paris with General Kutyepoff and other top counter-revolutionaries.

No communications passed between Reilly and the new SIS chief in London who had replaced Cumming. Only Boyce communicated with Reilly before he left the United States. Boyce urged him to cooperate with "The Trust," while stating clearly that neither he, the British Secret Service, nor the British Government would become involved if anything went wrong. Like all secret agents when trouble struck, Reilly would have to depend on his own wits and resources to escape.

Reilly was excited by Boyce's news and the opportunity to be involved in something worthwhile again. He considered it would be a good idea for the agents of "The Trust" to go to the United States where they could meet Henry Ford to obtain finance. He also recommended that Mr. Churchill's cooperation should be sought to canvass political support of anti-Communist governments across the world.

He wrote again to Boyce, "As regards a closer understanding with the international market, I think that to start with only one man is really important, and that is the irrepressible Marlborough. I have always remained on good terms with him . . . His ear would always be open to something really sound, especially if it emanated from the minority interests. He said as much in one of his very private and confidential letters to me."

"Marlborough" was, of course, their cover-name for Churchill. "Minority interests" meant the anti-Communists.

Although anxious as ever to tackle the Bolsheviks, Reilly became wary when it turned out that Maria Schultz did not know the identities of any of the leaders of "The Trust." Nor would the organization disclose any names at the top when pressed. Reilly lost patience at the purposelessness of attempting to merge all the anti-Bolshevik movements outside Russia into one movement with "The

Trust" inside Russia. It was not an option, since the anti-Bolsheviks were already a motley and irreconcilable collection of monarchists, bourgeoisie and social-revolutionaries. And who knew what "The Trust" was composed of? Or what "little list" they possessed for executing people they might consider undesirable?

He convinced Boyce that "The Trust" must first to be persuaded to agree to cooperate with foreign leaders before it would be possible to stage a successful counter-revolution. Otherwise there would be no solid foundation of trust. And, in particular, no financial one.

It turned out that although the leaders of "The Trust" had no intention of sending agents as far as the United States, they were anxious to have Reilly's advice, influence and help.

"Make contact directly with one of "The Trust's" more important agents in Helsinki," Boyce now directed him. "He is Nicolai Nicolaievich Bunakoff, who will answer any questions you want to ask—as long as you also send Bunakoff another letter to show Moscow Center or its representative that you are seriously interested in the so-called "commercial proposition."

They continued in their coded correspondence to refer to the political intrigue as if it were a business deal.

"Am I free to make suggestions?"

"Any suggestions you want. But you must, if possible, provide them with something to show that you are in a position to help them."

Reilly explained dismissively to Boyce in his next letter, "Our non-Russian supporters are already too impatient after waiting seven years, to accept the vague offers and promises in Bunakoff's communications."

He was disappointed and hesitated to go any further with Boyce's plan, in spite of Boyce's continually encouraging news of the strength of "The Trust." Had it not been for his poor financial position it was possible that Reilly would have gone no further at that stage. But he had always been a gambler, tempted by high rewards from taking high risks, so he replied again to Boyce's proposal.

"Much as I am concerned about my own personal affairs which, as you know, are in a hellish state, I am at any moment, if I see the right people and prospects of real action, prepared to chuck everything else and devote myself entirely to the Syndicate's interests.

"I was fifty-one yesterday and I want to do something worthwhile, whilst I can. All the rest does not matter. I am quite sure that you, although younger, feel likewise.

"Needless to say how deeply gratified I am to you for bringing me into this situation. I feel sure that if we are dealing with the right people, we will be able to work out something not only of the greatest interest generally, but possibly also of the greatest advantage to ourselves.

I shall write to you some more later.

Meantime—

Yours ever."

Reilly received a copy of a letter from Helsinki on April 4, which the leaders of "The Trust" had sent to Bunakoff as the go-between. It recommended that the best solution would be for Reilly to visit Russia and meet the executive of "The Trust" and make his own conclusions about its strength. Reilly wrote to Boyce right away:

"I am not only willing but anxious to do so and am prepared to come out as soon as I have arranged my affairs here."

Their letters were veiled to indicate that he was a businessman invited to investigate a manufacturing and distribution enterprise: "Of course I would undertake this tour of inspection only after very thorough consultation with you and Engineer B [Bunakoff]. Whilst there is no limit to which I am not prepared to go in order to help putting this new process on the market, I would naturally hate to provide a Roman holiday for the competitors. I think that I am not exaggerating in presuming that a successful inspection of the factory by me and the presentation of a fully substantiated technical report would produce a considerable impression in the interested quarters and generally facilitate realization of the scheme."

Boyce now made arrangements for a preliminary meeting two months later between Reilly and the representatives of "The Trust." But Reilly hesitated again, and gave his business problems as his reason. "I am struggling to restrain the people I owe money to, and want to put my affairs in to some sort of order before returning to the Continent of Europe."

Boyce finally met him when he reached Paris with Pepita on September 3. Once there, Reilly held long discussions with Boyce, General Kutyepoff, former chief of the Social-Revolutionary Secret Service, Burtzoff, and Grammatikoff. They all decided that the only way to be sure of whether cooperating with "The Trust" might result in a counter-revolution, would be if Reilly met its leaders in Helsinki, or somewhere close to the Russo-Finnish border.

"I am even prepared to risk travelling into Russia for a meeting," Reilly told them.

Reilly left for Helsinki a few days after their discussions, and stopped off to meet Vladimir Orloff in Berlin on the way. Orloff evidently respected the powers of "The Trust."

Reilly reached the venue in Helsinki on September 21 and met Bunakoff for the first time; also Maria Schultz and her husband. Boyce's assistant was present. He was as keen as Boyce on the enterprise. Reilly was encouraged still further by Maria Schultz's reports of the present situation in Russia.

He wrote from Helsinki, "If only twenty-five percent of what she said is based on facts (and not on self-induced delusion, as is so often the case when the wish is father to the will) then there is really something entirely new, powerful and worthwhile going on in Russia."

As expected, the leaders of "The Trust" failed to turn up. But Bunakoff received a message from Russia soon after Reilly's arrival. It stated that he should go on to Wyborg, which was close to the Russian border. The leaders would be waiting for him there on September 24.

When Reilly, Bunakoff and the Schultzes arrived in Wyborg, they were met by Yakushev with two other members of "The Trust."

Reilly cross-examined Yakushev intently, knowing that he had been spying for Boyce since 1921 and claimed to be in a senior post in Dzerzhinsky's GPU. He was one of the agents who had been sending intelligence reports on Russia to the Britain's Secret Service. Reilly was accustomed to the world of spies and double-agents, even triple-agents. He was satisfied that Yakushev was not an *agent-provocateur* under instructions from Dzerzhinsky, and that "The Trust" really was a powerful anti-Bolshevik underground movement.

6
Double-Cross

"STAY IN RUSSIA FOR A FEW DAYS and meet the Cabinet," Yakushev advised Reilly. "They may be the legitimate future Russian Government. They all have important top positions in the Soviet State. That's why it isn't possible for any of them to leave Russia: their absence would be noticed. In any case, if you want complete confidence in them, only a meeting with the top executives in Moscow will do that."

Reilly agreed to leave for Moscow the next day. Yakushev gave him a passport in the name of Nicolas Nicolaivich Steinberg before leaving for Russia himself.

"My colleagues will accompany you across the frontier. I'll meet you there."

Reilly had confided in Paul Dukes only the previous year that he intended to return to Russia to fight. But before leaving New York with his business position in poor shape, he had deliberately made financial arrangements for Pepita in case of his death, so he evidently believed the risk could be great. Only forty-eight hours before he knew for sure that he would be invited to Moscow, he had written to Pepita.

"Above all, don't worry about me. I feel perfectly well and my heart is overflowing with love for you. You are never out of my thoughts. We love each other so completely that it is impossible that such love should not reap its full reward both in spiritual and material happiness."

Reilly had made up his mind to the possibility that he might never return to the West.

In Reilly's continued obsession to be instrumental in overthrowing the Bolsheviks and restoring law and order to his beloved Russia, and bringing justice to the Russian people, this trip was an opportunity he could not resist whatever the risks. It seemed that "The Trust" was powerful enough to lead a counter-revolution. It only needed financial support from outside Russia to topple the Soviet Russian leaders. Apparently the leaders of "The Trust" needed his guidance and advice. How could he fail the millions of Russian people who were victims of Stalin's and Dzerzhinsky's Red Terror?

Reilly had waited seven years for this moment. At the very worst, he might lose his life. But, with his financial affairs in such poor shape, he was not afraid of that risk, particularly as "The Trust" had managed to save Savinkov's life, until he had decided to end it himself.

He gave the letter he had written for Pepita to their go-between, Bunakoff, with instructions to send it only if Reilly was unable to leave Russia.

He crossed into Russia with the two agents from "The Trust" and Maria's husband, George Radkevich, on September 25. Radkevich accompanied them for only a short distance before returning to Finland, where he reported that Reilly had boarded the train for Leningrad. That was the new name for Petrograd.

Boyce received a letter from Reilly, dated September 27, from Moscow, saying "All is well."

It was the last time that Boyce or anyone else in the West ever heard from Reilly.

Soon afterwards, a small announcement in *Izvestia* stated that, "On the night of September 28th/29th four smugglers attempted to cross the Finnish border. Two were killed, one, a Finnish soldier, taken prisoner and the fourth, mortally wounded, died on the way to Leningrad."

On the night when Reilly had been due to return to Finland, Finnish soldiers had heard shots. And a White Russian in the Finnish frontier police who was scheduled to escort Reilly back across the frontier had not returned. It appeared to be the end of the master-spy.

But who could tell in the shadowy world of secret agents, double-agents, forgeries and deceptions? Some people believed he was not dead, but was now working for, or maybe against, Soviet Russia. But that was mere supposition.

7

Pepita's Version

NEITHER BOYCE'S NOR GENERAL KUTYEPOFF'S AGENTS could find any evidence of Reilly's death after he vanished. Every enquiry hit a dead-end. Maria Schultz visited Russia to urge Edward Opperput in "The Trust" to obtain information for her. But he refused to say anything. Perhaps he knew nothing. Or perhaps he was afraid.

To Reilly's wife, Pepita, the silence was reassuring, because she was convinced that if the Russians had carried out Reilly's execution, they would have already reported it.

She phoned Thwaites at Britain's SIS, and also attempted to obtain Boyce's help. But Boyce had been far away in London when Reilly had disappeared in Moscow. All he could do now was send her reassuring letters from Helsinki and Stockholm.

Four weeks after Reilly's disappearance it was clear to Britain's Secret Service that something was not right. It now leapt into activity, hurriedly removing itself from a politically embarrassing situation. Always eager to use Reilly's skills in the past, now the SIS was anxious to deny any connection with him.

Boyce failed to turn up after arranging to meet Pepita in Paris. He wrote to her from London instead, to say,

"I have no recent information, and can't see how I could obtain any since my only possible source had already left Helsinki. He is on his way to meet you in Paris, so you will be advised of the situation sooner than I would. Unfortunately, I was prevented from seeing you in Paris because urgent business took me abroad again. It means I'll have no private address for a while. But I promise to let you know where I am later on, if you will arrange for letters to be forwarded from your present address. *Au revoir* and trusting you will soon get more definite and satisfactory information."

Bunakoff had no news either, but gave her Reilly's letter, as promised. Meanwhile, Pepita traced Boyce to *Berners Hotel* in London, but found he had been instructed that it would be unwise for a Secret Service agent to be seen with her.

"I will need all of Reilly's documents," he said when they arranged to meet in secret: "Private papers and correspondence, including the ones from me. Otherwise they could be valuable to the Communists, not only as propaganda, but to endanger our Secret Service operatives."

Alley and George Hill did whatever they could to discover the truth about why Reilly had disappeared. Hill visited Don Gregory at the Foreign Office and Sir Archibald Sinclair, the Member of Parliament who had been a Private Secretary to Winston Churchill. Sinclair hinted that the Government might pay compensation to Pepita for Reilly's death, but she received nothing, since payment could be interpreted as an official admission that Reilly had been on an assignment for the SIS when he vanished. In any case, Pepita was not Reilly's legal wife. When she complained that Cumming had known that and was a party to her bigamous marriage instead of preventing it, she was threatened into silence by a warning that her British passport could be taken from her.

Even though she now presumed that her husband was dead, she inserted a brief notice in the "Deaths" column of *The Times* on December 15, 1925, hoping that the authorities might be pressed into revealing something:

REILLY—On the 28th Sept., killed near the village of Allekul, Russia by G.P.U. troops, Captain Sidney George Reilly, M.C., late R.A.F., beloved husband of Pepita N. Reilly.

Britain's newspapers devoted considerable coverage in the following days to accounts of her husband's extraordinary exploits. One journalist wrote that he had even disguised himself as Lenin and undertaken an inspection of the Red Army. Why he would have bothered to do so was left unexplained. Many of the stories were complete fictions or exaggerations, or inaccurate sensationalism. The *Times* was more gentlemanly. It was the only newspaper not to display an editorial commentary. Harold Williams of the *Times* wrote to Pepita that Reilly "died well and in the best of causes," and claimed that they had published no comment because of "certain political complications."

The Foreign Office made no comment either, apart from admitting that they knew Reilly. They could not state if he was engaged in any work for the Foreign Office.

France mourned Reilly's presumed death, since he had provided the French and British Governments with information in December 1924, about a Communist rising planned to erupt in Paris and Northern France. The French Premier, Monsieur Herriot had ignored the warning at first, but was convinced by Baldwin's Government, which gave them conclusive proof, with the result that the Communist ringleaders were safely rounded up and deported from France.

La Liberté wrote, "Let France remember with gratitude this loyal servant of the Intelligence Service."

It was only later that Pepita Reilly divulged the strange and menacing experiences of being married to an international master-spy.

According to her, Reilly seldom spoke of the past. But she had no doubt that he was in love with his Russian homeland and dedicated to rehabilitating it. He was also captivated by England, which had adopted him. But he lived in the present and the future, not in the past. In spite of little of his history being forthcoming, Pepita gradually put together fragments of information that appeared in their conversations from time to time.

She knew her husband was involved in the conspiracies to restore Russia to a parliamentary democracy, and that their great hope as the instrument of that restoration was Boris Savinkov.

She insisted that Sidney was an ideal husband. But she was always made conscious of agents from the *Cheka* secret police who kept Savinkov and Reilly under their watchful eyes. Among Savinkov's donors was Sidney Reilly, who was known as a generous man. But, while Reilly gave funds which went largely to supporting Savinkov in a life of luxury, Sidney went into debt. There was nothing but worry for him and his failing business attempts, and the failure of his claim in the United States for funds owing to him that he desperately needed.

As she saw it, her husband had become a tormented and a sick man on the edge of a nervous breakdown. He was thinking more and more anxiously of returning to Russia, despite the possible danger to his life: he was still under sentence of death there. Sidney repeatedly warned her never to visit Russia herself, even if she received a letter inviting her to do so that might appear to come from him.

Then came the morning visit of a strange bearded Russian to their flat in Westminster. He announced himself as Mr. Warner. He spoke charmingly and seductively of Moscow and Petrograd, and the need of the oppressed Russian people for a leader like Reilly who could liberate them from the communists.

"When we have an idea," he said, "we have not a man who has the courage and resource to carry it out."

The stranger finally admitted that Warner was only his cover name, and introduced himself as Drebkoff. He claimed to be the head of a White Russian organization in Moscow. He showed Reilly an introductory letter from Savinkov in Paris, and others whose signatures Reilly knew.

Drebkoff had thought of everything to entice Sidney to Moscow. He showed Reilly a petition imploring him to come to Russia, and even produced a passport made out for him in a different name. Pepita argued with Drebkoff by pointing out Reilly's ill-health. And Reilly agreed with her that he would be worse than useless. Their Russian visitor left with regret.

After he left, Pepita said, "He's bound to be a messenger from the *Cheka* secret police."

But, when Reilly examined the documents, he said, "I think they're genuine."

The appeal to Reilly's generous heart and to his vanity, and the urgency of the invitation, had not failed to arouse Reilly's curiosity. He met Drebkoff for lunch at *The Savoy* the next day, and cancelled his intended vacation with Pepita, which she had planned as a much-needed rest for him.

Pepita described an attempt to kidnap Reilly in London that went wrong, and an incident when she was half-dragged into a fast-moving car with the window blinds down and an attempt to drug her by using a hypodermic needle. It too failed. But she had been scared that one or both of them would have been abducted to Russia and never heard of again.

Pepita had every reason to feel paranoid under watchful eyes, and see threats in everyone they met. The sensation that they were being watched followed her all the way to Paris.

"The problem," Sidney told her, "is that you never know who is with you and who is against you."

As she discovered in Paris, everybody involved with Russian politics was suspicious of everybody else. And with very good reason, since it seemed that no one was whom he or she made themselves out to be. And it was clearly evident that Reilly was being closely watched.

Pepita had observed the scenario unroll with its own momentum, but since most of the conversations she overheard were in Russian, the subtleties were lost on her. She had studied the two messengers during the arguments about Savinkov returning to Soviet Russia. One, she decided, was sardonic as he watched his colleague, while the other, who "was white and trembling and had hunted and despairing eyes," became more afraid the more that Reilly tried to persuade Savinkov not to go. He seemed to be "under the stress of some terrible threat." She was convinced that Savinkov would be caught in a trap.

Drebkoff was one of the watchers who followed them to the United States. Although he'd had a beard at first, he was now clean shaven. Pepita entered into conversation with him, and he was cynical enough almost to admit who he really was, although he now used the cover-name of Constantine. But he was so obvious that Reilly assured her he could not be the real threat: their watcher must be someone else whom they had not even noticed.

Reilly had done his best to lecture in the United States against the American loan to Soviet Russia. He received several anonymous letters warning him to desist, and was kept under close observation by *Cheka* agents. Nevertheless, he succeeded in preventing the loan. But he became a marked man when the hoped-for American loan was denied by Congress.

Reilly continued to send back intelligence information to the SIS about Bolshevik uprisings in different parts of the world, and his reports were distributed to other embassies too. Pepita could see that Sidney was impeding the operations of the Bolsheviks whenever he could.

All she had been left with was a mass of correspondence which was written to

Swedish Greta Garbo was Hollywood's idea of a Russian Commissar in Ernst Lubitch's satirical comedy movie, *Ninochka*, in 1939—in which Soviet officials seek an American loan.

and from her husband and his old friend Commander Ernest Boyce.

As months passed by, General Kutyepoff and others of Reilly's friends and associates, regretfully concluded that Reilly had been lured back to Russia by agents of the Soviet Government and was dead. Some suspected that "The Trust" was part of a Bolshevik plot. British Secret Service agents who had encouraged Reilly in his mission were dropped by the SIS, or reassigned elsewhere. Boyce retired from the Secret Service and was found another job with the *Société Française de Tabacs* by Alley in Paris. Rather than admit that they had been completely taken in by "The Trust," the SIS spread rumors that Reilly might have defected to the Communists, and might even have been a Soviet spy all along.

General Kutyepoff's right-hand man, General von Monkewitz, disappeared towards the end of 1926. No one knew whether he was a Red agent or had been lured to his destruction by "The Trust."

Maria Schultz, who was Kutyepoff's chief spy and the closest contact with "The Trust," through Opperput, was convinced of the strength of "The Trust" after seeing a mass of evidence of its anti-Bolshevick feelings. She had also seen anti-Bolshevik propaganda printed and circulated by them in Russia, and had even been present at secret meetings when its leaders had argued violently with members against Kremlin "murderers."

Although it was possible that it had been infiltrated by some GPU agents, she was certain of the integrity of the majority, and had enormous faith in Opperput, who was their Shadow Minister of Finance. She was also certain that Reilly was alive, although the leaders of "The Trust" would not confide in her.

The truth finally emerged in April 1927. Opperput—a tall red-headed man with a small beard who had served in the Tsar's army—confessed in neutral Finland that he had been a member of the OGPU counter-espionage all along.

Kutyepoff and Maria Schultz were shocked at his duplicity and treachery when they learned from him that "The Trust" was quite simply a Bolshevik plot to identify anti-Reds inside and outside Russia, and lure their leaders—Reilly in particular—into the GPU's hands, and murder them. As for "The Trust's" invisible leaders, they were all top GPU agents. The whole deceit had been designed by the chief of the KRO, Artuzoff, who was part of the GPU's counter-intelligence department.

To make "The Trust" thoroughly convincing, the GPU had deliberately printed anti-Bolshevik propaganda in Russia themselves, distributed their own anti-Soviet literature, and even organized genuine counter-revolutionary unrest. The leaders had always kept their operation under control, so that they could pounce on anyone they did not trust whenever they wanted to.

"What now?" Maria asked him.

"Since "The Trust's" main objective has now been reached," Opperput thought aloud that "it might be disbanded, or kept preserved to use again in future."

Feliks Dzerzhinsky died in mysterious circumstances in 1926. It was an occupational hazard for heads of secret police departments, since they knew who ordered the tortures and murders and where the bodies were buried. Menjinsky had replaced him as head of the GPU and, like Feliks, would liquidate any of his own agents at will, after they had served his purpose. It was said that he suffered from a persecution complex. He grew up in a wealthy family, trained as a lawyer and had only contempt for the working classes, whom he called "A stupidity discovered by the intelligentsia."

Opperput had defected to save his own skin.

According to him, "Reilly reached Moscow as planned. He had several discussions with Yakushev, Artuzoff, and Styrne—who was his right-hand man—innocently enough. I saw what happened. The OGPU did not intend to kill Reilly at first. They thought that if they did, anti-Bolsheviks outside Russia would become aware of the danger of "The Trust." It would have to be disbanded, and a considerable potential source of intelligence about anti-Bolshevik activities would be lost.

"Their original plan was to allow Reilly to return to Finland as evidence of the legitimacy and power of "The Trust." Then Reilly might lull Kutyepoff and the others counter-revolutionaries into a complacent view that "The Trust" was powerful enough on its own to create a counter-revolution, and its effectiveness should not be interfered with for fear of preventing a revolution from happening.

"But their attitude changed once Reilly reached Russia. He was their greatest enemy and should not be allowed to leave. The leaders of the secret police were divided on the issue and they argued. Reilly's fate was under discussion for two days after he had been quietly arrested and locked up in Butyrsky prison. To resolve the deadlock, the matter was referred to the Politbureau. Stalin decided that Reilly should not leave Russia alive."

Like Lenin before him, Stalin suffered from a deficit of feelings towards human beings, and was deeply involved in "the dirty business of politics."

Opperput told Maria that Reilly had been well-treated in prison for a while and even allowed to go for drives; even given his favorite brand of whisky. But he refused to answer questions, and there could be only one consequence, since no-one could resist the interrogations of the OGPU. So Reilly had finally been broken.

"When the secret police had squeezed all they could out of him, they staged a faked shooting accident on the Finnish frontier, to deceive the public that Reilly had been shot at a border post in mistake for a smuggler."

Although the circumstances of Opperput's admission had the appearance of truth, with all the deceit and double-talk it was more than likely that his story was a pack of lies—just another tactical move by the OGPU, who might be anxious that "The Trust" was blown.

In any case, Maria thought, "how could the traitor Opperput possibly be trusted to tell the truth?"

Maria Schultz was determined to find out what the truth really was. Suspicion of Opperput increased after he escorted her back into Russia and she failed to return when he did. Maria was never seen or heard of again.

8
The Hunt for Sidney Reilly

ONE OF THE ERRORS IN OPPERPUT'S ACCOUNT of what had happened to Reilly—even though only a tiny clue—was that Reilly never drank whisky. It indicated that Opperput's whole story and his flight to Finland was a double-cross. Even if everything else were true, his error over the whisky suggested that he had heard the story of what happened to Reilly at second-hand. That raised questions about what part of his tale had been true and whether all of it was a pack of lies.

Soon after Opperput fled from Soviet Russia, the Russians claimed they had uncovered an anti-Soviet plot by his chief, General Kutyepoff. The announcement was followed by mass executions across Russia.

Two years after Reilly disappeared, the Russian Minister in Warsaw, Voikoff, was assassinated, and the Russian news media claimed in an announcement in June 1927 that Reilly had been involved—that the assassination had been carried out by British secret agents. It raised the question: "Had Reilly been locked up in prison for two years, or had he been free the whole time?" And if neither of those possibilities was true, why did the Soviets wait for two years before making the announcement?

According to their news item, the true answer appeared to be connected to "the rupture by Great Britain of diplomatic relations with the USSR." It went on to say that "In the summer of 1925, a certain merchant carrying a Soviet passport with the name of Steinburg was wounded and arrested by the Frontier Guard while illegally crossing the Finnish frontier."

"During the enquiry a witness declared that his name was actually Sidney George Riley, [sic] and that he was an English spy, a captain of the Royal Air Force, one of the chief organizers of 'Lockhart's Plot,' who by sentence of the Tribunal of December 3rd, 1918, had been declared an outlaw.

"Riley[sic] declared that he came to Russia for the special purpose of organizing terrorist acts, arson and revolts, and that when coming from America he had seen Mr. Churchill, Chancellor of the Exchequer, who personally instructed him as to the reorganization of terroristic and other acts calculated to create a diversion."

Reilly's name was spelt incorrectly, and the announcement failed to mention his fate. Its story of the frontier incident differed from the original one released by the GPU, as well as from Opperput's story that he had been mortally wounded. But, by a strange coincidence, another press announcement stated that Léon Trotsky and Zinoviev had been expelled from the Communist Party. What was the connection, if any? Was it just a typical case of distracting the public from changes in leadership of the Soviet Union by confusing them?

Then, three months later, in September, *Izvestia* released some fairly harmless correspondence between Reilly and a former Russian officer named Bunakoff, in which Reilly was accused of writing "the only possibility of combating Bolshevism is to organize attacks on the Commissars."

Also in September, the Russian press announced the trial of five Russian terrorists accused of throwing bombs in the Communist Club in Leningrad three months previously. It quoted the Attorney-General for the GPU and Assistant Prosecutor, as having stated that the five terrorists had been "in close contact with the Secret Intelligence Service of England." It continued by announcing the imminent trial of six more alleged British spies. Reilly was named as "the British chief directing terrorist acts in Soviet Russia." He was described as a confidential agent of Churchill.

If the GPU had really executed Reilly in 1925, he could not possibly be directing terrorism in 1927, unless their original statement of his death was false and he had escaped and was now leading a counter-revolutionary group of partisans against the Communists.

Another report that Reilly was still alive came from a White Russian escapee from a Soviet prison who had managed to cross Siberia and reach Tientsin in October 1927. He maintained that Reilly was in the Orlovsky Prison, and that he was insane.

When the question of Reilly's activities was raised in Britain's House of Commons by a Communist M.P. named Mr. Saklatvala, the Parliamentary Under-Secretary of State for Foreign Affairs denied that Reilly had worked for Bruce Lockhart in 1918 or that he had tried to enter the Soviet Union in 1925 with the knowledge of the Foreign Office.

Mr. Locker-Lampson added: "I have no information regarding Mr. Reilly's alleged entry into Russia in 1925 beyond what has already appeared in the press."

He was entirely correct in that the Foreign Office never had any official dealings with Secret Service agents.

Another report—this one reached Riga from Moscow in November—stated that Reilly was still alive. It said that he had been tortured by the GPU and made a confession that had led to the arrest of a number of spies. It was impossible to resist confessing to anything under their crude and brutal torture. Many victims managed to commit suicide rather than submit to more torture. At the time when Reilly had disappeared, the number of executions by the Cheka and then the GPU was in excess of a quarter of a million. In addition, 1.3 million victims were imprisoned in about six thousand Russian gaols. Anyone who volunteered for the secret police and Russia's prison service was known for his or her sadism.

After those Soviet Russian press announcements in which Reilly's name was mentioned, there was only silence.

Reilly's wife Pepita and his former lover Caryll Houselander were left to wonder what had really happened to him and whether he was still alive. Caryll told friends that she was still in love with him and had experienced another mystical vision ten years after he had disappeared into Russia.

"I travelled far" she said, "and shared a prison cell with someone who suffered."

Evidently she was speaking of sharing Reilly's sufferings in 1935—ten years after he was said to have been executed. She gave her own account of her deep and abiding love for Sidney Reilly, which was very much what most, or all, of his other mistresses and wives had felt about him.

"In spite of my infidelity I still regarded myself as a Catholic and still regarded my sins as being sins . . . now I was tempted to turn my back on the Church once and for all, and to take what happiness life seemed to offer me outside it . . . the simple truth was that I was being swept by temptation as dry grass is swept by a flame of fire."

She wrote a posthumous poem in his honor, in which she likened him to "Christ on the Cross."

Rumors continued - sometimes that Reilly was still alive, sometimes that he was dead, and that he had escaped from one prison or another. Some British personnel of MI5 interpreted the official Soviet silence as meaning that he had made a deal with the Bolsheviks. If he was working for them, they would be unlikely to mention him again. He was, after all, Russian-born and with a great love for his country and its people. There were plausible rumors that he was working for them in China, which he knew at first-hand better than most westerners.

There was another possibility which was just as reasonable. It was that he had staged a suicide once again, as he had done when he had been nineteen years old, in order to assume a new identity. His life in the West was over and he was burdened with debts, whereas in Russia, he might well have realized his mistake over "The Trust" and finally recognized it in time as a trap to capture him. And so he had vanished again. Perhaps he had returned to the Amazon in South America, which he already knew. He spoke the language. Anything was possible with Reilly. And it would account for his silence and the Russian contradictions.

Much later on, the GPU appeared to know as little as the British Secret Service did about where Reilly was, since they gave out a vague story that they had captured Reilly and he had confessed. That news release appeared to have been driven by a desire to ensure that he would be permanently discredited if he ever turned up again in Britain or Russia. It indicated that their original story of his accidental death at a border post was false.

In 1931, a sensational serial appeared in the pages of the *Evening Standard* about Reilly's Russian adventures, under the byline of Pepita Reilly as "Sidney Reilly's wife." It prompted new questions in the House of Commons and a demand for the Foreign Office to pressure the Soviet Government for news about him. It brought Margaret out of hiding in Brussels to seize the opportunity to sue for libel, since she was the only legal Mrs. Reilly. The newspaper settled for a few thousand pounds in damages. The published book was withdrawn. And no one was any wiser about Reilly's bigamous marriage to Pepita.

Another incident that indicated Reilly might still be alive was that Pepita's flat in Paris was broken into several times and some of Reilly's papers, including a file on the Zinoviev Letter, were stolen.

Reports and rumors of Reilly being seen alive in Russia, in the United States, and in the Middle East, arrived at British Intelligence bureaus from time to time. One that emerged from a Polish official named Brunovsky, who had been released from Butyrsky Prison, claimed that a friend of his had discovered that an important British spy was locked up in the same prison. The name meant nothing to Brunovsky, but he had written it down on a scrap of linen which he had stitched into the lining of his coat. It read, "British officer Reilly. Persia. Father-in-law."

Few people remembered Reilly's connection with Persian oil by that time. Lockhart supposed that the Russian word for father-in-law was actually Reilly's code name in the Secret Service: S.T.1. It was plausible that the message had come from Reilly. But, if so, what could it mean?

In the same year that the Pepita's Reilly story had appeared in the *Evening Standard,* a British official in the Middle East reported that he had been approached by a Russian sailor on a tramp steamer, who told him in accentless English that he was anxious to desert from the ship; that his name was Reilly and he had escaped from Odessa. He needed money and clothing. The British official met him ashore and provided money and clothes, and a bed for the night.

A Liberal M.P. named Geoffrey Shakespeare asked the British Government in June of that year if there was any news of Reilly. The reply he received was; "No further information can be obtained."

At the end of the Second World War in 1945, when Russia was Britain's ally and George Hill liaised with the NKVD in Moscow, an NKVD agent told another member of the British Mission that Reilly was still alive, and that he was in prison but insane.

The NKVD was the successor to the OGPU.

9

Soviet Russia in a Hole

Three months after a 1966 article appeared in *Nedelya* about how the Soviet *Cheka* had bested Reilly and Lockhart by discovering the so-called "Lockhart Plot" in 1918 to overthrow Lenin and Trotsky, the file on Sidney Reilly was still not complete. No one in the West knew for sure whether he was alive or dead, or even if he was working for or against the West or the Soviet Union.

Nedelya was Russia's Sunday Magazine section of the government controlled *Izvestia,* and could not therefore be believed anyway. Then a book which claimed to provide the full story was published in Russia in the early part of June 1966. It sold about two million copies. Its Russian title was translated into English as *Troubled Waters.*

Until then, there had been numerous versions which described what had happened to Sidney Reilly after he was accompanied across the border into Russia by agents of "The Trust." He had been mistakenly shot dead as a smuggler in a misunderstanding at the border post. He had been arrested after meetings with the heads of the "The Trust," and executed. He had been imprisoned for two years and was still behind bars, but insane. He had escaped and was still fighting the

Bolsheviks in Europe. He had escaped to Brazil where he had changed his identity once again. And, just as likely—to some even more so—he had collaborated with the Bolsheviks to avoid torture and death. No one in the West knew which version was the true one.

Now the author of this new Russian publication provided yet another version of the Reilly saga. Apparently everyone had interpreted the information they had heard in very different ways, according to their own situation or attitudes, or their purpose. But this Russian author insisted that his version was the only "true" one. It was certainly different from the others.

Two thing which were abundantly clear from the outset was that this Russian version was written in a semi-literate bureaucratic form. Its writer was clearly no Tolstoy or Dostoyevsky, but an inept propagandist more accustomed to writing communist manifestos in a pretentious dialectical jargon which was often meaningless, largely in order to impress Russian readers with the legitimacy of the Soviet regime. It was also intended to impress on the general global public how efficient Soviet Russia's security services were.

There were very good reason for raking up the past and reinterpreting it, since Soviet Russia was seen by the general public through a haze of misinformation and disinformation which contributed its own myths and fantasies about contemporary life in the USSR. Which of all the mangled versions was true, and which was false? Apparently it was an attempt to set the records straight on the very existence of the Soviet Union.

What was clearly evident was that the Soviet leaders suffered from guilt. After they had finally turned away from concentrating on wreaking revenge against the previous regime they had overthrown, and had murdered their opponents, they feared they might be accused by the West of being simply subversive malcontents, and politically illegitimate—criminal traitors who had betrayed and destroyed their own country.

The situation was best expressed by the liberal statesman and a former Minister for War, Alexander Guchkov, who remarked, "It is now to be proved whether we are a nation of free men or a gang of mutinous slaves."

Russia had undergone a number of transformations since the early days of Sidney Reilly. After Marshal Stalin had died in mysterious circumstances, Malenkov became locked in a struggle for leadership with Nikita Khrushchev. Khrushchev became First Secretary of the Central Committee of the Communist Party and Soviet Union in September 1953. He, in turn, was toppled from power in October 1964—even officially fired from office. Unusually for Russia, he was not executed, but permitted to retire.

The next leader of Soviet Russia in 1964 was Leonid Brezhnev, who took the title of Chairman of the Presidium. He remained in office until his death in 1982. He was the leader from whom the publishers of this new account would have been obliged to obtain approval before they dared to print it. That meant every sentence and possible allusion in the book had been carefully examined beforehand by a number of people for its effect, in order to protect the USSR and its present leaders from the kinds of damaging accusations previously made against Marshal Stalin by Khrushchev.

It had been during Khrushchev's term in office that the awful crimes committed to millions of innocent people by Joseph Stalin's reign of terror had been admitted publicly by Russia's leaders. It had had a sobering effect on the Soviet image and its policies.

For one thing, although most of the uninformed Russian population refused to believe anything criminal of their revered former leader—who had, after all, saved Russia from annihilation by Nazi troops—leadership of the USSR had become an even more dangerous occupation after all the disclosures. Consequently Brezhnev took care not to act without the approval of all of the members of the Presidium. He was now merely the first among equals.

The Soviet military continued to expand under Brezhnev, and so did Russia's global influence. But, after Khrushchev withdrew ignominiously from the showdown with America's President Kennedy over the Russian-made nuclear missiles in Cuba, the Soviet leaders had been forced to recognize that the USSR had spent far too much on military and scientific expansion and nuclear power in order to compete with the United States for world domination. Now they could no longer continue to do so without American approval, even cooperation, since Soviet Russia had already, in effect, lost its independence.

The Soviet hedgehog had continued to dig itself into a deeper and deeper hole, and was now stuck in a dead-end. Concealed behind the assumed veneer of power, Russia's economy had declined to a state of stagnation (*zastoi*) as its Gross National Product dwindled.

"We know now that it was really decay," America's Condoliza Rice would write many years later when so much was public knowledge.

The new Russian book, with its alleged disclosures about what happened to Sidney Reilly, could therefore be viewed as a snatched opportunity to persuade Russians and the outside world of how efficient Soviet Russia really was at the time Reilly disappeared. It also acted as a prelude to reassuring the public that Communism was still a global force to be reckoned with. At the same time—although the world would not discover it for another three decades—the USSR was already collapsing economically and socially from within.

This most recent Russian version of Reilly's fate claimed to describe the entire story of Dzerzhinsky's success and that of the GPU in Reilly's capture in 1925. At least, the most recent before Robin Lockhart decided to publish a new book about Sidney Reilly to put the records straight. For reasons of policy and insecurity, the Russian leaders evidently felt a need to boast about their victory over Britain's Intelligence Services by using this new Russian book.

The motives behind Soviet Russian propaganda were not obvious then or later, due to Russia's very different history, its different values, and its ambiguous attitudes. Russia has always been uniquely Russia; as France was uniquely French, Germany uniquely German, and Britain uniquely British. But Brezhnev's Russia wanted global recognition and respect. Apparently the Soviet leaders thought they could obtain it by taking the legend of Sidney Reilly down a peg in public

Drawing in the May 1931 London *Evening Standard* "Master Spy" serial extolling Reilly's heroism as a British Secret Service agent known as Comrade Relinsky.

regard and exposing his weaknesses by painting him as a villain, while Russia's secret police were praised as patriotic heroes. This new version might even have been meant primarily for domestic consumption, as a warning for discontented Russians to behave, or be visited by secret police agents of Soviet Russia's efficient OGPU in the early grey and bleak hours of the morning when many people lie awake and meditate uneasily on the meaning of life.

The following narrative is taken from the translation of the Russian book and paraphrased to emphasize only those points necessary to explain the alleged fate of Sidney Reilly and the alleged failure of Britain's Secret Service. The obvious attempts to blacken Reilly in order to whitewash themselves would fool few people today, but evidently the Soviet authorities thought it would, with a new and naïve young generation in the mid-1960s—regardless of the situation where the narrative, with some minor details inserted to lend a sense of authenticity, gradually comes unstuck as we read it. This finally is the story from Russian officialdom's point of view, as seen through a very dark looking glass. It begins as follows;

"It was in the winter of 1917 that a certain Monsieur Massino appeared in aristocratic circles, his visiting card proclaiming him to be 'Agent for Turkish and Eastern Countries.' He was seen, that spring, in the cafés and gambling clubs where wine from the Imperial cellars could be ordered. As for his appearance; 'Monsieur Massino had the face of a man who has lived too well, his eyes are alive with an evil glint and his lips are sensual. He holds himself very straight, despite his years, and is very elegantly dressed.' Very few knew that his pseudonym concealed the identity of Sidney George Reilly, secret agent of the Intelligence Service.

"Reilly obtained false documents that brought him into a number of Soviet organizations. He possessed several different addresses, and was at home in all strata of society. Especially was he at home with women. As he asked his close friends, "If a lieutenant of artillery could manage to blow up the dying embers of the fire of French Revolution, why cannot a lieutenant of the Intelligence Service become dictator of Moscow?"

Evidently the Russian author had read Bruce Lockhart's comments in his own best-seller, but his narrative style appeared to have been influenced by Victorian stage melodramas. It declined steadily as the plot unrolled and the character assassination of Sidney Reilly by the Soviet propaganda continued relentlessly.

But to attempt to understand what it is really about, it is necessary first to catch up on the course of history by filling in some missing details, according to what we know from Reilly, from Robert Bruce Lockhart, and from several British secret agents who worked with Reilly.

10
A Marked Man

WHEN REILLY TEAMED UP WITH CROMIE to sabotage Russia's Baltic Fleet in the fall of 1918, he planned to mount a counter-revolution to create an opportunity for Allied troops to arrive and enter Petrograd in a bloodless coup, as they had already done, more or less, in Archangel.

Cromie transmitted the plan to the Admiralty in naval code, stating "Great discontent here in Red Army chiefly Let [Latvian] among whom we are agitating Bolsheviks (in) general very nervous."

If the naval code was intercepted—and historian Michael Kettle thought it was—it could have made Cromie a marked man by the Bolsheviks for "tampering with the loyalty of the Lettish troops at such a desperate moment."

Cromie reported in his next wire to General Poole, who commanded the Allied troops at Archangel, that allied officers were being prevented by the Bolsheviks from wiring either abroad or in Russia. Nor were they allowed to move from one town to any other. British subjects had been arrested in previous days without any charge. He had protested, and planned to tell the Soviets he had informed the British Government and requested Allied troops in Archangel to rescue British diplomats and citizens. As a consequence, those arrested by the Bolsheviks were released and were now under house arrest instead.

He also warned Poole that the local Russian commissar threatened to intern all allied subjects as soon as Allied troops occupied Vologda, which was midway between Archangel and Petrograd. He asked Poole to inform the Admiralty that "Position of Soviet power in Petrograd is becoming rapidly untenable."

Only then did it emerge that the number of Allied troops who had landed in Archangel was no more than 1,200. The limitations of the force changed the attitude of the Bolsheviks, since it was far too little to make much difference.

Reilly was aware of the contents of messages being wired between Moscow and Berlin about a treaty to withdraw Russia from the war against Germany, which he had been directed to do his best to avoid. He decided that the Latvians—who were the best fighting force—should arrest Lenin and Trotsky and march them through the street to public ridicule. After which he would organize Russian officers to set up a provisional military government. He would have Uritsky, who headed the *Cheka* in Petrograd, arrested. He would ensure that bridges would be blown up to prevent German troops from arriving in Archangel to outnumber Allied troops.

But Uritsky stated flatly that he knew what was going on in the old British Embassy. Consequently, the Bolsheviks now decided to use an *agent provocateur* to crush Reilly's plot before it was ready.

In the crisis of the moment, Cromie apparently became lax with his security by sending a note to Robert Bruce Lockhart through a young man named Smidchen, who would turn out to be a *Cheka* agent. The note stated that Cromie was making his way out of Russia. It added that Smidchen might be of use. Smidchen took the note to the Latvian Colonel Berzin. Berzin passed it to another Latvian named Peters, who was the deputy head of the *Cheka*.

Colonel Berzin was already in touch with the French and American Secret Services, and appeared to Lockhart, Reilly, and Hill, to be disillusioned with the Bolsheviks. Meanwhile, the allies now had troops outside Petrograd, and a fifth column inside. And the Latvian guard was under suspicion. It was evident that something significant was about to happen.

Berzin turned out to be the key to what followed. If the Bolsheviks won, the Latvians could denounce Lockhart for plotting against them. But if the Allies won, they could save themselves.

Reilly visited the American Consulate a few days later, where he met American Consul Poole, French Consul Grenard, and Colonel de Vertement. The Moscow correspondent of *Le Figaro*, Réné Marchand, was also present. Although Reilly left the room to talk privately with Colonel de Vertement, as it turned out, Marchand had quietly followed him into the room and listened to their conversation.

Marchand would turn out to be a double-agent who passed on whatever he learned to Feliks Dzerzhinsky.

By that time the populations of Russia's main towns were approaching starvation, and Izvestia claimed on August 25 that Allied agents had blown up several food trains. Marchand went to the Bolsheviks and informed them what he had heard - which was simply a proposal to blow up bridges on the Petrograd railway line where German forces planned to travel to the Allied front at Archangel.

Two days later, a treaty was signed between the Bolsheviks and Germany, in which the Russians would sell oil from Baku to the Germans and offer Germany the use of the Russian Fleet in the Black Sea. The day after that, Reilly and Berzin returned to Petrograd to complete Reilly's plans for an uprising against the Bolsheviks.

Next day, the *Cheka* raided the French Secret Service bureau's offices and arrested all French agents, except for Colonel de Vertement, who managed to escape by clambering across the rooftops. Hill broke off contact with the French and sent a warning to Reilly in Petrograd. But his agent was apparently arrested on the train before he could reach him.

It was then that *Cheka* agents entered the flat of the ballerina Dagmara, with whom Reilly generally stayed when in town. The result was that the *Cheka* arrested Colonel Friede that night and tortured him until he confessed that Reilly had copies of the trade treaty between the Russian Bolsheviks and Germany. Reilly had to be stopped from sending them to England.

Uritsky was assassinated in front of *Cheka* headquarters in Petrograd on August 30, and Lenin was shot by Dora Kaplan as he left a Moscow factory. Those two shootings and the exposure of Reilly's plans for a counter-revolution triggered the Bolshevik "Red Terror."

Robert Bruce Lockhart was taken from his bed by the *Cheka* after midnight.

"Where's Reilly?" they asked him. When he refused to answer, they arrested him.

Hundreds of Russian officers and members of the middle classes were shot out of hand. It was only the beginning.

When Reilly phoned Cromie at the Embassy for a meeting in a café on August 31, Cromie failed to turn up. Reilly rushed over to the old Embassy to find him, and discovered it was already surrounded by *Cheka* agents and troops who battered on the front door and tore it open. Cromie stood on the landing at the top of the staircase with a handgun, while the British Consul dashed upstairs to destroy any confidential and incriminating papers. *Cheka* agents mounted the stairs and Cromie opened fire, killing one and wounding another. The *Cheka* returned fire and their bullets struck Cromie, who fell headlong down the red carpeted staircase.

When the Embassy staff were escorted out, they saw Cromie's body lying at the foot of the stairs, with blood where he had struck his head.

Reilly slipped away among the *Cheka* agents outside and disappeared. When the news of Cromie's murder and Lockhart's arrest reached the War Cabinet in London, there was now no excuse not to intervene formally against the Bolsheviks.

Reilly returned to Moscow. Hill wrote that he was splendid, despite being hunted by the *Cheka*; "and yet he was absolutely cool, calm and collected, not in the least down-hearted, and only concerned in gathering together the broken threads and starting afresh."

After taking a ship out of Russia, Reilly landed in Estonia at Reval, where he had not planned to go, but arrived because of a misunderstanding. Reilly introduced himself as Lieutenant Sidney Reilly RFC to a Dutchman named Mr. van den Bosch, who had brought him out of Petrograd, and explained that he was an English officer on a special mission in Russia.

The Bolsheviks were not slow in setting up a tribunal to try Lockhart and Reilly for their counter-revolutionary activities. These were the findings of the Tribunal:

"This attempt at a counter-revolution was carried out with cynical disregard for international law and with criminal means to violate extra-territorial privileges. The whole onus rests in the first instance on the capitalist Governments, the responsibility for whose evil purposes lies with the indicted persons. The Revolutionary Tribunal finds R. Lockhart, Grenard and S. G. Reilly to be enemies of the working people and orders them to be shot on their first appearance on Russian territory."

Reilly managed to hide before the Tribunal commenced its sittings, while Lockhart and Grenard had already been expelled from Russia.

11
Reilly's Odyssey

TWO DAYS AFTER THE END OF THE WAR against Germany, Britain's policy had swung in Winston Churchill's favour, which was for military intervention against the Reds in Soviet Russia. It was in accordance with Lockhart's and Reilly's recommendations to support White Russian anti-Bolshevik forces in South Russia in order to prevent it from becoming a communist police state.

'C' ordered Reilly and Hill to return to the shores of the Black Sea and the territory occupied by the White Armies and the interventionists. They pretended to be businessmen engaged in commerce. They left England separately for South Russia by destroyer. The first information they sent back to the SIS was, "The original Russian anti-Bolshevik volunteer army is now under the command of General Anton Denikin, and the Don Cossacks are in action under the leadership of General Krasnov."

At more or less the same time, a British Military Mission led by General Poole headed for South Russia. First-hand reports from Reilly of Russian troop movements now came thick and fast to British Intelligence in London.

In the early part of 1918, the south had been roughly divided into French and British zones of interest and command, to enable them to support local White Russian forces. Admiral Kolchak had recently launched a coup in Omsk, the capital of Siberia, and called himself the military dictator. Now, according to Reilly's report, "Kolchak has agreed to cooperate with Denikin."

In another of Reilly's earlier reports, he advised that in his opinion, "the Reds cannot stand up to regular troops who are trained and experienced and better equipped."

He recommended fast and decisive action. It seems that his close friendships with the Polish Marshal Pilsudski and Boris Savinkov had discovered in him a military strategist and tactician, as his expertly detailed reports from the battlefronts now revealed. To judge from the impression they created in the SIS, it might even have been that Reilly had been trained in a military institution during those years in which he had claimed to have rescued a British Intelligence officer named Major Fothergill in the Amazon jungle.

His initial emphasis lay in deciding on unity of command.

"General Krasnov," he wrote, "is an opportunist. He has to be made to understand that supplies of equipment and arms and ammunition by the Allies depend on overall leadership by Denikin. He will do so with good grace because he is a clever man. The Cossacks will follow Krasnov in a campaign against Moscow, if it is short; otherwise not."

Perhaps his most significant warning was that "It will be fatal for Russia, and probably for Europe, if this task is not accomplished by next summer."

Reilly and Hill met with Denikin, who was a man of fifty. They described him as "possessing a dignified and cultured manner and a fine presence, of the higher staff officer type, rather than the fighting type: determined, well-balanced, broad-minded, high-thinking—but he lacked the characteristics that mark a ruler of men."

Nor did Denikin seem very optimistic. They quoted him as saying;

"In the old days, an army was victorious when it took the capital city and the church bells rang to announce it, while the army marched through the city to warn the population to behave."

"But," he said, "we cannot save Russia through Moscow: it must be conquered as a whole, and only with the assistance of the Allies."

To clarify what he meant, he added with more determination, "We will do all the fighting, but you must stand by, and protect us from being struck in the back."

Those were the type of first-hand reports that Reilly sent from the battlefronts. They continued to hearten Winston Churchill and encourage his stubbornness to fight on, regardless of Prime Minister Lloyd George's more parochial, or politically pragmatic approach to the Russian Civil War.

When Reilly paid a visit to Ataman Krasnov of the Cossacks, he found "bribery and corruption and suppression, typical of the old regime."

Reilly's first impression on meeting him was that he would not keep his word with Denikin. Krasnov believed firmly that it was too early to appoint a commander of all the forces: they should wait until the military position was clearer.

"What most of the generals really want," Reilly explained, "is the traditional tribal or provincial warlord type of power of the old agrarian or tribal regimes." Regardless of Reilly's doubts about him, he summed up Krasnov as "a genius of an entrepreneur and a soldier who was accustomed to speed, having fought with the Germans."

Krasnov could not understand why the Allies were so slow and hesitant. But they had, of course just fought, and almost lost, the biggest and most technological war in history, and they had had enough of war.

Reilly was convinced that the Volunteer Army was the only dependable force and represented unity—which was what he had been recommending from the outset. "But its success will depend on the amount and promptness of support from the Allies."

He recommended that a British Commissioner should be sent to General Denikin.

He passed through Sebastopol on the way back to Odessa on January 29, 1919, where he found the Bolsheviks taking great pains to seduce sailors and troops "with money, women and all forms of entertainment. Their major propaganda tactic is to make them feel nostalgic for their homes and families."

When Reilly returned to Odessa in early February, he found it in utter turmoil under French military occupation. Having investigated the spheres he had been asked to, and sent back his reports on the situation in each area, he had now completed his work in South Russia and was told to await instructions or return to London.

But, among all the paperwork passing back and forth about him, J. D. Gregory, who was head of the Russia department in the Foreign Office, added a note in his own handwriting; "I understand that Mr. Reilly is one of the most useful agents we could have in Russia, and it seems a great pity he should return."

The remark was approved and initialed by his superior, Sir Ronald Graham.

To judge from Reilly's observations about the anti-Bolshevik generals, it is clear that his reports were being read by Winston Churchill, who acted on them. And, despite Lloyd George's frustrated anger at what he considered Churchill's obsession with the Russians, and General Denikin in particular, Reilly's reports from the South Russian front made Churchill more determined than ever to crush the Bolsheviks before they could become established for good.

Finding no further use for his services in South Russia, after reporting on the French fiasco which continued in the Ukraine, Reilly returned to London, leaving the situation in South Russia shifting like a kaleidoscope.

1919 was a time of considerable frustration at the Paris Peace Conference, where Lloyd George, Clemenceau, and President Wilson, continued to quarrel with each other, patch up their differences and quarrel again. Reilly was expected there at the end of March. It was only a short visit, but at least he was able to discourage implementations of the Bullitt peace proposals to the Bolsheviks. He sailed to the United States and was reunited with Nadine in New York.

Reilly reported to the Foreign Office in London on his progress in New York on May 10, informing Picton Bagge—who was Britain's Commercial Secretary to Russia - that America's banks and industrialists were considering Russia as a potential market for goods and investment.

"What banks and corporate investors are waiting for," Reilly explained, "is the restoration of law and order in Russia."

Five days later, Reilly reported, "I have seen one of the foremost experts on the Russian economy, who provided considerable information, with statistics, maps and charts on Russia's natural resources and industrial and commercial potential. I advise inviting this expert to England, where he could also cooperate in the Jaroszynski situation."

That situation was one which the British Government had been reluctant to pursue.

Reilly boarded the SS *Baltic* for England on the same day.

Sir John Picton Bagge accepted his proposals and immediately prepared a program to take over the Russian banks. He attached Reilly's telegrams to his report, adding that Jaroszynski would be arriving in London in a few days' time. Sir Ronald Graham decided it looked like a financially and commercially sound scheme. Acting Foreign Secretary Lord Curzon agreed, without committing himself in any way.

Reilly arrived at the Foreign Office from New York on June 7, where he gave his views on the Russian situation. He explained that White Russian advances were very slow, and put forward a proposal to deal with that problem. It categorized, firstly, the best use to be made of General Denikin; then the influence of the Orthodox Church. And, lastly, how best to handle Ataman Gregoriev in the Ukraine.

His audience, including Rex Leeper, were all impressed with the success of his Intelligence mission, the details of his report, and his well thought out advice on possible strategies and tactics.

Reilly asked Winston Churchill for support. Churchill, who was now Secretary of State for War, proved enthusiastic and supportive, as usual. But Britain's Foreign Office appeared to be structured, as a matter of policy, to resist making decisions whenever possible. Churchill warned them that "If England will not give this assistance, Kolchak and Denikin will perish, and then Germany will step in."

Reilly's enemies in the Foreign Office referred obliquely to "somebody called Reilly," and marked him as a dangerous character who had been in the German Secret Service. But, since General Denikin was advancing with his troops, Britain's War Cabinet agreed to provide the General with further support for eight months, until March 1920.

Denikin's forces surged forward all through that summer and autumn. But Admiral Kolchak was retreating; and then running in headlong flight by the end of September. Unfortunately for them, they were not receiving supplies of war material promised by Britain. Nor was General Yudenitch. The Bolsheviks had rallied, and several bloody battles took place.

Yudenitch was beaten when Trotsky appeared with his Red Army. The Reds checked Denikin before Christmas 1919, and he began a steady retreat. The morale of the White Russians was broken when General Denikin was pushed back to the sea.

Many Russians had to be left behind at the port of Novorossick in March 1920, when they attempted to embark for other shores. There was a widespread epidemic of typhus at the Southern Front. The remains of Denikin's army was brought to the Crimea, where General Wrangel took charge of them.

The Crimean peninsula now served as a pocket for the final phase of the Civil War, in which all the defeated survivors of the White armies converged in May

1920. By October, Wrangel had collected an army of about 58,000, including some 17,000 cavalry troops. They were supported by a small number of tanks and armoured cars, even forty aeroplanes and two battleships, several destroyers, gunboats, and four submarines. His problem was how to break out of the peninsula where they were trapped.

It was too late by the time the Bolshevik General Frunze made a final assault on the Crimea in November and defeated this large major threat to the Communists. Some survivors managed to escape to Istanbul, Bulgaria and Yugoslavia, where they dissolved in the second half of November.

The Russian Civil War was over, and the anti-Bolsheviks were scattered all over the world.

Civilization collapsed in Russia, where only the bare essentials of staying alive for one more day or night had any significance, and most human lives had no value at all. Living in poverty and appeasing hunger pains were the priority. It also meant avoiding filth, squalor, corpses and disease, and striving daily against feelings of hopelessness:

"People took on the quality of wolves, and man often became the enemy of man in the most physical sense, as in a jungle."

Despite Churchill's support for Reilly's plans, Lloyd George would not back him anymore. And the British public were far too tired of war to support any more intervention in Russia.

Now that the Civil War was over in Russia, Reilly was left with the knowledge that he was the only leader of the cause left to continue fighting against the Bolsheviks. Nevertheless, Reilly was still convinced that the Bolsheviks could not last in a country so devastated from civil war: they were simply not skilled or experienced enough to establish law and order by means of a just and equitable government.

Reilly's future as a British Secret Service agent was now jeopardized as Churchill was protesting against a proposed reduction in funds for the Secret Service:

"With the world in its present condition of extreme unrest and changing friendships and antagonisms, and with our greatly reduced and weak military forces, it is more than ever vital to us to have good and timely information. The building up of Secret Service organizations is very slow. Five or ten years are required to create a good system. It can be swept away by a stroke of the pen. It would in my judgment be an act of the utmost imprudence to cripple our arrangements at the present most critical time. Before such a decision is taken, I must ask formally that the matter should be considered in the Committee of Imperial Defense or by a Cabinet Committee comprising the same personnel."

It would continually infuriate Churchill to find that most politicians and civil servants preferred their own uninformed personal opinions to hard facts that agents of the SIS had ferreted out while endangering their lives. Even some of the leaders in the War Office and the Admiralty were quick to express a personal opinion, or the opinion of a friend, or a member of their family, in order to form policy, without regard for on-the-ground intelligence information.

Churchill requested more funds for espionage and counter-espionage, for MI5 and the future MI6, and concluded by stating that "Taking into consideration the present unsettled state of the world generally . . . the General Staff can only regard as folly any proposal which would tend to render ineffective a weapon of defense which no other Power is able to dispense with at the present time, and is satisfied that a reduction of the grant to such a sum as £10,000 would, in fact, result in the practical crippling of the organization."

Disease and destitution spread across Poland and Russia, with typhus and cholera killing off those who would otherwise have died from starvation.

12
The Russian Version

THE INTENTION OF THE CAREFULLY WRITTEN YET CLUMSY NARRATIVE of *Troubled Waters,* was to give the Russian story a sort of legitimacy by creating an atmosphere more suited to a romantic Western novel or a Hollywood spy thriller, apparently to get the propaganda into as many hands as possible. It succeeded in making it a best-seller, in Russia at least. But the only reason that anyone in Britain's SIS or Foreign Office might read it would be to find out if it revealed what had really happened to Reilly after he had returned to Russia in 1925. Was he fighting the Reds, or was he dead? Had the Soviet secret police turned him? Or had he been a Russian mole all along?

For more sophisticated and discriminating readers in the West, the fictional opening roused instant suspicions of what the Russian propagandists were really up to.

It seemed that readers were meant to catch a young woman named Maria and a man named Yakushev by surprise at a secret lovers meeting. Perhaps the puritanic Bolsheviks thought that something prurient would appeal to Western readers. But they seemed to have no idea how people outside of the USSR thought or behaved. In any case, they made out the couple to appear to be husband and wife. Since this is the same Maria who vanished in Soviet Russia soon after Reilly disappeared, the reader's curiosity was bound to be aroused.

Perhaps more of interest to a reader in the West was the stilted dialogue the

Russian author wrote for them, since it was unnatural and unbelievable. So unbelievable that it was easy to imagine a government employee writing it – someone who had never been out of Russia and had no knowledge of how other people talked or behaved in a free democracy.

Added to that was the politicized translator of the text who was evidently more accustomed to copying out dogmatic Marxist tracts and bureaucratic rules and regulations than anything to do with human beings.

Despite its clumsy unnaturalness, we are obliged to read it because it is what Soviet Russia said *really* happened to Sidney Reilly. Never mind the derring-do of the Scottish Robert Bruce Lockhart, or the grandiose claims about Reilly by Lockhart's son Robin, or Reilly's Byronic account of his own actions, or the more laconic and unrevealing records of the British Secret Service. This, according to the Soviet Union's secret police, is "the truth." Everything else told by the West, they claimed, was lies.

It took no leap of the imagination to recognize that this chapter of the Russian book, at least, was a clumsy attempt to demonize Lockhart and Reilly and the British Secret Service, together with Maria, General Kutyepoff, Boris Savinkov, and any others of the usual Soviet suspects. All are set up for target practice, so that each one can be shot down verbally, one after the other, with machine-gun rapidity, again and again. There is little subtlety, except perhaps for characteristic details scattered throughout that were intended to lend their story authenticity and suspend disbelief.

"Why did the Finns manage to beat the Reds?" Maria asks out of the blue— apropos of absolutely nothing at all.

"How did the Finnish barons succeed in cutting of the hydra's head off a Finnish Revolution, while our own Denikin and Wrangel failed? What is your opinion Alexander Alexandrovich?"

Yakushev seems somewhat bemused. All he can say is, "What do you think?"

"It is because they started hanging too late," the puppet Maria reminds Yakushev, to give him his cue.

"How does one know when it's too late or too early to start?"

Maria: "They should have started hanging at the very beginning. Now we do not allow them to do so. But I do have confidence in Alexander Pavlovich."

Yakushev: "Of course one must use a heavy hand. I regret, Maria Vladimirovna, that in Paris we did not seize the general at the outset."

"Kutyepoff is a strong man. In Gallipoli he hanged all those who forgot their duty."

Yakushev laughs suddenly, apparently to make him seem more human and believable. "You are ruthless, Maria Vladimirovna, ruthless, although beautiful . . .

And you so full of female charms! But I forgive your complaints, because you have a minister's head on your shoulders. And because of your expression."

Maria: "What sort of expression?"

"Well, radiant . . . Radiant for the future of Russia, the Russia we lost, the Russia you and I knew and I believe we will restore."

"At the price of a great deal of blood," she adds sceptically. "Did you ever meet this man Reilly in Petrograd?"

Yakushev is apparently ready for the abrupt change of subject, providing he sticks to the lines allotted to him by the Department of Propaganda. "No. I met some other English officers—snobs who strutted about in dinner jackets."

Maria: "They say he is not like that—unflinchingly brave I'm told."

Yakushev grasps her hand and lowers his eyes with feeling. "Poor, poor Maria, you don't know what a viper you are nursing in your bosom!"

She turns away from him in embarrassment—most likely at his unnatural dialogue and the elaborate and wooden plot provided for them both by the dreadfully inept Russian author.

Yakushev is now obliged to draw Maria's attention to a man with a cigar at the next table who is listening to them, in order to provide them with an exit line: "Time to go!"

Readers have to put up with the ineptness, so far, of this account, in case some situation is revealed to enlighten us about where Sidney Reilly really is and what he is doing for or against the Soviet Union—or possibly even for Britain's Secret Service as a double-agent.

They are suddenly transported to Bunakoff's apartment at one o'clock, where the Russian-speaking British intelligence double-agent is waiting for them on time. Although Yakushev's dialogue begins in polite and general terms, he quickly turns to the business in hand:

"You are the one who suggested we should get in touch with the Englishman— how shall we go about it?"

Bunakoff: "Someone will come from England for preliminary discussions."

Yakushev: "I thought he was engaged in a business—why should he return to politics?"

Bunakoff: (shrugs). "It's taken him most of his life. I promise you, Soviet Russia has never had such a dangerous enemy."

His remark is evidently intended to educate the reader rather than Maria or Bunakoff. The author's aim is to build up Reilly before shooting him down. But, by now, the Soviet theatricals have something of a simplistic and eerie end-of-term school play about them.

"I hope you're right," Maria says meaninglessly, if only to remind us that she is still there.

Bunakoff shows them a letter signed with a code name: "The Iron One." It too is written in the same stilted and bureaucratic hand, as if preparing readers for a five-year Soviet industrial program.

"Red Power is slowly dying," the letter informs them. "The heroic period of the spring of 1921, which was followed by a period of consolidation, did not produce the anticipated results in view of the terrible national famine and economic breakdown. It is the Red Army which, up to now, seems to me to be the enigma . . . "

And so on and so on . . . It is not worthwhile quoting the rest of the letter because of its unbelievability and its tedium. It was impossible to believe that Reilly would have written such a clumsy letter in the pedantic way that communist party members wrote their political pamphlets. But it is a reminder of how they even spoke to each other in a stilted Bolshevik jargon of their own, using an imposed formula with which they repeatedly scorned the bourgeoisie and praised the workers at every opportunity.

Secret Service readers and those from Britain's Foreign Office would hardly be likely to continue reading this clumsy Russian propaganda if it were not for the fact that—apart from depicting Reilly in an unpleasant light as a scoundrel whose word cannot be trusted, and an "enemy of the people"—it is gradually inching Reilly in small stages to land up in a locked cell in the Kremlin.

According to the Russian script, Reilly wants to meet leading members of "The Trust" as early as May, but is delayed from doing so because of his pharmaceutical enterprise.

So Kutyepoff arrives in Helsinki in the middle of August 1925 to renew his contacts with "The Trust" and discuss the line he should take to trap Reilly. Since Reilly is expected soon in Paris, that is where he is told to meet Reilly and send him on to Finland. Then he or Yakushev should invite Reilly to Moscow.

Narrative and dialogue continue to be very complicated in the typical bureaucratic communist manner, added to which are all the confusing Russian names, with which most Western readers have great difficulty struggling to get the upper hand. Nevertheless, Reilly does arrive in Paris, where he meets Kutyepoff.

According to the Russian script, Reilly is disillusioned with the inaction of White émigrés and has no good opinion of them. He pins his hopes instead on "The Trust."

Maria sends a message to Yakushev in Moscow that Reilly is expected in Helsinki at the end of September.

Yakushev is ready at the Finnish frontier on September 21, 1925. After which he meets Reilly at Bunakoff's flat. Reilly appears to trust Yakushev; so that Yakushev can boast in a letter to the GPU how clever he was to make friends with him.

When Reilly declares he intends to leave on Saturday on the ship for Stettin, apparently there was nothing he could achieve in the short time available to them; so they were left to improvise.

13
Reilly's Downfall

YAKUSHEV WRITES IN HIS REPORT, "When Reilly announced that at the present time he could not make the journey, I said as quickly as possible, that if it was a question of speed, I was prepared to arrange the trip to Moscow in such a way that he could be in Leningrad on Sunday morning and leave there for Moscow the same evening. A whole day would be ample to get acquainted with the Political Council of "The Trust." Then in the evening he could return to Leningrad, spend Monday there, and that night, pass through "The Window" back to Helsinki. That would be on the Tuesday, and on the Wednesday there was a ship leaving for Stettin."

Reilly apparently considers his suggestion seriously, because he is keen to go to Moscow. But then readers are reminded of the death sentence still hovering over him since 1918. In spite of that, he was impressed by Maria and Kutyepoff and evidently has confidence in "The Trust" - although readers might be excused for wondering why.

Before they have time to question it, they are returned to Yakushev's report on Reilly:

After thinking for a while, Reilly says, "All right, you have convinced me. I'll go with you."

Bunakoff rises in surprise—as well he might! But perhaps it is to allay any suspicion that he might be a British secret service agent, working for Commander Boyce. But true loyalties are difficult to sort out and never satisfactorily explained in a world of double and triple agents whose loyalties require flexibility to stay alive. Nor is it made easy in the Russian narrative to remember who is a double agent and who is not, or who is who, or who else knows what they are up to. There is even considerable uncertainty whether they know themselves.

"I suggested we should discuss arrangements for the journey," Yakushev notes for the records. He says to Reilly, "Your overcoat and suit will attract attention in Russia—take Radkevich's overcoat. We must also buy a cap and top boots. Leave your things with Bunakoff. You will only need a small suitcase. I can promise you quite a comfortable journey and a completely safe one."

All that appears to be missing is for him to add, "Trust me!" And give a sly wink to an invisible audience.

Now that all has been decided, Reilly suddenly becomes voluble. He asks questions about "The Trust," about life in Russia, and even about the Soviet attitude towards religion. The subject is introduced so that Reilly can reveal his villainy by making out a case for the inevitability of planned attacks on the Jews after a counter-revolution. It is a crafty way for the communist hierarchy to transfer their own racist prejudices on to Reilly—who represents the Monarchists or the West according to their propaganda. So they put words into his mouth that a Monarchy or a dictatorship will be necessary to restore order. In other words, Reilly's real intentions are tarnished to be claimed as an attempt by him to restore the old oppressive imperial regime.

Yakushev, pretending to be a senior member of the counter-revolutionary organization, says that "The Trust" is relying on Reilly's assistance to obtain funds, which are needed to continue fermenting unrest and bribing officials. Reilly replies that he has plans ready and will give full details of them to the Political Council in Moscow.

Now Reilly sends a letter to his wife, Pepita, through Bunakoff: "I am leaving tonight and will return on Tuesday morning. There is no risk at all. If by chance I should be arrested in Russia it will be merely an unimportant coincidence. My new friends are so powerful that they will succeed in freeing me."

Then Reilly takes leave of Bunakoff; and Maria and her husband Radkevich, who remain in Finland.

According to the Russian account, Rusensterm and Radkevich escort Reilly to the frontier—reminding readers ominously of the villainous Rosencrantz and Guildenstern about to betray Hamlet in Shakespeare's play. Perhaps it was a Freudian slip by the author.

They arrive at Kuokalla Station at ten o'clock at night on September 25, and make their way to the frontier at midnight. "Reilly's top-boots squeaked," according to the Russian account, and he wets the soles in a ditch to silence them.

On arrival at the River Seatri, a shadow appears on the river bank. It turns out to be Toivo Vjahi, one of the most experienced agents of the Soviet frontier service, and one of the stars in this version of Reilly's downfall. He pretends to be a border guard who had been bribed. He has been precisely instructed to take Reilly by cart from the frontier to Pargolovo Station, seventeen kilometers further on. If Reilly changes his mind at this point and begins to resist, Vjahi has instructions to use his gun.

But Reilly only pauses to talk in English to his Finnish guides, and stops when

Vjahi tells him this is no place for chatter. Then they begin an exhausting walk to the cart that is waiting for them in the forest. The muddy roads are terrible and the cart jolts Reilly so badly that he jumps out and decides rather to trudge through the squelching mud for the entire seventeen kilometers to reach Pargolovo Station, where Vjahi sees him off on the train for Leningrad. Schukin gives Reilly a passport in the name of Steinberg.

Sidney Reilly arrives in Leningrad on the morning of September 26, where he spends the day in the GPU agent Schukin's flat with Yakushev. He is introduced to a factory hand named Staroff, who is a deputy of the Moscow Soviet. Staroff gives Reilly accounts of working conditions in Soviet Russia. Also Mukaloff, who is present as one of Wrangel's representatives.

Reilly, Yakushev and Mukaloff leave that evening by train on an International Sleeping Car for Moscow. Staroff preceded them.

Waiting to meet them on the platform in Moscow, for this scenario, on Sunday September 27, are supposed 'delegates of the monarchist organization,' namely Dorojinsky, Schadkorsky and Staroff – apparently another trio of comics. In fact all are agents of the GPU, pretending to be Monarchists in order to tarnish Reilly in the records.

That is the Sunday when a conference takes place with the Political Council of "The Trust" in a dacha at Malahovka. According to this record, Lieutenant-General Nicailovich Potapoff makes a great impression on Reilly. Alexander Langovoi is present also, as Commander of the Red Army. After they finish lunch, they retire into the woods, where they settle down on the grass for a discussion in the shade of a tree, and Yakushev sets up Reilly for his fate by asking him about financial aid.

Reilly continues to talk like a ventriloquist's wooden doll seated on the author's lap and using the strange stilted tones which, apparently, all members of the Communist Party have already become accustomed to.

"No Government will give you money. Today, everyone's house is on fire. Churchill believes, as I do, in the speedy overthrow of Soviet power, but he is not in a position to supply funds. He has been keenly disappointed on a number of occasions. For us, the most important thing is to put out the fire in our own house. There is unrest in the colonies. Due to the influence of Moscow, the workers are moving to the left. Money must, therefore, be sought inside Russia. My plans to raise money are crude and will probably repel you."

That is, of course, the intention.

"In Russia there are great treasures of immense value. I am thinking of old master paintings, engravings, precious stones, gems. To remove these from the museums will not be too difficult. Just think of the money—which would amount to many thousands of pounds! Abroad, such treasures have a tremendous value. It is true that it is difficult to steal from the public rooms of the museums, but in the basements, ready and packed, are some amazing works of art. We must arrange to send these abroad. I myself, without the help of any intermediaries, can organize the sale. In this way, we can obtain very substantial sums."

Potapoff pretends to be shocked, and exclaims, "But we are not museum robbers! It would ruin the reputation of our whole organization."

Reilly: "For the sake of money, a reputation may have to be sacrificed. In any case, it will not be necessary to let more than a few into the secret."

He informs them he has already made a note of what should be stolen:

1. Pictures of famous Dutch painters, also French masters and important Rembrandts.

2. Engravings of French and English masters of the XVIIIth century, and miniatures of the XVIIIth and XIXth centuries.

3. Antique coins of gold, silver and bronze.

4. Italian and Flemish primitives.

5. Works of the great masters of the Italian and Spanish Schools.

Potapoff and Yakushev have difficulty in restraining their shock when they hear his proposals.

According to the Russian script, Reilly enjoys being treated like a V.I.P in Moscow, and being listened to by the chiefs of "The Trust," as if he is an oracle.

They return to the dacha when the sun begins to set and the grass turns damp. Reilly draws Yakushev aside on the way and remarks, "You have the good manners of a gentleman who looks at things more realistically than the rest of the members of The Trust."

Pledging Yakushev to secrecy, this caricature made of Reilly informs him that he could obtain fifty thousand dollars towards organizing the theft of pictures and other valuables from museums and also for infiltrating into the Comintern.

Reilly: "General Potapoff is clearly too scrupulous. I must tell you that you will never succeed in a counter-revolution if you observe the rules of morality. Take terrorism for instance, Savinkov once told me that one of his terrorists failed to throw a bomb in a carriage because there were children inside. If you are going to be influenced by principles, you will achieve nothing in your fight with the Soviets. I view my activities from a much wider perspective, not only for the politics but also as a businessman. You won't overthrow Soviet power in three months. We must prepare a thorough plan for the 'export' of art treasures. I have personal influence with the press. When I return from Moscow, I will offer *The Times* a series of articles under the title of "The Great Bluff."

In reality, of course, despite all the clowning of pretending to be shocked by Reilly's suggestions, the Bolsheviks had already been selling Russian treasures to the West for cash since the October Revolution about a decade earlier.

But now—having successfully condemned himself by the words placed in his mouth by the Russian novelist—the phoney Reilly glances at his wristwatch. He has to leave for Leningrad by the evening train, cross the frontier during the night and proceed to Helsinki in order to catch the Wednesday boat to Stettin.

Two motor cars are waiting outside as Reilly takes leave of Rakushev, Potapoff, and the others. He takes a seat in the first car together with Staroff, and Puzitsky—an experienced Chekist who took part in Savinkov's arrest.

Potapoff and Yakushev are in the second vehicle. Now, according to the script, they are able to give vent to their real feelings.

"What a terrible man!" says Potapoff.

According to the Russian narrative, both men are visibly shaken.

Reilly was supposed to be arrested in the car while on the way to Moscow. But he wants to send a postcard to his friends abroad, and to put it with his own hands into the pillar-box to prove that he visited Moscow. He is taken to the flat of one of the GPU agents who wants to know the address on the card.

While Reilly writes a message on his postcard, Staroff telephones GPU headquarters to report the delay. He is given orders to arrest Reilly as soon as he has mailed the postcard.

Reilly is arrested and taken to GPU headquarters, where he admits his identity at the preliminary interrogation conducted by Pilar (or possibly Stryne). Reilly also admits that he entered Soviet territory illegally with the aid of "The Trust," a counter-revolutionary monarchist organization. He refuses to explain his criminal behaviour.

When, in the course of the interrogation, Reilly learns that "The Trust" is an operation of Soviet Intelligence, according to the Russian script he loses his self-control and cannot conceal his distress. He is then locked up in solitary confinement in the 'Inner Prison' of the Lubianka.

So—at any rate, according to the Russian version of what happened to him—Reilly remained in his cell for just over a month.

14
The Lubianka Prison

Still according to the Russian narrative, Yakushev learns of Reilly's arrest in Staunitz's flat on the Moroseika. His first thought is for the future of "The Trust." Reilly's arrest would cause the counter-revolutionaries to lose confidence in it, and in Yakushev.

Therefore, on the night of September 28/29, Puzitsky and several of his colleagues leave for Leningrad to fake a shooting incident on the frontier with Finland near Allekul. Firing and considerable noise is staged to suggest that Reilly and his companions have been ambushed, and that Reilly has been killed in the ensuing mêlée near the frontier post.

Part of the prearranged plan was that all genuine members of "The Trust" were not to be told anything immediately about the incident at the frontier. The intention was to ensure that the first news about the catastrophe should come from Finland. Only then would there be an alarm sounded among members of "The Trust."

Maria sent a telegram to the heads of "The Trust" in their agreed code on September 29, saying "The parcel has disappeared. We await explanation."

Reilly would have been kept long enough in solitary confinement to reflect on many of the circumstances and their details which had led him to a prison cell in Moscow. He might even have hoped that the British Government or the Secret Service would insist on his release from the Lubianka prison in the Kremlin by making a political issue of his arrest. He would have dwelt on what was happening far away in London and wondered who, if anyone, had even noticed his disappearance. Waiting for something to break the monotony and anxiety of his sleepless nights and days lying on his bunk and dwelling on what he would say during his interrogation by the GPU, he would have returned in his mind to the grim failure of his attempted counter-revolution, on his lost political and business opportunities, and his financial losses.

He would have felt disappointment at the way he had allowed himself to be deceived and trapped by "The Trust" when his self-confidence had been at a low ebb. He might even have consoled himself with the thought that he had not been the only one to have been taken in by their overtures, since other people had believed in its legitimacy too. Even Boyce in the British Secret Service had believed in "The Trust." So had the intelligence services of France and the Baltic countries.

He would certainly have considered and reconsidered his position again and again. Reilly had always thought of British Intelligence as the best in the world. And yet the crude and brutal *Cheka* had managed to make fools of them and him, even though the Soviet secret police had been in existence for only seven years. Since neither he nor Boyce had seen through their well-planned and well-executed plot, how could Maria Schultz be expected to? He felt sure that she was still innocent of the deceit and that she still trusted in the legitimacy of "The Trust" as a force to overthrow the Soviet Government.

Reilly was treated well at first by the GPU. He expected that would change during interrogation by Feliks Dzerzhinsky. But all that happened when they met so that Feliks could identify him with certainty, was a triumphant smile when the Chief of the Soviet secret police recognized him.

All Dzerzhinsky said while he gazed at Reilly's features was, "What took you so long?"

Reilly soon occupied the same well-appointed cell where Savinkov had been accommodated before his alleged suicide. The GPU spent hours talking to Reilly, and there was no point in attempting to deny what they accused him of. All the while, he watched his interrogator and listened carefully for clues that there might be some way he could find to be released. He was an optimist and a gambler, always ready to believe in the next throw of a dice or turn of a card as his mind opened up to an opportunity by means of his astuteness, or his sense of romantic fantasy that saw himself as the hero of his own epic drama.

He had always wanted to be recognized as a hero, and either be awarded a medal by a grateful Tsar or patted on the back by 'C.' But Cumming was no longer there to watch his back. More than anything else, he had wanted to be thanked by a grateful Russian people for saving them from tyranny. So it is likely that he took his unfortunate situation coolly and calmly, as he did most things when on the edge of danger, particularly when taking death defying risks. He was a master of the calm and rational appraisal.

There are several accounts that "He probably was not tortured himself, but simply made to witness some horrific torture and execution scenes."

The Soviet secret police became brutal only when he refused to talk about his spying activities for the SIS. Despite the British Secret Service often seeming amateurish to him, it was by far the best espionage service in the world, and Russia's GPU were anxious to know its structure and personnel, and how it functioned. So that, in the end, Reilly had no other choice but to cooperate with them.

After he had revealed everything he knew about the Foreign Office and the British Secret Service, he was of no further use to them. Whatever Reilly told his interrogator would form the basis of the future Soviet State Security System and become the best secret police force in the world - or at least second-best only to Britain's MI5 and MI6.

According to the Russian narrative, the following documents reveal his fate.

FROM THE PROTOCOL OF THE INTERROGATION OF
S. G. REILLY ON OCTOBER 7th, 1925.

On October 7th, 1925, I interrogated in the capacity of Prosecutor, Reilly, Sidney George, born 1874, British subject, born Connemara (Ireland); father, captain in the navy. Permanent residence, London and, more recently, New York. Captain in the British army. Wife abroad. Education: university; studied at Heidelberg in the faculty of philosophy; in London, the Royal Institute of Mines, specializing in chemistry. Party: active Conservative. Was judged in absentia in the matter of Lockhart in 1918.

Later in the protocol, the story is told of Reilly's activities after he had managed to escape from Russia in 1918.

Afterwards, I was appointed political officer for South Russia and went to Denikin's Headquarters; I was in the Crimea, in the South-east and at Odessa. I remained in Odessa until the end of March 1919. By order of the British High Commissioner in Constantinople, I was instructed to report on Denikin's front and on South Russia generally. Afterwards, I was sent to the Peace Conference in Paris.

From 1919 to 1920 I had close links with various émigré groups. At the same time, for the British Government, I undertook negotiations with Jasoschinsky and Bark for very important financial plans for backing commercial undertakings and industrial schemes etc. All this time I was in the employ of the Secret Service, my main duties being to advise the ruling circles of England on Russian questions and problems.

At the end of 1920 I was in close contact with Savinkoff and went to Warsaw where he was organizing an expedition into White Russia. I took part in this expedition and was in Soviet Russian territory. I received orders to return to London.

In 1923 and 1924, I had to give a lot of my time to my own affairs. In the fight against the Soviet powers, I was less active, although I wrote a good deal for the papers (English) and supported Savinkoff. I continued to advise ruling circles in England on Russian questions and in America also, as in those years I was often in the United States. I spent 1925 in New York.

At the end of 1925, I illegally crossed the Finish frontier, proceeded to Leningrad and after that came to Moscow, where I was arrested.

FROM THE PROTOCOL OF INTERROGATION OF
S. G. REILLY ON OCTOBER 9th, 1925

I arrived in Soviet Russia on my own initiative, hearing from Bunakoff of the existence of an apparently important anti-Soviet group.

I have always been actively engaged in anti-Bolshevik matters and to these I have given much time and my personal funds. I can state that the years 1920-4, for instance, cost me at a very minimum calculation fifteen thousand to twenty thousand pounds.

I was well-informed about Russian affairs from information sent to me by various sources in Russia and by English and American intelligence sources.

In this deposition, it should be noted that Reilly arrived in Russia 'on his own initiative.' Later he was to reveal his ties with London. It seems that the initiative of "The Trust" was only a stimulant to the trip.

Prior to his arrest, Reilly once again said to Yakushev that he knew all the English secret agents working in Soviet offices, but during his cross-examination he stubbornly denied this. He talked much of general subjects, forgetting that he was the accused and not a consultant on Russian affairs. Those he used to advise were no longer interested in his fate. But when Reilly was told of the decision of the G.P.U. to carry out the death sentence passed on him in 1918, his former courage failed him. On October 13th he wrote the following statement:

TO THE PRESIDENT OF THE G.P.U. F. E. DZERJINSKY
After prolonged deliberation, I express willingness to give you complete and open acknowledgment and information on matters of interest to the G.P.U. concerning the organization and personnel of the British Intelligence Service and, so far as I know it, similar information on American Intelligence and likewise about Russian émigrés with whom I have had business.
Moscow. The Inner Prison
30th October, 1925.   Sidney Reilly

A cryptic sentence added a final note after so many questions and answers embodying so much subterfuge: "Sentence of execution of the Revolutionary Tribunal was carried out on November 5, 1925."

Much of the Russian story of what led up to Reilly's arrest, which was published during Brezhnev's time in office, was written in the language of Soviet Russian communist propaganda. It aimed at whitewashing the USSR and blackening the British Secret Service, while diminishing the importance of Sidney Reilly in particular. But it was not an official document of the Soviet Government, but a book written by an author for the purpose of spreading disinformation that had to be approved by the Communist Presidium.

A very different book from another Russian author that impressed western critics far more for its knowledge and candor when translated in 1974, was *The Gulag Archipelago* about the Soviet forced labor camps. Its author was Alexandr

Solzhenitsyn. He stated that one of the Finnish Red Guards at the frontier was Richard Ohola who participated "in the capture of British agent Sidney Reilly." And that Reilly was "killed while crossing the Soviet-Finnish border

Evidently Solzhenitsyn was only repeating what he had heard, since Reilly was taken to GPU officer Roman Pilar, who had previously ordered the execution of Reilly's friend Savinkov in the previous year. So despite Soviet propaganda claiming that Reilly had been shot at the frontier, he was in fact being interrogated by Pilar at the moment of the fake disturbance and shooting at the border crossing.

Reilly—his quick-witted mind always working at top speed, even during his interrogation - was making mental notes of the GPU's interrogation techniques which he then wrote down in tiny notes on cigarette papers and hid in the walls of his cell. They were discovered afterwards by Soviet guards. GPU technicians made photographic enhancements of them. Evidently Reilly felt they would be useful for the British Secret Service to know. Some of his notes included a daily diary describing events between interrogations. Contrary to the false GPU documents in the Russian book, which should perhaps be described as a novel, they ended on an optimistic note with a conviction that "I see great things ahead."

Evidently Reilly still hoped to achieve something extraordinary in his life which would benefit the Russian people.

We are left with the difficulty of imagining all the different facets of Reilly's complex and subtle character as described by friends and foe, colleagues, wives and lovers, and official documents from the British Government, and from Soviet propaganda.

British Intelligence documents, released in 2000, would state that Reilly was executed in a forest near Moscow on Wednesday November 5, 1925. That account was taken from an alleged eye-witness named Boris Gudz who said the execution was supervised by a GPU officer named Grigory Fedoleev, and that George Syroeezhkin fired the last shot into Reilly's chest.

There can be no doubt that Reilly's skills as a spy were far more professional than those of other "harmless" British Secret Service agents in those early days which were a prelude to MI6. There is also no doubt that he was a very brave man and a Russian patriot who admired Britain and the English. Although Russia was the country he was born in, Britain was the country that recognized his talents and awarded him with a medal for exceptional courage. His belief in himself had encouraged him to imagine that he could provide funding for a counter-revolution by exploiting political opportunities to raise money for business, and business opportunities to raise funds for a counter-revolution.

Reilly's main problem appears to have been that he lost his focus in the excitement and danger of intermittent crises, and failed to recognize the difference between a political coup and a business venture. There was also a quality that many women were drawn to, including his three wives. It was a heightened self-confidence that gave him an appearance of power. On the other hand, at its extremes, there were moments when he acted from delusions of grandeur. It might even be said that, as with many self-confident men with powerful personalities, overweening belief in himself led to his downfall from *hubris*.

Behind his facade of self-confidence and power, Sidney Reilly possessed flaws like any other human being. And he was so multifaceted that even he sometimes became lost in trying to catch his reflection, since it seemed that a different man gazed back at him from every looking glass.

15
Dark Loneliness

ROBERT BRUCE LOCKHART KNEW SIDNEY REILLY better than most people from having worked with him in deadly dangerous situations. He admired his courage, and continued the story even after Reilly's presumed death, by explaining how "The Trust" passed through a difficult period in the aftermath to Reilly's arrest by the GPU. Which of its members was genuine? Who could be trusted? Which were traitors? And, if traitors, to whom? Most importantly in Reilly's ambiguous situation, what could he do to turn a dire problem into an opportunity to fulfill what he considered to be his destiny?

Maria tried to reach Moscow, hoping that Reilly was only wounded in the rumored shooting on the Finnish border. She thought he might be in hospital, and wanted to save him. She wrote to Yakushev, "There is a torturing, dark, loneliness, full of the unknown . . ."

Her expression aptly described the lonely and isolated feelings of millions of people who were uprooted by war or revolution, as were most of the Russian people at that time, crushed and lost beneath an oppressive tyranny without the power to change events in their own favour. And with the life-shattering conflicts between Communists and anti-Communists, there was something worse that she needed to confront:

"I cannot get rid of the feeling that I somehow betrayed Reilly and was responsible for his death myself. I was responsible for "The Window." For the sake of the movement, I ask to be allowed to work inside Russia."

Maria did not know that, although she might be asking the right question, she was asking the wrong people. Even so, she did receive a reply, and a promise that she would be recalled to Moscow.

Another woman who was so concerned about Reilly that she travelled to Helsinki was Reilly's bigamous wife, Pepita, who made a point of meeting Maria there. She showed Maria the last letter that Reilly had written to her, which she had received from the British Secret Service agent known as Bunakoff, in which her husband had warned her that he might be arrested but not to be concerned if he was, because of the power of "The Trust" to have him released. Maria, who still believed in the authenticity of "The Trust," assured Pepita that it was not responsible for her husband's disappearance.

Pepita believed what Maria told her. That was the occasion when she had decided to insert a notice of his death on the Finnish frontier in *The Times*, in a faint hope that somebody, somewhere, might respond to it.

Meanwhile, immediately after Reilly's arrest, the alarm was sounded in Staunitz's flat in Finland. Staunitz was the cover-name for Opperput.

Yakushev, Langovoi, Suboff, Staunitz and Makaloff held a hurried meeting. But, like everything in "The Trust," it was staged by one group of actors for the benefit of an audience composed of another group of actors on whom their lives depended. Who knew who was who, and who could be trusted not to be spying on each other? Bolsheviks continued to deceive anti-Bolsheviks and anti-Bolsheviks deceived Bolsheviks. It was a set-up to continue fooling Mukaloff and Staunitz, who did not know what had happened to Reilly after he left. They chain-smoked nervously, their cigarette butts dropped carelessly on the floor, while they burnt incriminating papers. Mukaloff was a wreck of his former self.

Yakushev was as nervous as the others. He wanted to go to Leningrad, but was held back because he was needed where he was by "The Trust." Suboff and Mukaloff were instructed to find out what had happened at the frontier that night on September 25.

Mukaloff was also shown the telegram sent by Maria that needed a response from "The Trust." Staunitz drafted a coded reply to her, after agreement with the others. It said simply, "The illness ended with the death of the children."

In other words, the mission to trap Sidney Reilly was over.

Although Maria was expected in Finland, it was her husband Radkevich who turned up instead, and insisted on an explanation of the coded message from Staunitz. Radkevich looked severe, and Staunitz thought the hand in his coat pocket was holding a gun. He was overcome, and asked Radkevich for whatever details he knew of Reilly's fate from the Finnish side of the frontier.

Radkevich tried to calm himself while he struggled to explain what little he knew. He and Captain Rusensterm had walked to the frontier and waited there, then heard sudden screams and gunshots. They had rushed to the bank of the river, imagining someone was coming across. He had decided that the shots must have been aimed at bandits, never imagining for a moment that something had happened to Reilly. They waited on the riverbank until morning.

Staunitz accepted his account of what had happened, and Radkevich was permitted to re-cross the frontier through "The Window" in the area of Stolpzoff.

This and several other accounts of Reilly's disappearance provided echoes of truth, but they could not all be true. Some echoes were misinterpreted. There were so many inconsistencies with the earlier accounts and, even if the whole truth were known inside Russia, according to Robin Bruce Lockhart there were so many obvious and unnecessary inaccuracies.

The obvious, clumsy propaganda attempts to praise Soviet skills in capturing Reilly, and the deliberate attempts to blacken his character, were only to be expected. The exposure by the Russians of Staunitz/ Opperput, who played only a minor role in the GPU operation, was also understandable, since he defected soon afterwards.

The Russian account is nightmarishly accurate on one hand, and surrealistically inaccurate on the other. For example, Reilly's alleged confession that his father was a captain in the navy was absurd—it was Margaret who had pretended her father was a naval captain. Nor had Reilly studied at Heidelberg, as he had allegedly confessed under interrogation. He was not in Moscow in the winter of 1917. Nor, apparently, did he use the name of Sidney Berns in the United States.

Although his execution is said to have taken place on November 5, 1925, the previous date given in *Izvestia's* September 27 edition for his death was in June. All other Russian references to Reilly indicated that he was alive in 1926. One even suggested that he was not only free but at large in 1927. So the statement that he was executed in November 1925 is unconvincing. Robin Bruce Lockhart concluded that perhaps the Russians did not know the real truth. Or, with something they considered was so important to hide, they preferred to maintain a smokescreen over Reilly's fate by deliberately issuing false statements.

He added another ironic possibility by referring to Savinkov, who returned to Russia in 1924. Reilly had written to the *Morning Post* that Savinkov had not been captured by the Bolsheviks, and had theorized that he was killed on the Russian frontier instead—although the GPU had staged a mock trial in order to tarnish Savinkov's name as a turncoat. Perhaps the GPU had noted Reilly's theory about Savinkov and transferred it to Reilly instead.

Since Lenin died in the same year that Reilly vanished, it is possible that the Russian story was a smokescreen intended to divert attention from the struggle for leadership of the USSR. Behind that smokescreen was a battle for power between Trotsky who led the Red Army and Stalin who headed the Communist Party.

According to Churchill, what advanced Trotsky was a cold and detached intelligence like Machiavelli, the organizing ability and command of Carnot, oratory that appealed to the bloodthirsty emotions of mobs, toughness and ferocity, and a complete absence of humanity or passion—all the qualities required to destroy an entire culture and replace it with an unproven theory concocted in the circular reading room of the British Library by a hard-up freelance journalist named Karl Marx.

Trotsky was cold and chilling towards his mother and a complete disappointment to his father. He abandoned his wife and children. He was prepared to sacrifice anyone and everything in order to indulge his ego. All of that served him well in the soulless regime of communism, which did not concern itself with human beings or human values: it had been simply an excuse to seize and hold power.

The army which he had remade was fed, clothed, and better treated than anyone else in Russia, and drew officers from the old Tsarist forces, with the single-minded aim of saving Russia. Although the military were grateful for Trotsky, he was outmanoeuvred by Stalin when it came to political power. Lenin recognized in Trotsky his own icy determination and viewed him as his heir. Trotsky was the head of the Russian Army, which he had reconstructed amid indescribable difficulties and perils, and now stood very near the vacant throne left by the inept Romanov dynasty.

But Lenin never recovered from the attempt on his life and died in 1924.

Trotsky had made the revolution for his own ends, just as Lenin had. It was now his turn. But there was one fatal problem—he was a Jew. And there was no room for Jews in anti-Semitic Soviet Russia. By the time that Trotsky managed to extricate himself from leading the Red Army, Stalin was in charge. The implacable Georgian administrator knew that the real power lay in being Chairman of the Communist Party. Under Stalin, Russia's secret police would become virtually his own personal spy ring from which he appeared to know everything worth knowing about everyone who was ambitious for power or leadership. He was quick to denounce them as traitors and they were instantly wiped off of the slate and forgotten—either imprisoned for life in the Lubianka or shot by a firing squad. Trotsky found a wall of opposition already built against him.

Instead of being the dictator of Soviet Russia, as he'd hoped, Trotsky was invited to take a holiday. While he was absent, Stalin removed officers known to be loyal to Trotsky in the Red Army. Trotsky's holiday continued until the Red

Army forgot about him. He was assassinated in Mexico several years later by one of Stalin's agents.

Stalin was also skillful at accusing opponents of attempting to restore capitalist elements in Soviet Russia, as if it were the biggest crime of all. But one of the problems of industrialization that exploded from time to time in the USSR, just as it did in the West, was the awful working conditions in the factories, where productivity was considered more important than the health and safety of industrial workers. It provided opportunities for unrest, strikes and rebellion, just like in all newly industrialized countries.

Churchill had to deal with it also in the coal mines of Wales. But, whereas there was an economic recovery in Britain, it was not the case in Soviet Russia, where Russians were starving while Britons were well-fed.

Churchill could also congratulate himself and proclaim to his constituents that over a million Britons now drew welfare benefits, including 236,800 widows, 344,800 children, and 450,000 seniors over the age of sixty-five.

1925 was also the year that Adolf Hitler relinquished his Austrian citizenship and began writing an inflammatory book to stir up the uncontrollable passions of bitter German ex-servicemen and the vast army of unemployed in Germany, where there was a sharp distinction between the rich minority and the poor masses, with deep social unrest as a consequence. All were reasons why Britain was obliged to retain its Intelligence on Germany, Austria and Soviet Russia.

Tensions still simmered from the results of the "Great War," which appeared to have created a mental and emotional sickness that spread across Europe and resulted in various forms of neurosis and psychosis, leading to violence and a resultant growth in psychiatric care in Vienna. Mental disorders were virtually uncharted territory. Even so, it was considered that neither paranoia nor schizophrenia could be cured by psychiatry. Psychiatric wards were burdened with rebellious political agitators with mental problems.

Women and children had had to cope and survive on their own during the war, without husbands or fathers to fend for them. Traditional families came under considerable strain after the war. There were something like half a million war widows in Germany alone, and most would never marry. Of the millions of soldiers who returned home from the battlefronts, many were "destroyed men," who could not settle down into family life or civilian routines.

The streets and homes and beer cellars were filled with haunted men reliving shocking scenes of butchery day and night, and riddled by guilt and anxiety. Many committed suicide, others drank themselves into a kind of living death, or attempted to reassert their authority over frightened wives and children by beating them.

Mutilated veterans begged at street corners. Most could not find work. The early days of peace were confused by irrational behaviour and violence, insurrections, revolution, and mutinies. All provoked the collapse of social order.

Since there was no reliable information, Stalin was caught by surprise by what he called the "peasants' strike." It was a shortage of grain that caused massive and widespread starvation. Soviet leaders became adept at blaming others for their own mistakes—it was the fault of the peasants, or the kulaks, or the bourgeoisie, the White Russians, incompetent local officials, or the Jews, or unproductive workers. Blame was distributed freely when things did not go according to Stalin's plans. In any case, Lenin's accelerated industrialization program was only possible by using forced labor.

The biggest cause of the food shortage was simply the breakdown in the economy. Cities faced starvation because peasants did not market enough grain, and the peasants did not bother to grow enough because there was nothing to buy with the proceeds.

As for a probable reason why the Brezhnev administration took so much care to use the Russian book for propaganda purposes after Stalin's death, they undoubtedly knew—long before Gorbachev—of the ineffectual and stagnant condition of the USSR which had foolishly followed an unproven theory that did not work. There was little they could do about it, except use propaganda to continue with their pretense that Russia was still a major world power.

Like all police states, it tended to be sensitive about its deficiencies. So did the leaders, who continually looked for ways to deflect criticism from themselves by blaming others. In essence, the story in the Russian book was a witch-hunt. And Reilly, with all his publicity in the news media, was an ideal scapegoat to ridicule and demonize, and blame for the social and industrial unrest, the political rebellions, the economic failures, America's turn-down of their application for a desperately-needed loan, and the failure of their secret police to provide intelligence information that might have helped them avoid most of their failures.

THE GADFLY

1
The New 'C'

ONE OF THE RESULTS OF THE ZINOVIEV LETTER SCANDAL in Britain was that Whitehall tightened its security procedures under the newly elected Conservative Government. Prime Minister Stanley Baldwin was informed that intercepts and Special Branch reports would no longer be circulated after it took office. Winston Churchill, who was now back in office as Chancellor of the Exchequer, was anxious to catch up on Soviet intercepts, and was frustrated and angry when he discovered that he no longer had access to them. He protested to the new Foreign Secretary, Austin Chamberlain, about "such serious changes in the system which was in vogue when we were last colleagues."

"I have studied this information" he wrote, "over a longer period and more attentively than probably any other minister has done. All the years I have been in office since it began in the autumn of 1914. I have read every one of those flimsies and I attach more importance to them as a means of forming a true judgment of public policy in these spheres than to any other source of knowledge at the disposal of the state."

He was referring to the secret "Room 40" with which he had been involved at its inception. It was still a section of the British Admiralty involved in crypto-analysis; still breaking enemy codes in order to obtain secrets of their military policy and strategies, tactics, new technologies, and battle plans and movements of their armed forces. No one knew more than Winston Churchill what it could be aimed at in order to obtain top secret information and to counter terrorism. Unlike most politicians, who either could not grasp its importance or its scope, or dismissed it as ungentlemanly "double-cross," Churchill may have obtained more useful information that led to the Allied victory in the Great War than anyone else ever had.

But, in spite of Churchill's protest, only the Foreign Office received a complete set of intercepts thereafter.

SIS and GC & CS moved from their previously separate headquarters early in 1925 to adjacent offices in Broadway Buildings at 54 Broadway, opposite the St. James's Park subway station in Westminster. Commencing on the third and fourth floors, they gradually spread upwards in the eight storey building.

The Chief, known as 'C,' was now Admiral "Quex" Sinclair. His office was situated in the center of the fourth floor, guarded by one of his secretaries. The address gave him direct access to his home at the rear of the building in Queen

Anne's Gate. He sought as much secrecy as Cumming had previously done. On the other hand, he was well-known as a *bon vivant* and nicknamed after *The Gay Lord Quex* in Pinero's popular comedy.

Hugh "Quex" Sinclair was described by Paul Dukes as "The most unusual person I had ever seen. He was a short man with a Jewish face and keen eyes. He had a hard-brimmed hat in his hand and below a blue suit with a red tie he had light brown shoes."

For a naval officer previously accustomed to wearing an impressive uniform, this was an extraordinary transformation. Particularly the light brown shoes, which were considered to be in bad sartorial taste and never worn with a dark suit.

"My first impression was that how clever the authorities were to head the SS with an American gangster."

The new 'C's immediate emphasis was on improving the quality of information by hiring more agents, and showing that he was fully in charge by promoting an amalgamation of the SIS and MI5 for greater efficiency and economy. But the existing authorities shrewdly saw an empire-builder and were fearful of placing too much power in his hands. They preferred the present system: and so it remained.

With the Locarno non-aggression pact planned between France, Germany and Belgium—and guaranteed by Britain and Italy—Austin Chamberlain and his Foreign Office were keen to avoid any new disputes with Soviet Russia that might upset its implementation. He wrote to Prime Minister Baldwin in July;

"A great mass of information has accumulated in this office proving the continuous hostile activities of Soviet Agencies against the British Empire, more particularly in the east. Nearly all this information is of the most highly secret character, which I do not circulate to Ministers lest any carelessness in the handling of the papers should endanger our sources of information . . . The provocation offered as shown by this secret information is such as I suppose we have never tolerated from any government and it becomes increasingly difficult to maintain the attitude [of preserving diplomatic relations] which I have thought it right to recommend to the Cabinet."

He continued to believe that Britain "would be justified as a consequence of the facts now known to us in breaking off [diplomatic relations with Soviet Russia] *if we thought it expedient to do so.*"

The head of the Foreign Office's Northern Department, J.D. Gregory, explained to Prime Minister Stanley Baldwin how that policy worked, when he said, "Peace is the paramount international need and a definitely outlawed Russia would be bound to seek an increased means of disturbing it."

The modern name of Britain's intelligence service gradually became known more publically in the 1920s when the report of the 1925 Cabinet Secret Service

Committee spoke of the "Secret Intelligence Service, commonly known as SIS." A police Special Branch memorandum described SIS. as the Special Intelligence section of the Foreign Office, although its usage in Whitehall and the SIS itself still varied from time to time. A common phrase like 'C's organization' was sometimes used, and the shorthand term of MIII was still being used in August 1939. A new cover name, MI6, was adopted early in the Second World War and became more commonly used from then on.

The Government's budget cutbacks for intelligence services were a continual sore point with Winston Churchill in his various positions as a Minister of the Crown. A proposed budget cut greatly alarmed Winston Churchill when Secretary of State for War. He had protested about such budget cuts to his senior Cabinet colleagues as early as 1920. But the tradition of cutting back budgets for intelligence gathering as soon as a war ended continued.

Churchill had a greater faith in, and fascination for, secret intelligence than any of his predecessors. During his early adventures on the outposts of empire as Colonial Secretary, he had acquired a fascination for cloaks and daggers which never left him. While Home Secretary in 1910-1911 he had followed closely the development of SIS to MI5. As First Lord of the Admiralty in 1914 he had been personally involved in the new practice of wireless interceptions and code-breaking in "Room 40." As Minister for War during the 1920s, he considered the Soviet intercepts to be more helpful for making judgments than any other minister. Many of them came from Sidney Reilly.

Churchill grudgingly accepted an appointment by Lloyd George to the Colonial Office after his predecessor Lord Milner was due to retire. His task now would be to sweep up whatever remained of the old disintegrated Ottoman Empire and reshape it as a possession or mandate of the British Empire. He said he took it up in 1921 "as a stopgap." What he really wanted to be was Chancellor of the Exchequer, a position at 11 Downing Street, which was next door to Number Ten and often second only to being Prime Minister.

2
Sidney Reilly's Narrative

WHATEVER WAS KNOWN BY BRITAIN'S SECRET SERVICE in 1925, Reilly's whereabouts were apparently not among their secrets. Churchill continued to read reports by Reilly, through 'C,' and Reilly corresponded with Churchill, until he had vanished from sight in 1924. That means we cannot know the contents of any private conversations between Sidney Reilly and Winston Churchill—including one that Churchill mentioned took place at Checkers—because they were Top Secret. It also means we cannot know whether or not Reilly's return to Soviet Russia and his disappearance there had anything to do with their former political tactics towards the Bolsheviks.

For example, could Reilly have been acting in accordance with Churchill's instructions, as Boris Savinkov might previously have been? We don't know.

Reilly's whereabouts were still unknown in 1933 when his widow, Pepita, decided to publish her own account of her husband's life as an espionage agent, under the title *Adventures of a British Master Spy: the Memoirs of Sidney Reilly.*

She remarked in the foreword, "What his fate was no one knows."

An introduction to the memoirs by Michael Smith—who served in British Army Intelligence and is an award-winning journalist—warned readers that Reilly's reputation as a British master-spy was badly tarnished by historians who dismissed some of the stories told about him. Smith rated Reilly as "a superb agent" And the accounts in this book by his widow, about British espionage operations in Petrograd and Moscow, had been adequately confirmed by Captain George Hill of Britain's Secret Service, whom we know often worked alongside Reilly. Although it might lead to a conclusion that it was Hill who wrote Pepita Reilly's book, in fact, said Smith, "it includes details that Hill clearly did not know and could not have known and which we now know to be true."

Readers of Reilly's Odyssey had already fallen deeply into the shadowy world of rumor and gossip, deceit, conjecture, unsubstantiated conclusions, wishful thinking, and outright lies. In this case they were not the result of political propaganda or counter-propaganda, or a deliberate intention to deceive the public. A third party was involved in writing the narrative. His job was to put Reilly's story together for a serial in the *Evening Standard* in 1931 and a book purporting to portray the courageous and scary adventures of a master spy two years later.

Lockhart helped Mrs. Reilly publish her book and the serialization in the *Evening Standard*, but apparently did not write any of it.

Pepita Reilly's experience of her husband had lasted for little more than two years, and she would have known only what he chose to tell her about his espionage exploits. It would hardly have amounted to much, since he was accomplished at compartmentalizing his life with rigid security precautions. But apparently he had already made notes for a possible memoir to be published after he retired from the British Secret Intelligence Service.

Even so, neither Hill nor Reilly could have released much information, because they would have been obliged to sign the Official Secrets Act. And anything Reilly planned to write would have had to be vetted by 'C' before he could obtain permission to publish it. Or he could even be arrested and imprisoned under the terms of the Act.

Whoever was the ghost-writer for Pepita's book had to create what amounted to an authentic account of Reilly's life as a super-spy from the bits and pieces of information she provided.

Mrs. Reilly claimed that one of the three accounts in the 1932 edition (and a new one in 2014) was based on memoirs written by her husband. Her faith in her husband is touching, but open to interpretation, since he might have fooled her as he fooled everyone else.

"Who was Sidney Reilly?" she asked. But she was not necessarily the best person to find out. At least, whoever it was wrote the foreword to her book was determined to correct some of the inaccuracies in "the section devoted to him in Winfried Ludecke's standard work Behind the Scenes of Espionage." Readers were also cautioned on Page XV that "The work of Saugann, widely read in France but forbidden in England, which affects to be an exposure of British secret service methods, is false from start to finish."

The author pointed out that the public knew nothing about Reilly's private life; by which she meant the personal life "of Sidney the ideal husband." She evidently considered that to be her trump card as his biographer.

It seemed from Pepita's account that first and foremost Reilly was a patriot. And he obtained psychological satisfaction from gambling dangerously when the odds were hugely against his winning. Evidently she accompanied him on his trips and at his meetings whenever she could, and was a first-hand witness to Reilly's heroism while he lived continually on the edge between the possibility of success or disaster.

We are on more familiar ground when we pass on to "Sidney Reilly's Narrative." Here is the Reilly we have come to know—or thought we knew—in one of his more typical situations in Moscow in the middle of summer, disguised as "Comrade Relinsky" a *Cheka* police agent whose identity papers enabled him to move freely about the city.

The glimpses he describes of extreme poverty and neglect of the population in the streets of this major city are revealing, with such poverty that it had reached the point of hopelessness, starvation and stagnation. It was normal then to see people collapse and drop dead while lining up in the bread queues, which were "long, silent, listless, apathetic." As for the mass starvation in rural areas that wiped out whole villages or towns, no one knew or cared about them at the time, since, even to Russians, they were as remote as foreign countries.

Dignified men and women of the middle-classes who were now forced laborers watched over by an armed guard were "tired, emaciated, starving, weary." And were deliberately prevented from joining the food queues.

There is much more of this as secret agent Sidney Reilly expresses some of the reasons for his hatred of the Bolsheviks who had stolen his country and turned it into a pig-sty.

For those who chose to disbelieve in Sidney Reilly, his exploits, his claims, and his motives, everything he described in his notes which his widow called a memoir, was verified by Sir Paul Dukes who managed to have his own memoirs as a Secret Service agent published in 1922. Dukes called his account *Red Dusk and the Morrow*. It is a first-hand memoir of his return as an agent of the Secret Service to Petrograd, where he had previously lived and worked in the *Marinsky Theater* before the Revolution.

Since he observed the October Revolution unfold when he was a civilian, and revisited it during the Civil War, his account is featured in a following chapter, to show that what he saw and experienced was much the same as Reilly did. But his more detailed narrative was published.

Reilly wrote, "I had not been prepared for the full extent of the change which had come over my birthplace. Petrograd, which once could challenge comparison with any city in the world, bore a ruinous and tumbledown aspect. The streets were dirty, reeking, squalid. Houses here and there lay in ruins. No attempt was made to clean the streets, which were strewn with litter and garbage. There was no police except for the secret police which held the country in thrall, no municipal administration, no sanitary arrangements, no shops open, no busy passengers [sic] on the pavements, no hustle of traffic on the roads. The place had sunk into utter stagnation, and all normal life seemed to have ceased in the city."

Those images of Moscow and Petrograd lay at the heart of Reilly's determination to find a way to overthrow the Communist Government before they could become a permanent and dominating feature not only of Russia, but throughout the whole of Europe.

As his friend Grammatikoff declared, Russia was "in the hands of the criminal classes and of lunatics released from the asylums. Nobody did any work. There was a growing want of all the necessities of life. People were starving."

Wherever Reilly was now, it was left to the imagination of his widow, his mistresses, his friends and his former colleagues, to fathom from what little was known, what he could possibly be doing about it in Soviet Russia.

3
Diplomacy

REILLY WAS AMBITIOUS AT A DANGEROUS TIME in a dangerous career and a dangerous world. From time to time, it may have required a little boasting, a little exaggeration or storytelling, and a certain amount of unpredictability, to succeed and survive; just as with any diplomat. In his case, it required a great deal more audacity. And lying on certain occasions would be essential for a spy to protect his cover. Those are all fairly common characteristics when undertaken in the field of diplomacy, or in a business venture. As the enemy spy, Captain Franz von Rintelen of German Naval Intelligence, remarked wryly after World War One;

"The secret service agent is a spy if he is on the other side but an intelligence officer if working for you."

In Reilly's case, as a secret agent, those characteristics would have been essential in order to achieve patriotic ends in times of war. Diplomacy was among his many attributes as a secret agent.

Who better to define the job of a professional diplomat than Soviet Ambassador Maisky, among the careful notes he made in *The Maisky Diaries*. According to him, the priority of a diplomat is to acquire vital information that might influence national policy. It meant establishing close contacts with at least five hundred influential political leaders or social leaders.

It was "not enough to have a nodding acquaintance with a person, and to meet him once or twice a year at some official function or in the corridors of parliament. One must meet him on a regular basis, invite him to breakfast or dinner, visit him at home, invite him to the theatre occasionally, attend the wedding of his son or his daughter, wish him many happy returns on his birthday, sympathize with him when he is ill.

"It is only when your acquaintance has come a little closer to you (and Englishmen need to scrutinize with someone for quite a while before they count him among their "friends") that his tongue starts to loosen, and only then may you start to glean things from him, or else start to put the necessary ideas into his head."

Maisky's diary entries are a fair description of the way that Reilly worked as an Intelligence Agent, And yet, as far as could be ascertained so far, it had led him into a cell in the Lubianka prison in Moscow's Kremlin, which was notorious for its indifference to its inmates.

4
Civilian Spy

Paul Dukes became a secret agent with British Intelligence at the same time as Reilly did, and knew him intimately—or as closely as anyone could—since they were undertaking the same sort of activities for Britain. Dukes was born in Somerset to a creative family in which his brother was the playwright Ashley Dukes and his father a clergyman. It had probably given him a taste for theatricals. Dukes became a teacher of languages in Riga, Latvia, and was a fluent Russian speaker. It was claimed that he was only appointed to the British Secret Service by Cumming because Reilly recommended him.

Dukes had been a concert pianist and a deputy conductor at the Petrograd Conservatoire. He would help prominent White Russians to escape from Bolshevik prisons, and smuggle them out of Russia through Finland. He would even eventually be fictionalized on film as a "Scarlet Pimpernel" named Smith, for his uncanny ability to merge with Soviet Russian officials and appear to possess the authority to have their prisoners released.

He loved disguising himself and was evidently masterly at assuming a great number of new identities which enabled him to infiltrate several Bolshevik organizations, like the Soviet Communist Party, the Comintern, The Communist International, and even the *Cheka* secret police. He passed on information from the Politburo to 'C' in London. On returning to England he was knighted by King George the Fifth; the only British spy ever to be awarded a knighthood.

Dukes would write a book on the rise and fall of Bolshevism called *Red Dusk and the Morrow*, as well as other books about the Reds, and later on about the Gestapo. He had no illusions about either totalitarian ideology, and recognized that the language of both was designed to conceal what was really happening and what was planned to happen under the tyranny of a totalitarian police state. Dukes claimed that people had been beguiled into joining the Communist Party by its purposeful use of a language that said the opposite of what was happening and what was intended to happen: it was part of their strategic recipe for obtaining power by stifling resistance.

As Dukes explained, he went to Russia not to conspire but to inquire. He had been warned by the Foreign Office at the end of 1920 that someone named Mr. Charles Davison, whom he had never heard of, had been executed in Moscow, and the explanation the Soviet Government gave for his murder was that "Mr. Davison was shot as an accomplice of my *provocative activities*." And yet, Dukes had never even met him and had no idea who or what he was.

It was those types of rumored but invisible so-called "connections" that were also used to discredit Sidney Reilly by authors like Deacon and his imitator. Dukes claimed numerous instances of that type of so-called "conclusive evidence" that turned out to be gossip or rumor, or even false news. The main purpose of Dukes' mission was to investigate what was happening in Bolshevik Russia, and what exactly Bolshevism was; what the Reds and their leaders were doing and planned to do in future, and what their ideology was supposed to mean—since Lloyd George's Government had no idea what a Bolshevist was. Nor, apparently, did anyone else. And yet, Britain had to decide whether to recognize the new Bolshevik government in Russia or not, and whether to support them or defeat them.

Despite that, Winston Churchill, with his sense of history and his perceptiveness of social Darwinism, possessed a fairly clear idea of what Russia's leaders were up to, and knew that they posed a threat, not only to Europe, but to the whole world, because of their brainwashing techniques. Ideological illusions were on a par with medieval superstitions and religious fixations that drew society back to tyranny and barbarism. It had taken the West thousands of years to achieve liberty, human rights and freedom of speech, which would all be lost. But impressionable people with credulous minds readily accepted false impressions and ideas because of the frailty of reason, and the human need to believe in something.

One of the images that Dukes observed in the final days of Tsarist Russia, when he counted the hours to the inevitable and final eruption of a revolution, was when, in March 1917, many of the soldiers sided with police who dressed in the uniforms of soldiers to deceive the public. There they lay, prostrate across the roadways, firing their rifles at intervals. He saw the first revolutionary regiments appear and watched the sacking of the arsenal by the mobs, while other soldiers broke into the *Kresty* Prison across the river. After the Tsarist police had been scattered by the mobs in the *Nevsky Prospect*, a murmur arose from the angry crowds and erupted into a roar with the one word on their lips—"*Revolyutsia!*"

Dukes reasoned that it would all end in a Declaration of Independence of Russia. He imagined the pent-up miseries and woes of 180 million people emerging and set in motion. But in which direction would this mass of energy go? It was centered at the *Tauride Palace* late at night, where entry through the gates was only possible with an official pass. He climbed over the railings and found friends and comrades among the bushes on the other side. Soldiers lay sleeping in heaps on the floors of hallways and corridors. Arms and ammunition were piled almost as high as the ceilings. The revolution had begun with hopes of freedom, at last, from an oppressive and corrupt regime which had maintained a stranglehold on the lives of the entire population for centuries.

Germany had sent Lenin and his Bolshevik revolutionaries to Russia in a guarded train because they had agreed to remove Russia from fighting in the war against them.

One year later Dukes was in the eastern city of Samara, with the winter snow melting and spring sunshine beginning to appear, and "the new proletarian lawgivers" watching his group suspiciously. But the revolutionaries were, so far, too preoccupied in stealing whatever they could from the middle-classes and vandalizing property, or setting it on fire, to pay much attention to possible counter-revolutionaries.

Dukes was suddenly ordered back from Moscow to London by an unexpected telegram from the War Office. He set off through the turbulence and the political arguments, and the growing hunger and bread queues in the city, to Archangel, from where he took a steamer to Murmansk on the eastern shore of the Barents Sea, with its perpetual daylight. He boarded a destroyer there for Patchenga; "a tug to the Norwegian frontier, a ten-day journey round the North Cape," and by the fjords to Bergen; surging finally in "a zig-zag course across the North Sea, dodging submarines, to Scotland."

Once back in the British Isles, Dukes took the first train to London. A car awaited him at Kings Cross station. He was driven to a building in a side street off of Trafalgar Square. His driver led him through the entrance, and they were carried in an elevator to the top level. He followed his driver through a maze of passages and past a rabbit-warren of nooks and alcoves piled heavily in the war-emergency offices on the roof. His guide led him further through narrow passageways and up flights of steps and down again, under low wooden archways and around unexpected corners, up another flight of steps that led to the roof again, and across a short iron bridge into another maze, where he was shown into a tiny room and greeted by a colonel in uniform who rose from behind a desk. His driver announced him and slipped away.

Colonel Frederick Browning shook his hand. "Good afternoon Mr. Dukes! I am glad to see you."

It was here and then that he was offered a post in the British Secret Intelligence Service. After cautiously asking what it implied, he was told,

"We have reason to believe that Russia will not long continue to be open to foreigners. We wish someone to remain there to keep us informed of the march of events."

Dukes' instructions were to return at 4.00 p.m. the next day to make up his mind. The army officer rang a bell, and a lady escorted Dukes out. When he asked her what sort of establishment this was, she shrugged her shoulders amicably and pressed the button for an elevator without replying.

The following day he was escorted again by a different woman, through the narrow corridors and staircases to the same colonel. He told Dukes that, after he returned to Soviet Russia, the Foreign Office wanted to be accurately informed about the attitude of every section of the community; on the amount of support the Bolshevik Government enjoyed, and the development and modification of its policy; the possibility of altering the regime or mounting a counter-revolution; and what part Germany was playing in the affair.

It would be left to Dukes to decide where and how he made his way back across Russia and what cover he decided to use; also how he would send reports to them afterwards. Since he knew the conditions better than most, it would be up to him to make his own suggestions. The Colonel gave his own views on Russia, and asked for his corroboration or corrections. He also mentioned a few names of English people whom Dukes might encounter. Then he went to see if the Chief was ready to receive them.

When the colonel returned, he asked Dukes to come back again on the following day, since the Chief was now unavailable. One of the young ladies showed him out again without comment or expression.

Dukes returned the next day. No sooner had he arrived when Colonel Browning led him through the rabbit warren of passageways to meet the Chief.

He caught glimpses of tree tops through windows on the way to the Chief's quarters, then of the Embankment Gardens, the Thames at Tower Bridge, and Westminster. Whisked around another corner, he was led into a large study, where the Colonel knocked on a door and stepped into a dark room with a low ceiling at the top of the building. Dukes was confused before he even entered, but not entirely disoriented. He saw a writing desk placed before a window that put everything in silhouette for a moment, so that he could not immediately distinguish any other objects, except for a row of telephones on one side of a desk and a pile of papers on the other.

He began to note a number of maps and drawings lying on a side-table, with models of aeroplanes, submarines and miscellaneous mechanical devices. A rack of test tubes gradually emerged to show chemical experiments had been in operation. Seated in a swing chair behind the desk, and writing with hunched shoulders, while his head was supported on one hand, was the Chief in shirt-sleeves.

Dukes went no further in describing the Chief, except to say he was "a British officer and an English gentleman of the finest stamp, absolutely fearless and gifted with limitless resources of subtle ingenuity, and I count it one of the greatest privileges of my life to have been brought within the circle of his acquaintanceship."

'C' stopped writing after a moment and studied him. "So I understand you want to go back to Soviet Russia, do you?"

He was brief and precise, naming a few English people in places like Archangel,

Stockholm, Riga, Helsingfors, and Petrograd. It was left to Dukes to decide how he would get back and send in his reports. 'C' smiled and directed the Colonel to teach Dukes the ciphers and take him to the laboratory to learn about inks. Paul Dukes' code name was now ST25.

'C' gave him an engaging smile when they were about to leave, and said, "Don't go and get killed."

Three weeks later Dukes was on his way back to Petrograd on a troopship with American soldiers, heading for Archangel. Movement was more difficult than he had expected at Archangel, where he was obliged to travel on foot through moorland and forest for 600 miles to Petrograd. Everywhere the roads were watched. The autumn rains made moors and marshes impassable, obliging him to choose alternative routes. He let his beard grow, and soon looked anonymous, like every other Russian.

He tried out a pathway in the direction of Helsingfors, the capital of Finland. News here in this isolated area came only through rumors, gossip, slander and scandal—as it had always done in rural areas set far apart from each other. It came from word-of-mouth, which was often false and misleading, even contrary to what was really happening. But it was swallowed wholesale and without criticism by everyone, in much the same way that communism was being gobbled up by the masses in Russia although they had no idea what it was.

5
Parting of the Ways

DUKES KNEW HELSINGFORS as one of the unhealthiest spots in Europe, and generally tried to avoid it. Its population of German-speaking peoples and Russians of the old regime could be dangerous. In any accidental encounter with strangers it was safer to tell people the exact opposite of what you intended.

He soon found the British Consulate, where he was introduced to an agent of the American Secret Service who had only just managed to escape from Russia. He gave Dukes a letter of introduction to a Russian officer in Viborg called Melnikoff, which was not his real name. Many of the people in those parts had a variety of different names to suit different situations and occasions—hence the inaccuracy of searching for official information, which might be under a different name, or had already been prudently removed.

Melnikoff turned out to be "a Russian naval officer of the finest stamp"—an expression that Dukes used for those he respected. He had worked with Britain's

Naval Attaché, Captain Cromie, who had been murdered by the Bolsheviks at the British Embassy. Melnikoff's parents had been brutally shot by the Bolsheviks. He had only just managed to escape death. Not surprisingly, he hated the Bolsheviks. His life from then on was directed solely at avenging the murders of his parents.

Since Melnikoff was a monarchist, Dukes avoided talking politics with him, but they enjoyed their friendship. Melnikoff offered to make arrangements for him to cross the Finnish frontier at night and return secretly to Soviet Russia. Each side of the border was guarded suspiciously with constant skirmishes because of the hostility between Finland and the new Soviet Government which had taken power in Russia, its dominating neighbor.

Melnikoff promised he would reach Petrograd ahead of Dukes and prepare a place of shelter for him there. He gave two addresses where he could be found—a hospital, and a small café which was concealed in a private home, unknown, so far, by the Bolshevik authorities.

After three days of drinking whisky, Melnikoff was ready to leave. Dukes was to follow him two days later. Melnikoff gave him a piece of paper with a password on it for the Finnish border guards. Then he withdrew to his room to transform himself into someone else, with a seaman's cap pulled down over his eyes and dirt smeared on his face. He changed into a shabby coat and dark trousers, and wound a muffler tight round his neck, then shoved a huge Colt revolver inside his trousers.

At the last moment before leaving, Melnikoff and Dukes sat down silently and gazed at each other, in accordance with the old Russian custom when friends took leave of each other; since it could be for the last time. Then they wished each other a safe journey and prosperity, as if parting for a long and hazardous journey to the other side of the world. Would Melnikoff vanish forever in the vast wastes of the Russian continent, Dukes wondered. And would he himself simply disappear into the immensity of the Russian countryside? Neither knew with any sense of certainty what would happen from day to day.

When Melnikoff said "Good-bye" to Dukes, he hesitated and glanced back briefly at him, then instinctively crossed himself in the Russian Orthodox style, before adding, "Sunday evening—without fail."

Once outside the street door, the Russian looked piercingly in both directions and pulled his cap even further down his brow to his eyes before making the leap and vanishing into the darkness.

It was Saturday when Dukes rose the next morning, so the Jewish booths in the marketplace were shut. Only the Finnish ones were open. But he had already bought the few odds and ends he needed for his own disguise. He decided to buy a few more items from the Jewish stores when they opened on Sunday morning.

By the time Ivan Sergeievitch arrived to meet him early on Sunday, Dukes wore a Russian shirt with black leather breeches, black knee-boots, a shabby tunic, and an old leather cap with a fur brim and a little tassel on top. It was an old style worn by the Finns in a district north of Petrograd. His dark beard was now profuse and shaggy, and his unkempt hair hung over his face. His new friend was a refugee from Russia and obliged to make occasional small amounts of money smuggling whatever he could to support his wife and children. The present currency was either money or butter.

"Remember, you are a speculator," Ivan advised Dukes.

It was the Bolsheviks' description for anyone who sold their clothing or furniture, or icons, or jewelry, for food. Although they suffered if they were caught trading privately, it was safer than being accused of being a spy. Ivan gave him the address of his flat in Petrograd:

"Tell the housekeeper I sent you, but avoid being seen by the porter, who's a Bolshevik, or the house committee"

He accompanied Dukes to the train station at Viborg, where they sat separately and pretended they did not know each other, so that they would not be connected by the *Cheka*. After Ivan left, Dukes sank down in his seat, imagining that everyone was watching him.

It was pitch dark when the train finally stopped with a screech at Rajajoki on the Finnish side of the border. He had to walk along the tracks for half a mile to reach the frontier post over a wooden bridge across the Sestro River, where a Finnish sentry stood at his post at the barrier. The Soviet sentry on the other side of the frontier was only twenty paces away from them.

Dukes left the bridge as he'd been directed and searched for the wooden house where the Finnish patrols were located. He knocked timidly on the front door and, as soon as it was opened, handed over the slip of paper that Melnikoff had given him.

The Finn examined the scrap of paper by a greasy oil lamp and then lifted the lamp to study the newcomer's face. Satisfied, the Finn invited Dukes in and shut the door to keep the cold out and the heat in.

"What name do you want on the papers?" the Finn asked, as he seated himself busily at a table.

When he had finished typing out the document, he held it out for Dukes to read. It was headed in the top left-hand corner; "Extraordinary Commissar of the Central Executive Committee of the Petrograd Soviet of Workers and Red Armymen's Deputies" The text followed:

CERTIFICATE

This is to certify that Joseph Afirenko is in the services of the Extraordinary Commissar of the Central Executive Committee of the Petrograd Soviet of Workers' and Red Armymen's Deputies in the capacity of office clerk, as the accompanying signatures and seal attest.

Dukes scribbled in the names he was told to, and was given another similar paper to sign, on the grounds that two documents were better than one, particularly when examined by illiterate guards. The seal was the most important item that was always viewed with awe and respect. It was stamped on the small photo of himself that he provided. Dukes was also directed to sign himself as Tihonov and as Friedmann, his secretary or witness or guarantor. He did whatever the Finn told him, as Melnikoff had already instructed him to.

As soon as the paperwork was concluded, they crossed over to the other side of the river by boat. Stepping over the thin layer of ice along the edge, he climbed the bank while the boat he'd left behind was hurriedly rowed back across the river to Finland.

Dukes was now on his own in Soviet Russia. Only a short walk away was a silent train station. He slept in the bushes until daylight to avoid suspicion. It began to snow as dawn broke through.

He travelled second class to Petrograd. It took him twenty-five minutes while the train stopped at every station on the way. There was a crush at the Finland Station when they arrived, and his paper was studied again. He felt a mixture of relief and apprehension to be back. He was homeless, helpless and friendless in what had once been his home town. But the dejection he had felt when left on his own in the carriage was gone at the familiar landmarks around him.

This was the journey he had embarked on in a spirit of adventure. All he wanted now was to merge anonymously with the common crowd in the familiar streets, while he observed what the greatest social experiment the world had ever witnessed did for the common people. Dukes was, after all, a genuine Christian brought up in the Church and sympathetic towards the poor and dispossessed.

The life that the new SIS agent Dukes now lived, always on the edge of danger, was similar and yet somewhat different from the life that Sidney Reilly lived as a secret service agent for the same British Intelligence bureau. The difference was that, for the moment at least, Dukes was an observer of the new Soviet regime, studying it objectively like an anthropologist for his own academic interest and the SIS, who would inform the British Government. It was a huge adventure, a bit of a game for him, which he observed almost dispassionately, whereas Reilly lived twice as dangerously in his valiant attempt to organize a counter-revolution in order to overthrow the Soviet regime before its tentacles could spread across Europe.

If Dukes was a philosophical observer taking his first analytical look at what the so-called Bolsheviks were up to in Russia, Reilly had already seen what the Bolsheviks had done to his country and was unforgiving in his determination to topple the communists from power.

6
The Dystopian City

DUKES HAD BARELY EMERGED FROM THE TRAIN STATION when he encountered another sign of what the new Bolshevik paradise had to offer—an old man leaning with his face against a wall and sobbing desperately. He had not eaten for three days and could find nowhere to keep warm for the night. Petrograd was a dying city. Its population had been reduced to the very basic functions of animals—eating and sleeping and attempting to keep warm in some snatched temporary shelter to stay alive for one more night.

He handed the man an old twenty-rouble note. The Russian looked bewildered and hesitated before attempting to thank him. He could only mumble; "What use is money, when there's nowhere to get bread?"

Dukes passed him a piece of bread from his pocket.

The only movement in the streets was from pedestrians. The roads were filthy and strewn with litter and an occasional dead horse with its ribs showing. It had evidently been whipped to get the last ounce of energy out of it before it had dropped. Remnants of tattered and faded red flags still hung across streets and in between some houses, left from a celebration of the Bolshevik victory. Small random groups of people came in to sight, evidently of an educated class; elderly ladies and gentlemen in worn-out clothes, shovelling away the early snow and slush under the supervision of a guard who stood still and did nothing.

Dukes could read the dilemma of the revolution in the faces of the well-behaved men and women doing all the work stiffly, as if unaccustomed to heavy labor. They knew, like most of the middle-classes, that the peasants and working classes had been treated shabbily and unjustly under Romanov rule, but were unable to do anything about it. Now they did not know how to convey their sympathy other than by politely accepting their fate at the hands of layabouts, hooligans, bullies, criminals, and sadists, who enjoying bossing them about and watching them suffer.

Everyone had known the evils of the Tsarist regime, but no one had any idea how to make changes that would establish some sort of dignity and equality in a just society. It meant an imaginative transformation that was completely beyond their reach after centuries of oppression. And yet, as they gazed around at the shabbiness and disorganization, they knew that this was no paradise. But they were wise enough to hold their tongues.

Dukes gazed at the familiar view from the *Liteiny Bridge* over the *Neva River*, admiring the slender gilded spire of the cathedral, and the fortress of St Peter and St Paul, wondering who was now incarcerated in its subterranean dungeons.

His first destination was the home of an Englishman known only as Mr. Marsh, allegedly a prominent business man in Petrograd and a former friend of Captain Cromie. Marsh was thought to be still at liberty. He lived on the quay of a branch of the *Neva* that flowed through the city. Melnikoff had promised to prepare him for Dukes' arrival.

He found the house, but first assured himself that no one was watching it or him before entering. An unfriendly-looking man hovered in the hallway. He let Dukes in but then stood with his back barring the closed door.

"What do you want with him?" he said suspiciously.

Dukes affected to be lost and, although he knew the number, asked "Can you tell me the number of Mr. Marsh's flat?"

"Marsh is in prison," the man told him. "His flat is sealed up. Do you know him?"

"I *don't* know him," Dukes replied. "I've never even seen him. I just brought him a few things he left behind."

He showed the man a small parcel of socks, handkerchiefs and biscuits from his coat pocket.

"Give it here," the man said gruffly.

Dukes did so reluctantly while the man barred his way to the exit.

He hurried out and headed for the hospital that Melnikoff had told him about, at the far end of *Kamenostrovsky Prospect* in the delta of the river. The few street-cars visible were too overcrowded and overflowing to board, so he had to walk. On arrival, he found that, although Melnikoff was supposed to be related to one of the doctors, he was nowhere to be found. He asked an old woman at the lodge.

"Which Melnikoff?"

He gave her a description. "Nicolas," he added.

"He was here last night," she told him. "He left this morning. Hasn't been back since."

All he could do now was wait until afternoon and then try the hidden café in the private flat that Melnikoff had told him about.

He trudged slowly back into the center of town through the shabbiness around him—past the odd dead horse in the road, past the ladies who were made to sweep the streets but were not strong enough to remove the corpses of the horses, past a few stores that still remained open but had little to sell, except for sheet-music, books and flowers. Soviet licenses were now required to buy anything except Soviet propaganda. The flowers were too expensive for most people, who needed their money for the basics needed to stay alive.

Hawkers unloaded second-hand books and whatever else they had been able to steal from private homes, while private vendors displayed anything that might bring them a few roubles for bread or milk. Dukes could see that evidently life in general was stagnating, and the world as he had previously known it was gone.

Government announcements and other public notices were displayed on walls, some about Red Army mobilization, others about compulsory labor for the middle-classes, and some others about the distribution of food. He bought all the newspapers he could handle, and pamphlets by Lenin, Zinoviev, and other communist leaders. He found a cab with a horse still standing and drove back to the Finland Station where he had seen a buffet when he'd arrived, with bits of herring and tiny pieces of black bread. He was glad to have somewhere to sit and read the newspapers and, hopefully, discover what was going on.

While drinking artificial tea, he saw that all news was evidently filtered through the Soviet monopoly of all communications, which was propaganda. In March 1918, the Bolsheviks had changed their official name to the "Communist Party of Bolsheviks." Although the western press talked of peace, these newspapers and Soviet journals wrote of creating a mighty Soviet Red Army that would set Europe and the whole world aflame with international revolutions.

At three o'clock, he felt he had absorbed what important information to send back to London. He was uneasily aware that what was true about what was happening here would be kept secret by the SIS, whereas the distortion of reality from the false propaganda would be believed by the public in England because they knew no better.

He got up and gazed around him. This, he realized, was how England would look, too, if socialism was not crushed at the outset. It was obsessed with class hatred, and determined to punish everyone for imaginary offenses.

He resumes his search for Melnikoff by finding the tiny café at the top of a building in a street off of the *Nevsky Prospect*. As soon as he rang the bell the door was opened a crack, through which he saw the fearful and suspicious eye of a woman. She was about to close it firmly again when he pushed his foot into the opening and hurriedly asked for Melnikoff.

"What Melnikoff?"

He described him as best he could, and the door opened somewhat wider, through which he saw two ladies; the first one plump and elderly, the other young and good-looking. The young one asked cautiously, "What is his first name and patronymic?"

"Nicolas Nicolaevitch."

She nodded and told the other woman, "He said someone might be coming this afternoon."

"Come in," she said to Dukes. "He was here Saturday and said he'd return yesterday but didn't come. He might be here any minute."

Dukes was ushered into a sitting room where several small tables were set out in some kind of order. The charming young woman introduced herself as Vera Alexandrovna, and served him delicious little cakes at a corner table on his own, with a cup of what looked like coffee.

"Coffee," she said. "Well, a mixture of my own. I hope you find it acceptable?"

He nodded cautiously.

"I'm sorry I can't offer you hot chocolate" she added.

He began to apologise self-consciously, in turn, for his grubby appearance.

"Don't excuse yourself," she said. "We all look shabby nowadays. Nicolas Nicolaevitch told me you were coming and were a friend of his. But I shall ask no questions. You may feel yourself quite safe and at home here and nobody will notice you."

The empty room gradually began to fill with about a dozen middle-class visitors, and several bumptious young men who swaggered in and talked in raucous voices, laughing loudly. They appeared to be former army officers and had money to spend on expensive delicacies. He learned later that the tiny café was a rendezvous for conspirators who received funds for counter-revolutionary work from representatives of the Allies.

He saw four of the self-important and loud-mouthed young officers studying him with interest from their table.

"How do you manage to keep the café going?" he asked Vera Alexandrovna.

"With difficulty," she said cautiously. Then, remembering he was a friend of a friend, she explained; "We have two girls we send into the villages twice a week for flour and milk. And we buy sugar in the Jewish market. But I don't think we can keep going much longer, in case we are found out. We've already had Reds speaking to the porter. But we gave him flour to shut him up."

Dukes felt uncomfortable at the attention he was causing from the others, when a fat man came in, bowed and kissed Vera Alexandrovna's hand politely and introduced himself.

"Well," he said, "our Reds won't last much longer. They say they are going to mobilize! With what? All it needs is a little push from outside and they'll burst like a bubble."

A tall thin man with sunken eyes and a black moustache separated himself from his friends at the next table and approached Dukes, introducing himself as Captain Zorinsky.

"You are waiting for Melnikoff, are you not? I am a friend of his."

They shook hands.

"He didn't come here today," Zorinsky added. "But if I can do anything for you at any time I shall be glad."

Dukes nodded but did not encourage him, and Zorinsky returned to his own table. Dukes decided to leave, since he found the atmosphere in the confines of the small room made him apprehensive. He got up to go.

"I am sorry you missed him," Vera Alexandrovna said at the door. "Will you come tomorrow?"

He had no intention of doing so, but said he would. He decided to visit the flat of Ivan Sergeievitch, who was Melnikoff's friend, the one who had accompanied him to Viborg station.

As he left the building, he found so few street lamps alight that the road-ways were bathed in gloom. He began to worry about finding a night's shelter, already falling into the pattern of being occupied solely with the basic function of surviving - the next meal, the next place of shelter where it might be warm, and avoiding people who might be enemies and places that might turn out to be traps.

He saw a hoarding round one side of the *Kazan Cathedral* and peered inside, to find piles of lumber and rubbish. It might be a good place to spend a night if he failed to find anywhere else.

The house he was searching for was in a small street at the end of *Kazanskaya*, in a flat on the top floor. When he reached it, the entire house looked deserted. He met no one on the stairs and nobody answered his ring at the door of the upstairs flat.

He was turning away when he heard footsteps advancing from inside and a female voice asking from behind the door who was calling.

He put his mouth to the door and answered quietly, "From Ivan Sergeievitch."

After a moment's caution, the voice asked, "From which Ivan Sergeievitch?"

He lowered his voice further now that the other person was listening intently, and spoke into the keyhole. "Yours. In Viborg."

After another cautious pause for consideration, she asked him, "But who are you?"

"Don't be alarmed," he said. "I have a message from him."

The footsteps receded and he heard the murmur of voices conferring with each other. Then he heard two locks turn, and the door was opened on a short chain-bolt. He repeated what he'd said and whispered that he had just arrived from Finland and would probably go back there shortly. The chain-bolt was removed for him to enter.

"I'm the housekeeper," the woman said.

She hurriedly closed the door and locked it firmly again behind him. He saw her little figure trembling with fear as she studied him carefully. Beside her was a girl whom Ivan Sergeievitch had described as the nanny of his children in Finland. Dukes attempted to put them at ease by describing his new acquaintance as an old friend who had asked him to come and see them.

The housekeeper invited him into the kitchen, which was the only room which was warmed.

He sat down gladly, feeling very tired by now.

"Ivan Sergeievitch is well," he told them. "So are his wife and children. They send their greetings."

They stared at him wordlessly.

"Impossible to get passports to come back," he explained, and got up again with a formal bow. "Allow me to introduce myself, I am Ivan Pavlovitch."

The housekeeper offered him some food.

"Thank you, but I'm afraid you won't have enough for yourselves."

"We only have soup," she told him apologetically. "But there is enough for all of us."

The nanny's name was Varia. When the housekeeper left the room to heat the soup, she took the opportunity of confiding in him why her companion was so frightened.

"She had an awful shock this morning - she nearly got arrested by the Reds at the market. She's been terrified ever since. They came to arrest anyone buying or selling food."

Finding that Varia was a self-possessed and sensible young woman, Dukes explained that he'd found his house locked that afternoon with no one there. It was a long way to go back to see if his housekeeper had returned or not. Would they mind if he slept on their sofa just for the night?

Varia left the room to ask the housekeeper. Then she returned and told him they had agreed.

While they were eating their cabbage soup at the kitchen table, a soldier let himself into the flat and sat down silently with them on a box against the wall.

"This is my nephew Dmitri," the housekeeper explained.

The two men nodded wordlessly to each other. Dukes thought he seemed like a good-natured young man with little to say for himself.

Dmitri watched them with twinkling eyes and rosy cheeks, while he cut off square chunks of black bread from a loaf and dealt them out. The housekeeper explained that Dmitri had volunteered in order to obtain Red Army rations. Dmitri smiled but said nothing.

Dukes was shown a sofa for him to sleep on in the study.

Varia woke him in the morning with a glass of real tea from Dmitri's rations. Dukes had to reorient himself to his surroundings and felt bewildered for a moment. Then he recalled that he had not found Melnikoff. Although he had only just woken up, he was already anxious about where he could find a place to sleep for the night.

When he returned to the kitchen for another glass of tea and to wash his hands under the tap, he encountered a family atmosphere. Dmitri was sitting on his box and munching a crust of bread in complacent silence. Dukes decide to find out about the Red Army.

"Been in long?"

"Three weeks."

"Is there much for you to do?"

"Done nothing yet."

"No drill?"

"No."

"No marching?"

"No."

"So what do you do?"

He smiled contentedly. "I draw rations."

There was a long pause in the conversation while Dmitri helped himself to more tea, without having much more to say.

"Were you in the old army?"

"Yes."

"What did you do?"

"Orderly."

"And now?"

"Driver."

"Who are your officers?"

"We all have a commissar."

Dukes knew this was an armed Bolshevik official attached to each regiment to ensure that officers were loyal and obeyed communist rules and regulations.

"Who is he?"

"Who knows? He's just one like the rest," Dmitri said disdainfully.

"Well . . . what is the Red Army?" he asked finally, feeling he'd not learnt much.

"Who knows?" Dmitri replied with a careless shrug.

Trotsky knew. Reilly had reported what he had said about his new Red Army:

"The Red Army is formed for the only kind of justifiable warfare, namely civil war on the bourgeoisie and all revolutionary armies that don't agree with us. The bourgeoisie must never again be allowed to possess weapons." He had also declared that "Using army officers of the old regime is only a temporary measure. They will be dispensed with as soon as we train enough proletariat officers."

7
A Search for Melnikoff

DUKES HAD ALREADY DECIDED THAT DMITRI was just one of many who rarely questioned anything and regarded the new Bolshevik Government as just another accident of fate. Why bother to ask about anything, since it would only be temporary, and destined very soon to disappear like all the other incidents in life? There was little else you could do in Russia than endure in silence.

Dukes insisted on paying for the food before he left to search for Melnikoff. Varia told him at the door that he was welcome to return.

Dukes would report back to 'C' that the Imperial Russian Army—officers and men alike—had been no match for modern German troops and did not possess enough munitions or equipment for a determined war. Desertions took place nearly everywhere by the thousands, so that anyone who goes near the army must come away with an impression of moral disintegration of the troops.

The peasant infantry were the first to fall apart. The artillery, with its high numbers of industrial workers, suffered fewer losses and retained its spirit, as did other specialized troops. But in the end the artillery yielded too. A secret order was given during the retreat from Galicia to flog the soldiers for desertion and other crimes. Rodzianko admitted—and he was in close touch with officers, and visited the front himself—"The ground for the final disintegration of the army was prepared long before the revolution."

"There are at least two sides to every situation," Dukes thought to himself as he trudged along the street uncertainly, and unsure in his own mind what to make of the situation.

Whatever the opinions held of the arrogant and cold-hearted intellectual Trotsky, he performed an almost impossible task in creating and leading an entirely new Red Army by imposing training and discipline, inculcating dedication, and motivating his men by his leadership. He put together an effective war machine in only twelve months.

The early morning weather was raw outside the friendliness and warmth of the flat. Snow began to fall as people hurried down the streets holding bundles and small parcels. Line-ups of working women stood patiently outside un-named small stores whose signs over the door simply said, "First Communal Booth," or "Second Communal Booth." It was all anyone needed to know to identify them as depots where bread was distributed to the population in very small amounts according to individual ration cards. People grumbled about having to wait in queues:

"Does Trotsky have to wait in a queue?"

Having received their ration for the day, the women shuffled off and trudged back home for the warmth, with their meagre rations sheltered from the falling snow beneath their shawls.

Dukes, too, trudged on in the piled-up snow, crossing the river at the bridge and along the *Kamenostrovsky Prospect* to the hospital where Melnikoff had said he could be found. But he had still not returned and no one knew anything about him.

Dukes wandered aimlessly about the city until he found himself in the neighborhood where he had lived before. Turning into a side street, he noticed a window with a slip of paper stuck on it and one word, "Dinners," written in pencil. Evidently it was not an official communal eating house, where people needed an official ticket to enter.

He peered in and found a single room on the ground floor that had once been a store but had been emptied of everything and now featured three small tables, barely enabling seating for more than a dozen diners. There were none there at the moment. At least it looked clean.

A woman immediately appeared from behind a curtain.

"Dinner?" she said. She asked him to sit down and wait since it was too early. After a while, she brought him a bowl of gruel. "Bread," she said, "is extra,"

"Can I get dinner here every day?"

"As long as they don't close us down."

She told him, "Our premises have shrunk and shrunk again each time they were closed down, from what my father once ran as a smart restaurant on Sadovaya Street. Look for the paper in the window. Don't enter if it isn't there. It will mean the Reds have taken us over."

The second course was carrots.

He bought three small white loaves and returned that afternoon to Varia and Dmitri and the housekeeper, who were delighted at his contribution. When he telephoned Vera Alexandrovna to enquire about Melnikoff, she said he wasn't there.

What he found particularly interesting was hearing them discuss among themselves—like many other people in Russia—whether or not the British or their Allies from the war would arrive in the country and relieve them of the Reds. It was a frequent subject of gossip and rumor: so he decided to confide in them that he was British.

After a moment of apprehension, even fear—because he did not look like an Englishman in his disguise—the possibility that the rumors of intervention by the Allies in the war might be true, as evinced by the reality of an Englishman face-to-face in Petrograd, began to perk the women up.

Dmitri sat with a broad smile spreading over his good-natured face while Dukes explained. Then, to celebrate, the women put up a fairly good dinner with meat and potatoes in his honor.

"Where did you manage to get meat?" he said with surprise. It turned out to be Dmitri's army ration.

That night Varia made up a proper bed for him, and Dukes lay back to consider his first two days on returning to Petrograd. He had lived from minute to minute and hour to hour, unnoticed among a population who were also living from hand to mouth. He began to feel satisfied that he had managed to merge successfully with the crowds. Only occasionally had he caught a look of envy from someone at his black leather breeches. But he was safe because commissars wore good leather clothes. Even so, he decided to smear some dirt on them tomorrow, since everyone else looked shabby, except for the peasants who wore their usual sheepskin coats and bast shoes.

In one of the propaganda pamphlets he'd bought was an appeal to the peasants to "Join the Communes." It sounded reasonable for the peasants to work, not for gain, but to provide the workers in the towns with bread in exchange for goods from them. But, as he'd seen, there were no goods. And he had discovered how the regime deliberately provoked class hatred, perhaps because the intellectual leadership despised the middle-classes, the peasants, and the workers equally.

He was woken suddenly in the morning by a loud ring of the doorbell, and got up hurriedly, already preparing several possible defences or attacks according to who might be at the front door. But when it was opened cautiously with the chain bolt still on, and then withdrawn, and the door opened wide, he had only time to reach for his passport before Melnikoff burst in.

Melnikoff had altered his appearance with a pair of spectacles and different clothes. He was accompanied by a huge man with a jolly face, dressed in a ragged brown suit and a dirty hat, whom he introduced as "Marsh." They all shook hands.

"I thought you were in prison," Dukes said to Marsh with relief.

"I had a lucky escape—slid down a drainpipe into the next yard as the Reds came in the front door." He had cut his hair and beard short since then. "They were searching for me everywhere. I had to knock one of the blighters down. Then I heard Melnikoff shouting for me."

"How did you find me?" Dukes asked Melnikoff.

"Lucky guess," Melnikoff said. "But I'm being followed too. Can't stay long. Meet me at the 15th Communal Eating House in the Nevsky at three. You won't need an entry ticket. I'll talk to you then. But," he warned, "don't stay anywhere for more than two nights."

On the way out, he called "And don't go to Vera's again. Something's wrong there."

Marsh told him to get dressed and he'd take him to a regular safe house. He gave him the names of several people who could be trusted, including one in the Ministry of War and one in the Admiralty.

The housekeeper was so overwhelmed to have two English visitors that she brought in some tea.

Evidently the Bolsheviks suspected Marsh, and any other Englishmen, for assisting allies whose passports had been taken away, to escape from Soviet Russia secretly.

"Any number of foreigners have been arrested," Marsh told him, "including my wife. She was seized by the Reds and taken as a hostage for my obedience."

"What do you plan to do about her?"

"I don't know. I feel guilty. I can't make up my mind what's best. She's imprisoned in the notorious Extraordinary Commission at No. 2 Goróhovaya Street."

He was waiting for a man he knew who had connections. He also had a wide circle of acquaintances and friends, some of whom managed to live an unobtrusive life working regular hours for wages in Soviet offices.

They finished their tea and Marsh left ahead of him, so that they would not be seen together.

"Follow me in five minutes. I'll be at the hoarding round the Kazan Cathedral."

8
Captain Zorinsky

DUKES LEFT MARSH, after arranging that if Melnikoff could not find him a place to sleep he would return to him, and set off to meet Melnikoff at the communal eating-house, as arranged. He directed his steps by following people moving hurriedly across the street towards a concourse of other people gathered outside an eating-house, where he saw two sailors on guard outside the entrance with fixed bayonets. He hesitated, to watch some other people filing out, led by militiamen. Some others were having their documents examined, or being searched in the dark lobby. He looked round in the dim light for Melnikoff, and was startled to feel a tap on his arm. When he turned round to see who it was, he found himself confronted by Zorinsky, the officer who had accosted him in the private café.

"I expect you planned to meet Melnikoff here?" he asked. "Lucky you didn't go into the restaurant. It's being raided. Melnikoff was one of the first to be arrested. They took him away."

"Why did they raid it?" Dukes asked him.

"Who knows? What will you do?"

Dukes did not wish to confide his movements to Zorinsky. "I don't know," he said.

"We must think of a way of getting him out. He was a great friend of mine. Come home with me and we'll talk it over. I live nearby."

Dukes nodded agreeably, since he wanted to save Melnikoff, They passed into *Troitzkaya Street* and entered a large house on the right.

"What shall I call you?" Zorinsky said.

"Pavel Ivanich."

Zorinsky's flat was large, luxuriously furnished, and meticulously tidy. It showed no sign of being searched and turned upside-down. The Captain invited his guest wordlessly to sit in a deep leather armchair.

"You live comfortably," Dukes observed as he gazed around him.

"My wife is an actress. She gets as much food as she wants and our flat is immune from requisition of furniture or interference by workmen. We can go to see her dance together one evening. She registered me as an assistant manager of the theater, so I am really a gentleman at large." He locked eyes with Dukes. "I spend my time in counter-espionage. You look surprised. It's just a question of whether to be active or passive in these circumstances."

Zorinsky showed him a piece of paper from a drawer. When Dukes glanced at it, it appeared to be a badly-typed document full of errors, as if typed in extreme haste. Dated two days earlier, it was a report of confidential negotiations between the Bolshevist Government and leaders of non-Bolshevist parties about forming a possible coalition government. Nothing had apparently come of it, but it revealed the nervousness, or deceit, of the Bolshevik leaders who were negotiating with the Social-Revolutionaries and the Menshevik party.

"Is it authentic?" Dukes said dubiously.

"The Menshevik delegation drew it up and sent it secretly to the Bolshevists. I saw the original and obtained a copy two hours before it reached them."

Dukes handed it back to him.

"Keep it," said Zorinsky dismissively. "I intended to give it to Melnikoff—he would have given it to you. It's an amusing game, counter-espionage. I used to provide information to Captain Cromie. But I keep in the background."

He offered Dukes a cigarette from a large box, and rang a bell to order tea.

"Whatever the Allies are doing," he remarked, as he offered him a light, "you might as well leave us alone as bungle things as you are doing. But all sorts of people here imagine they are conducting espionage underground or planning to overthrow the Reds. Are you interested?"

"Very."

Zorinsky launched into an exposition on the counter-revolutionary movement, as if he knew it intimately.

"There are belligerent groups," he said, "planning to seize army stores, blow up bridges or raid treasuries. Of course, they will never *do* anything," he sneered, "because they organize like idiots. The Social-Revolutionaries are best—they are fanatics like the Bolsheviks. The others don't know what they want."

Zorinsky carried on talking, while a neatly-attired maid in a clean white pinafore brought in tea and served it with biscuits, sugar and lemon.

"Cromie was a fine fellow," the Captain said. "Pity he got killed. The French and Americans have all gone now. Marsh had bad luck, didn't he?"

Dukes pretended innocence. "Marsh?"

Zorinsky leaned back in his chair and glanced indifferently out of the window. "You don't happen to know where he is, do you?"

"No idea," Dukes said. "I heard in Finland that he was arrested. But I imagine you would have followed his movements."

"Aha," he said with a cynical and crooked smile, "but I do my best to avoid *No. 2 Goróhovaya!* When people get arrested I leave them alone. It's wiser to avoid the mysteries of that institution."

"Is Melnikoff there?"

"Yes," the Captain said seriously. He looked hard in Dukes' face. "Melnikoff is different—we must act at once. I know just the man to investigate, and I'll get him on to it tonight. Will you stay to dinner? My wife will be delighted to meet you. She is very discreet."

Dukes accepted the invitation. When Zorinsky left the room, he heard him on the telephone, arranging for someone to call about nine o'clock.

Zorinsky's wife, Elena Ivanovna, was a jolly little creature but like a spoilt child. She appeared for dinner in a pink Japanese kimono. The table was so beautifully set that Dukes felt out of place in his shabby clothes and uncouth appearance.

"Oh, don't excuse yourself," she said. "Everyone looks shabby nowadays. Have the olden days gone forever, do you think? Will these horrid people never be overthrown? Is it the end of our world?"

"You don't appear to have suffered much, Elena Ivanovna," Dukes remarked.

"No, our troupe is treated really well. But the theater is filled with those horrible sailors every night."

Dukes noted the abundance of vodka as Zorinsky drank a toast to him. His host acknowledged his glance by saying, "I am not a Communist, but there's plenty to be had even if you are not a member of the Communist Party. And I hold the door open. But you Allies had better arrive before the Bolsheviks make Communism work. Or it *will* be the end of the world."

They drank another toast to the Allies, and Zorinsky held forth with his views on Russia and the revolution.

"The Russian peasant is a brute. What he wants is a good hiding, and unless I'm much mistaken the Communists are going to give it to him – otherwise they'll go under. In my regiment we used to smash a jaw now and again on principle. It's the only way to make Russian peasants fight. Now Comrade Trotsky has already abolished his Red officers and has invited us—yes, us, the counter-revolutionary Tsarist officer swine—to fill posts in the new Red Army. Trotsky will order me to flog the peasants to my heart's content. I would make a career in no time under Trotsky."

Within five days after Duke's return to Petrograd, Marsh had fled the country, leaving his wife in a cell with thirty-eight other women and believing she would be released from prison if he were no longer in the city. Melnikoff had vanished after his arrest, perhaps for good.

The reports that Paul Dukes sent to his new Chief in London would have been carefully scrutinized by 'C' before being sent on to Prime Minister Lloyd George in his despatch box. Lloyd George would study them thoroughly, since Dukes was the only voluminous literary British Secret Service agent in Russia at the time, and the Prime Minister had to make up his mind, as a priority, whether to intervene in the Russian revolution by using Allied troops, or make a deal with the new Bolshevik Government and turn a blind eye to their human rights violations and their barbarism.

Winston Churchill received copies of all intelligence reports – the "flimsies," as they were known - and was passionate about intervening. But the British Prime Minister was still hesitant. He was a shrewd politician who always kept an eye open to his own political future.

While Paul Dukes reported on the conditions and attitudes among the masses, it was the time when Bruce Lockhart was still in Moscow officially. He was directly in touch with the Bolshevik leaders - with Trotsky in particular, and also secretly with the counter-revolutionary Boris Savinkov. Lockhart recommended that

Britain should intervene. But Lloyd George was dismissive of Lockhart's personal views and formal recommendations, and dissatisfied with his reports. Regardless of what was actually going on, as Prime Minister he had to find the best way to deal with uninformed public opinion.

That was the point when 'C' sent Reilly to Moscow to report on the political and military situation, and Reilly went straight to the gates of the Kremlin to meet Lenin.

Secret Service agent ST/1 had travelled to north Russia prior to the end of March in 1918. He reported from Petrograd on 16 April that the Bolsheviks were 'the only real power in Russia,' and that some arrangement would have to be made with them to secure the Allied bases at Murmansk and Archangel, and prevent Russia's Baltic fleet from being acquired by Germany. It would have to be destroyed. Apart from that, Reilly was confident that opposition to the Bolsheviks, if effectively supported, would finally result in their overthrow.

Reilly's famous adventure with Lockhart, which became named "The Lockhart Plot" was already part of Britain's and Russia's history when viewed from the perspective of 1925, when no one in the West knew what had happened to him since he had returned to his homeland. Or whether his return had been voluntary or forced.

9
The Gadfly

THE ONLY WAY to find out what really happened to Reilly in 1925 would have been to know what was taking place in his cell in the Lubianka prison, where he had been locked up after his arrest. But before the outcome of his arrest and imprisonment under threat of torture by the Soviet secret police could be fully meaningful to anyone interested in his fate, his early life needs to be reconsidered. So much that is derogatory has been written about him by people who did not know the whole truth, or were intent on blackening him for reasons of personal prejudice, that another description is required from someone who knew him better than they did. Once we possess a third-dimensional image of the real man in full, we can decide whether he was a hero of Britain's Secret Service or a Soviet spy who defected to Communist Russia.

Important facets of Sidney Reilly's character have been withheld from the public until now, by writers who dismissed them as sheer fantasy and those who sought to discredit him. And yet we have it on the best authority from Robert

Bruce Lockhart, who worked with him in the Secret Service and knew him intimately, that the key to his true character and his real aims are wrapped up in a story by the one person who had been closest to him in his formative years when she had been his lover. This too was dismissed until indisputable archival evidence was found in 2016 confirming Edith Voynich's sexual relations with Reilly in Italy.

She was the successful novelist who became his mistress when he had been barely out of his teens. She was the older married woman whom he had originally spied on for Britain's Secret Service. Or it might have been Edith's accomplice, who appears to have been a colleague of her husband Wilfred Voynich, alias Kelchevsky. All three were being watched, not only by Britain's Secret Intelligence Bureau, but also by Russia's imperial secret police, the *Okrhana*.

The Lockharts claimed she had portrayed Reilly in her best-selling novel which she had called *The Gadfly*. Most importantly, perhaps, she knew him when he was twenty-three—a time when his ambitions were formed and set for how he would live out the rest of his life. His close and confiding relationship with Voynich had resulted in his becoming the central figure in her best-selling novel which sold more than 2.5 million copies in Russia alone. It was subsequently filmed in Russia with Dmitri Shostakovich's film score which is known popularly as *The Gadfly Suite*.

Of course, she'd had to give her fictional hero an entirely different name. It is significant that she chose to call her romantic hero Arthur, since dedicated novelists generally choose the name of their leading character with special care, so that it can convey the spirit of the novel's main theme.

Even in Russia, most readers would have been likely to identify the name of Arthur with the famous classical romances about a hero who seeks justice for all. He is the legendary English king of the poetical romances of the "Knights of the Round Table." The Arthurian legends have been translated into numerous languages in a number of different countries.

In the ancient, and still compelling legend of *Le Morte d'Arthur*, King Arthur takes an oath to devote his life for the greater good, and swears to "defend those who cannot defend themselves;" to uphold justice by being fair to all and loyal in friendship. He will be "generous to the poor and those who need help."

That summarizes how one of Reilly's very first lovers saw him as the legendary "knight in shining armor." It is also likely, in the very close and intimate circumstances, that the young and romantic Sidney would have spoken to her of his ambition to help the oppressed and suffering Russian people. And so, she evidently could not resist depicting him in her best-selling historical romance about injustice and heroism in the turmoil of a revolution. She transposed the situation of the tremors of a real impending Russian revolution to her novel, which she set in Italy in the 1840s. The story in her highly successful novel launched Ethel Voynich's career as a popular novelist, although she never again made another such success with her writing.

Before displaying a suitable extract from her historical romance, we need to recall that the last news we discovered of Reilly by our detection claimed he was in a cell in the Lubianka prison in Moscow's Kremlin. He was about to be interrogated by a leading member of the Soviet secret police named Roman Pilar. Or it may have been by Stryne, since they took turns.

According to one account of his interrogation and its aftermath, by an alleged eye-witness named Boris Gudz—who claimed to have witnessed Reilly's execution—he saw and heard the final shot in the chest, which he claimed was undertaken by a sharpshooter named George Syroeezhkin.

That account was questionable, whereas the following narrative takes us one step further in our inquiry. It is quoted word-for-word from the epilogue of E. L. Voynich's novel. If we ignore the names as pseudonyms for other people, we cannot help but remark on the similarities between the novelist's story and characters, and Sidney Reilly's own life when he was in his early twenties.

There are fundamental differences too, but Edith was a cautious Russian émigré being watched by the police of at least two nations. She would have considered them to be artistic license to protect Reilly's cover after he became a British Secret Service agent, and possibly even a double-agent or Russian spy.

In *Reilly: The First Man*, Robin Lockhart established the moment when Reilly decided to become a double agent, even a triple agent "supplying intelligence not only to Britain but to Japan and Russia as well."

Robin Lockhart stated that it was confirmed by Richard Deacon—author of *The History of British Secret Service*—who had been told it by journalist Richard Hughes, former Tokyo correspondent for *The Times* of London and *The Financial Times*.

ALIVE AND KICKING

"Gemma, there's a man downstairs who wants to see you." Martini spoke in the subdued tone which they had both unconsciously adopted during these last ten days. That, and a certain slow evenness of speech and movement, were the sole expression which either of them gave to their grief.

Gemma, with bare arms and an apron over her dress, was standing at a table, putting up little packages of cartridges for distribution. She had stood over the work since early morning; and now, in the glaring afternoon, her face looked haggard with fatigue.

"A man, Cesare? What does he want?"

"I don't know, dear. He wouldn't tell me. He said he must speak to you alone."

"Very well." She took off her apron and pulled down the sleeves of her dress. "I must go to him, I suppose; but very likely it's only a spy."

"In any case, I shall be in the next room, within call. As soon as you get rid of him you had better go and lie down a bit. You have been standing too long to-day."

"Oh, no! I would rather go on working."

She went slowly down the stairs, Martini following in silence. She had grown to look ten years older in these few days, and the grey streak across her hair had widened into a broad band. She mostly kept her eyes lowered now; but when, by chance, she raised them, he shivered at the horror in their shadows.

In the little parlor she found a clumsy-looking man standing with his heels together in the middle of the floor. His whole figure and the half-frightened way he looked up when she came in, suggested to her that he must be one of the Swiss guards. He wore a countryman's blouse, which evidently did not belong to him, and kept glancing round as though afraid of detection.

"Can you speak German?" he asked in the heavy Zurich patois.

"A little. I hear you want to see me."

"You are Signora Bolla? I've brought you a letter."

"A—letter?" She was beginning to tremble, and rested one hand on the table to steady herself.

"I'm one of the guard over there." He pointed out of the window to the fortress on the hill. "It's from—the man that was shot last week. He wrote it the night before. I promised him I'd give it into your own hands myself."

She bent her head down. So he had written after all.

"That's why I've been so long bringing it," the soldier went on. "He said I was not to give it to anyone but you, and I couldn't get off before—they watched me so. I had to borrow these things to come in."

He was fumbling in the breast of his blouse. The weather was hot, and the sheet of folded paper that he pulled out was not only dirty and crumpled, but damp. He stood for a moment shuffling his feet uneasily; then he put up one hand and scratched the back of his head.

"You won't say anything," he began again timidly, with a distrustful glance at her. "It's as much as my life's worth to have come here."

"Of course I shall not say anything. No, wait a minute—"

As he turned to go, she stopped him, feeling for her purse; but he drew back, offended.

"I don't want your money," he said roughly. "I did it for him—because he asked me to. I'd have done more than that for him. He'd been good to me—God help me!"

The little catch in his voice made her look up. He was slowly rubbing a grimy sleeve across his eyes.

"We had to shoot," he went on under his breath; "my mates and I. A man must obey orders. We bungled it, and had to fire again—and he laughed at us—he called us the awkward squad—and he'd been good to me—"

There was silence in the room. A moment later he straightened himself up, made a clumsy military salute, and went away.

She stood still for a little while with the paper in her hand; then sat down by the open window to read. The letter was closely written in pencil, and in some parts hardly legible. But the first two words stood out quite clear upon the page; and they were in English.

"Dear Jim."

The writing grew suddenly blurred and misty. And she had lost him again— had lost him again! At the sight of the familiar childish nickname all the hopelessness of her bereavement came over her afresh, and she put out her hands in blind desperation, as though the weight of the earth-clods that lay above him were pressing on her heart.

Presently she took up the paper again and went on reading:

"I am to be shot at sunrise tomorrow. So if I am to keep all my promise to tell you everything, I must keep it now. But, after all, there is not much need of explanations between you and me. We always understood each other without many words, even when we were little things.

"And so, you see, my dear, you had no need to break your heart over that old story of the blow. It was a hard hit, of course; but I have had plenty of others as hard, and yet I have managed to get over them,—even to pay back a few of them,—and here I am still, like the mackerel in our nursery-book (I forget its name), 'Alive and kicking, oh!' This is my last kick, though; and then, tomorrow morning, and—'Finita la Commedia!' You and I will translate that: 'The variety show is over:' and will give thanks to the gods that they have had, at least, so much mercy on us. It is not much, but it is something; and for this and all other blessings may we be truly thankful!

"About that same tomorrow morning, I want both you and Martini to understand clearly that I am quite happy and satisfied, and could ask no better thing of Fate. Tell that to Martini as a message from me; he is a good fellow and a good comrade, and he will understand. You see, dear, I know that the stick-in-the-mud people are doing us a good turn and themselves a bad one by going back to secret trials and executions so soon, and I know that if you who are left stand together steadily and hit hard, you will see great things. As for me, I shall go out into the courtyard with as light a heart as any child starting home for the holidays. I have done my share of the work, and this death-sentence is the proof that I have done it thoroughly. They kill me because they are afraid of me; and what more can any man's heart desire?

"I desire just one more thing, though. A man who is going to die has a right to a personal fancy, and mine is that you should see why I have always been such a sulky brute to you, and so slow to forget old scores. Of course, though, you understand why, and I tell you only for the pleasure of writing the words. I loved you, Gemma, when you were an ugly little girl in a gingham frock, with a scratch tucker and your hair in a pig-tail down your back; and I love you still. Do you remember that day when I kissed your hand, and when you so piteously begged me 'never to do that again'? It was a scoundrelly trick to play, I know; but you must forgive that; and now I kiss the paper where I have written your name. So I have kissed you twice, and both times without your consent.

"That is all. Good-bye, my dear."

There was no signature, but a verse which they had learned together as children was written under the letter:

> "Then I am
> A happy fly,
> If I live
> Or if I die."

Voynich's famous novel was Soviet Russia's beloved best-seller of all-time. Was its hero the real Sidney Reilly at age 19?

Half an hour later Martini entered the room and, startled out of the silence of half a life-time, threw down the placard he was carrying and flung his arms about her.

"Gemma! What is it, for God's sake? Don't sob like that—you that never cry! Gemma! Gemma, my darling!"

"Nothing, Cesare; I will tell you afterwards—I—can't talk about it just now."

She hurriedly slipped the tear-stained letter into her pocket; and, rising, leaned out of the window to hide her face. Martini held his tongue and bit his moustache. After all these years he had betrayed himself like a schoolboy – and she had not even noticed it!

"The Cathedral bell is tolling," she said after a little while, looking round with recovered self-command. "Someone must be dead."

10
Felicia

I F WE WISH TO FIND THE MOST LIKELY WOMAN whom Voynich named "Gemma" in her book, it is most likely to have been Reilly's first-cousin Felicia Rosenbloom. In Michael Kettle's short but convincing account of Sidney Reilly, he describes how the Rosenbloom family was photographed in 1890, after which young Sigmund fell violently in love with his first cousin. The two families forbade the match, and he left home and severed all connections with his family. But apparently he did not abandon Felicia: "In fact," wrote historian Kettle, "the cousins never lost touch."

According to another historian, Felicia left Russian Poland for Vienna in the 1890s when young Sigi was a student there. He visited her in the old quarter whenever he could. But he kept her existence a secret from everyone he knew. It is more than likely that there was some truth in Lockhart's claim that he revealed his relationship with his cousin to Ethel Voynich. If so, then "Gemma" could have been Ethel Voynich's pseudonym for Felicia.

Felicia appeared again in Reilly's life. In fact, she may never have left it. One author suggests they might have been married before Reilly met and married Margaret. But no evidence has been found for that claim. What we are told is that Felicia was a widow when she lived in Warsaw in 1911.

Several sources remark on Reilly sending her a copy of the *Rubaiyat of Omar Khayyam*, and translating a particular verse in German for her:

> Into this universe, and why not knowing,
> Nor whence, like water, willy-nilly flowing,
> And out of it, as wind along the waste,
> I know not whither, willy-nilly blowing.

Evidently something was going on between Reilly and his cousin Felicia which was kept secret all the time, except for his blurted out confessions to Voynich. Her novel was published two years after Reilly and Voynich met.

If the fictional Gemma was drawn on what Reilly told Edith Voynich about his secret life, and if Arthur was based on Sidney, what of the other clues about Reilly which inspired her novel and were recorded in it?

As for any connection between the fictional death of her revolutionary hero Arthur at the end of her book, and the real Sidney Reilly, he was alleged by several sources to have been executed thirty-eight years later in the Lubianka prison, in 1925. Evidently Ethel Voynich had pictured Reilly as a swashbuckling young hero who, with his courage and audacity and dreams of leading a counter-revolution against the Bolsheviks, would be likely to end up in front of a Soviet firing squad, or be executed in a Lubianka cell by a bullet fired into the back of his head, as was customary in Soviet Russia.

Her prediction about Sidney Reilly's fate thirty-eight years later would be uncanny, if indeed he *was* executed in cell number 73 in 1925.

It is impossible to tell how close her fictional tale was to the truth about Reilly. But the similarities of his own life to the events and characters she created in her book are too many and too significant for them to be merely coincidences, even though she obscured them by using different names. She also transformed his story by setting it, not in revolutionary Russia in 1917, but in revolutionary Italy in the 1840s, when it was dominated by Austria, which the revolutionaries attempt, and finally manage, to overthrow.

The story of *The Gadfly* focuses on a young Catholic named Arthur Burton, who is disgusted at the hypocrisy and lies of the Church he had been taught to believe in. He realizes he has been duped and renounces his Catholicism, fakes his death, and leaves his homeland for Brazil. When we hear of him again, he has become a journalist writing a column under the byline of "The Gadfly." He becomes a member of a revolutionary youth movement and fights against the

Catholic Church and a Father Montanelli whom he discovers is his biological father. The authorities are dedicated to capturing him because of the damage he is doing to their regime. It is a story of faith, disillusionment, and revolution - also of romance, adventure and heroism.

As for the title of her novel, a gadfly can be defined as "a person who hovers or dashes around provoking people into action." And, as the extract from the novel shows, he is finally captured by the authorities and executed by a firing squad, to become a martyr instead of a saviour. Here appears to be the origin of his delusion of grandeur by viewing himself later on with Caryll Houselander as "Christ the Compassionate."

Even so, the way the real Reilly dies at the hands of the Soviet secret police in Moscow is unconvincing—partly because the sources of his death appear to have copied each other, as if instructed to conform to a propaganda

Poster for Soviet Russian film of *The Gadfly*, for which Dmitri Shostakovich composed the musical score.

strategy, while at the same time giving different dates for his execution. In addition, historian Michael Kettle claimed it was not true that George Syroeezhkin fired the last shot into Reilly's chest. His version of the event differs:

"One morning, while Reilly was taking a walk in the Lenin Hills," Kettle wrote, "he was shot in the back by a man named Ibrahim, the O.G.P.U.'s crack marksman."

Unfortunately, Kettle refrained from naming his source when he wrote that in 1984. His caution is understandable, since it left open a possibility for more information to be discovered and revealed—which it was only three years later—about what really happened to Sidney Reilly, and whether he was alive or dead.

11
The Soviet Mole

ROBIN BRUCE LOCKHART wrote his second book about Sidney Reilly in 1987, in an attempt to tie up the many loose ends in his story. It also provided new facts and thoughts. It clarified the contradictions between authors. And it attempted to fill in any gaps left by Kettle's very short 1984 book, which was intended only to correct the errors, omissions and fabrications in the 1983 BBC—TV's fictional series called *The Ace of Spies*.

Robin had initiated the spate of books about his father's hero with his first publication called *Reilly Ace of Spies* in 1967. Now, two decades later, he wished to explain the reasons for the remarkable number of conjectures, errors, and contradictions in all of the subsequent biographies of Reilly.

"What became of him is a mystery to this day," he wrote in the preface to his new book. "In the final episode of the television series, Reilly is seen being executed by a firing squad. This is roughly in line with one of the many contradictory stories about Reilly put out by the Russians in unofficial accounts. The Soviets have never issued any official statement about him at all."

Numerous true or fabricated reports came from others that Reilly was either alive and well, or had become insane in prison, or he had escaped and was continuing the fight against the Bolsheviks, or he was working with them, or he had been shot in the chest by a Soviet assassin, or in the back of the head by a single executioner. Those contradictory rumors were typical of Soviet Russia's disinformation policy to influence the outside world. Even so, Robin Lockhart remarked, "But that the GPU should 'kill' him in the media several times over on several different dates also indicates that the Soviets "were worried that first reports of his 'death' had not been believed."

Robin Lockhart's hypothesis now in *Reilly: The First Man* was that Reilly, who was a master of deception, confusion, obfuscation, and manipulation, had defected and was alive and controlling all the stories himself.

Lockhart quoted from a letter he found after writing Reilly's biography, which he believed supported his most recent conclusion. It was written by Reilly to Lockhart's father, and set out to explain the evolutionary process of so-called "Bolshevism." Reilly ended his letter by stating, "the much decried little understood 'Soviets' which are the outward expression of Bolshevism as applied to practical government, are the nearest approach, I know of, to a real democracy based upon true social justice and that they may be destined to lead the world to the highest idea of statesmanship—Internationalism."

Lockhart now began to believe that Reilly, who had allegedly been educated at Trinity College in Cambridge a generation before Kim Philby, Guy Burgess, and Donald Maclean (part of the group known later on as the "Cambridge Five") was the first Soviet spy to defect to the USSR. They were communist 'moles' who had infiltrated MI5, MI6 and the Foreign Office.

Of course, their time and the circumstances were somewhat different from Reilly's earlier judgment and choices. What they rebelled against was the rise of the Nazis in Germany and Austria, and the friendly connections with them by Lord Halifax and Chamberlain who controlled Britain's government, and other influential figures in the Foreign Office and the Secret Service. Their choices were made because the idea of living in Britain under Nazi domination was too horrible to contemplate. Reilly made his choice because he could not accept a Communist-controlled Russia.

Most importantly, in his latest book, Lockhart was convinced that Reilly was still alive.

Baroness Maura Budberg had sent a message to Lockhart senior from Estonia in 1932—seven or eight years after his 1925 disappearance—confirming it as a fact. She had been one of Robert Bruce Lockhart's mistresses.

Robin Lockhart also claimed that, after his first book about Reilly had been published, he'd heard that NKVD Major Ossipov had told George Hill (now Brigadier Hill and a British Army liaison officer to the NKVD in the Second World War, when Russia was still one of Britain's allies) that "Reilly was still alive but 'unwell.' He would say no more.

Lockhart's point was that, when Allied secret service agents disappeared after entering the Soviet Union, no one outside knew whether they had been captured and executed as spies, or turned into double spies, or defected, or kept to swap with enemy spies on suitable occasions. All was speculation.

Meanwhile, of course, incriminating documents were destroyed.

Among other people curious about the inconsistencies in most news items about Reilly, a Russian academic named Revolt Pimenov also noticed the number

244 The Greatest Spy

of contradictions. He wrote an underground publication called "My Search for Reilly the Spy" in 1968. He made the observation in it that since so much remained unexplained about Reilly, he must be a double-agent. If so, he was one of the heroes of the Soviet Union's Intelligence Service and on a par with Kim Philby. He thought the Soviet Union should put up a statue of Reilly.

Pimenov was immediately arrested, tried in Russia, and exiled to Syktyvkar, where he still remained when Lockhart revealed his situation in 1987. Evidently the reason for his exile was to prevent the Soviet deception about Reilly from being made public. Soviet Russia had always had all sorts of different ways for troublesome people to disappear from its very beginning.

But what *was* "the Soviet deception about Reilly?" Robin Lockhart claimed that Reilly had been a Russian mole all along. He was convinced that Reilly had got together with Dzerzhinsky, the chief of the *Cheka* secret police, and planned everything with him.

He maintained that Reilly deliberately returned to Moscow "not in counter-revolutionary guise but to help, in his own way, in the building of the new Russia."

It is certainly inconceivable that Reilly could ever have been deceived by "The Trust." So Lockhart sought, and thought he'd found, the real reason why Reilly returned to his Russian roots. Like the romantic Michael Strogoff, the Courier of the Tsar in Jules Verne's famous novel, Reilly was a fervent patriot, and a passionate romantic. And, like the "Gadfly" of novelist Voynich's book, he was driven to be a hero of his country.

There is yet another possibility, which only came to light as recently as 2007— too late to be mentioned by any of the previous biographers. It supports the obvious fact that, of course, Reilly knew enough not to trust "The Trust." And it is neither a theory of political dedication, nor lost love, or disillusionment with religion. It is, instead, about psychological fulfilment. Reilly was a teenage rebel in search of a cause and an identity, a romantic finding his own sense of meaning and purpose in fulfilment. He became the hero of his own adventure.

The universal theme of the hero remains much the same: he lives in an ordinary world but is called to embark on a mission. The legend of Odysseus is an example. And every culture in every era has its own folk story of a young man seeking his destiny and finding it, often by returning home at the end of his life's journeys. There is *Sinuhe the Egyptian* and the engrossing tale of *Peer Gynt*. They take the reader out of anonymity and transform him into an individual by making him the hero of his own adventure story. In short, they provide him with a purpose.

The enigma of the double-agent poses the question: "How can the same person devote his loyalty to one regime and also to the revolutionary regime that works so passionately to overthrow it?"

The short answer was *sentimental romanticism*. It is our escape route from grim circumstances and immature follies. Romanticism lends point to the apparent pointlessness of life, and provides us with hope.

When Sir Robert Bruce Lockhart sought to describe what it was that motivated his own adventurous impulses, he explained it as "ineradicable romanticism"—as if it were an innate drive in men of action. He was not the only one. History reveals a whole gallery of adventurous young men seeking and acquiring power of one kind or another, all over the world.

12
The Emotional Threshold

As SOON AS ROBIN LOCKHART analyzed the circumstantial evidence, all of his convictions became adapted to embrace any, or all possibilities - and rationality was flung out of the window. Views on heroism versus treachery trigger emotional responses. Even a biographer or a historian is forced to take sides. As Dostoyevsky remarked of his own membership in the Petrashevsky Circle of romantic and idealistic revolutionaries, "it is not easy to step back before crossing the emotional threshold and making a total commitment."

Robin Lockhart theorised that, after returning to Russia in Savinkov's footsteps, Reilly would have known that he'd be blackened as a traitor by Britain and have to disappear—as we now know double-agent Kim Philby of both Britain's MI6 and Russia's KGB was forced to defect to Russia when he was exposed after twenty-five years of successful subterfuge. So, according to Robin Lockhart, Reilly would fake another "death," as he had done before at the age of nineteen and left a suicide note with his clothes beside the sea.

Typical of that type of guesswork are Lockhart's justifications, protestations, and suppositions, like "How Reilly made his approach to Dzerzhinsky is not clear," followed by vague alternative speculations like "he was disillusioned with capitalist society." It is nothing more than supposition, certainly not history. From what we already know of Reilly the smooth dealmaker, we could equally claim that he enjoyed capitalism because he made millions from it.

On the other hand, if we examine some of Reilly's letters more closely, particularly those to Commander Boyce, they are couched in a strange tone, as of a "bleeding heart." And yet, he would surely never expose his emotions in such a "Latin" way. The English of that time avoided volatile emotions and fickle sentimentality. They were still distant, cool, and reserved. They did not make friends easily. And when they did, they kept them at a distance, embarrassed by the flow of human affection. They took pains to avoid intimacy whenever they could.

Since Reilly was always on guard as a double agent and never gave himself away or revealed his vulnerability, he would surely never have genuinely claimed to an Englishmen like Boyce that all he had ever wanted was to serve his country. However true it might be, it would have been considered mawkish to say it, or write it, at that time in England. Only a romantic poet like Rupert Brooke could get away with jingoism—and then only if it rhymed, and the poet died.

As Sir Roger Scruton wrote, at that time in England, "Ironic laughter would interrupt their most solemn deliberations . . . "

It was his elegant way of saying that claiming such lofty emotions would compel listeners to burst out into incredulous laughter, to the blushing embarrassment of whoever made the error of expressing such high-minded thoughts about himself.

As Reilly had faked his death when an adolescent, now—according to Robin Lockhart's scenario—he faked it again by vanishing into the Soviet Union.

According to Robin Lockhart, to fake it a second time, he crossed the Finnish frontier with Yakushev and met Toivo Vjaki, one of the more senior border guards who drove them to Pavgolovo railway station in Russian territory. Then Reilly and Yakushev took a train to Leningrad. After that, came the faked shooting incident at the border crossing.

In a strange coincidence, Toivo Vjaki would also "die" soon afterwards as a "traitor," and turn up again forty years later as KGB Colonel I. M. Petrov. Those types of personal transformations were typical of the ambiguous form of the new regime in Russia.

Subsequent Russian reports that Reilly resurrected a previous pseudonym as Relinsky fail to ring true. More probably he was given the highly unremarkable name of Sidorov, which he had used before. But that was mere speculation. All that was actually known was that Reilly had returned home to Russia.

Despite Robin Lockhart's reference in his second book to "the overwhelming evidence that Reilly lived on for at least twenty years after his return to Russia in 1925," much of what Lockhart provides is no more than imaginative speculations which he had convinced himself were evidence for his theory that Reilly had *not* been executed, as had been assumed up until then.

Whether we choose to believe him or not, Robin Lockhart dropped some useful hints in between his numerous repetitions of his own "convictions"—as if thinking aloud while attempting to persuade himself that they must be true. Reilly's charisma was so seductive that men and women alike found themselves almost driven to believe whatever he wanted them to believe about him, and also about what happened to him. So that more information is still necessary to convince readers of what *really* happened.

Strangely enough, Lockhart and all the other biographers of Sidney Reilly, with their wild surmise based on incomplete information and mere circumstantial evidence, missed the most obvious historical fact, which might solve the major problems in all, or most, of Reilly's mysteries and ambiguities. Among all the uncertainties and paradoxes, the history of the times around 1925 provides us with the real reason for his return to his homeland. It also explains what most probably occurred after he arrived in Moscow.

According to the Finnish Captain van Narvig, who was a former officer of the Russian Imperial Army in Finland in 1925, Reilly was fully aware that The Trust was a cover for Russian counter-intelligence agents.

"There is no question at all that Reilly did not know he was entering a wolves' lair," van Narvig told Richard Deacon. But Reilly was "romantically eager to re-organise Bolshevism, if he could not defeat it." According to him, Reilly was disgusted with the pro-German attitude in the British Secret Service. It was why he defected to Soviet Russia.

Twenty-five years later, the "Cambridge Five" double agents were disgusted not only with the barbaric behaviour of the Nazis in Germany, but also with the pro-Germans in Britain's Foreign Office, in the SIS, and even in the Conservative Government. Moreover, personal friendships were being formed by then, between influential British leaders, like Lord Halifax and Goering - who was the leading Nazi in Germany - and other Government Ministers in Britain with their opposite numbers in Germany, who were deliberately entertaining them lavishly and enticing them into the Nazi fold.

The upshot was that, only five years later, not only had it become inevitable that Hitler would make war in Europe, but Britain might ally itself with Germany. The thought of a Nazi Britain was abhorrent to the "Cambridge Five." And yet, there was no other country sizeable and powerful enough to stand up to Nazi Germany, except for Soviet Russia—a fact that both Winston Churchill and President Roosevelt recognized when the circumstances and timing were right.

Once we remove the mysteries of Reilly's apparently contradictory statements and behaviour from his own moment in time and, instead, apply it to the scenario that followed with the "Cambridge Five" spies later on, then work our thinking backwards, we arrive at the crux of the problem and the main reason for Reilly's actions: it was patriotism.

With the gradual unrolling of the future came the inevitability of a Second World War. Philby, Burgess and Maclean sided with Soviet Russia because they were convinced that the Nazis would persuade Britain's appeasers in the government, the army, and the Foreign Office, and other pro-Germans, to join forces with them, or at least accept the Nazi domination of Europe and Russia, and become a Nazi-dominated British Empire.

For Nazi Germany, the years prior to war were simply a preparation for it. There was no question of compromise by Germany, or turning back, or ever agreeing with any of Britain's proposals at any time.

If we return our thinking to Reilly's time, Adolf Hitler had been arrested for high treason in 1923. He was tried in 1924, and sentenced to five years in Landsberg Prison. While in prison, he wrote *Mein Kampf,* in which he spelt out his intentions to invade Russia and enslave and then slaughter its entire population in order to steal the territory for a Greater Germany. Hitler's book was published in 1925. It was the same year that Reilly disappeared after returning to Soviet Russia.

Stalin was the shrewdest of all the Soviet leaders. If he had not realized it before then, he would have known with certainty now, that he had only a limited time to industrialize and arm the backward and disorganized Soviet Russia in order to defend its population and territory from invasion by powerful German forces. That required, as a minimum, parity in tanks, bomber and fighter aircraft, troops, anti-aircraft guns, and ammunition. Soviet industry had to be developed to produce them.

For Reilly, the situation would have been like a *déjà vu* moment. He had helped Tsarist Russia before, when his homeland had needed to industrialize in order to replace its fleet of battleships destroyed by the Japanese in the Russo-Japanese war. He had helped to defend his country from more heavily armed potential enemies before, and he could do it again. Soviet Russia would have less than fifteen years to organize its own industries and manufacture all the necessary war materiel to protect itself.

Industrialized Britain was about four years behind Germany, in terms of industrial and military potential before World War 2. It was therefore reasonable to speculate that the new and economically shaky Bolshevik Government could have been about twenty years behind Germany in the manufacture of enough fighter and bomber aircraft, tanks and artillery, trucks and shells, and small arms, to reach parity with a militant Germany. If so, there was no time to lose.

It would have been a challenge to Reilly to make a patriotic gesture once again. Such heroic efforts seem to have been in his genetic make-up. He had not been rewarded by the Tsar for his help on the first occasion, but now he could earn the gratitude of Stalin and his homeland.

In short, Reilly could well have had a change of mind and heart on recognizing the urgency of the situation at the same time as Stalin was forced to face up to the enormous challenge of a *renaissance*.

Reilly would surely have wanted, as a patriot, to save his homeland and his family from destruction and slavery. And Stalin might well have decided that he needed Reilly's unique talents, which he had already demonstrated, in analyzing and reporting on complex situations, diplomacy, organizing industry to manufacture war material, planning future strategies and tactics, and foreign policy, and reorganising Soviet Russia's secret police.

Reilly was the most experienced and skillful secret agent in the world. He knew more about the West than anyone else in the Soviet Union. He would have wanted to cooperate in strengthening Russia now, rather than continue to compete with the Reds, who had become too entrenched and powerful by then. It was time for truth and reconciliation with Soviet Russia's leadership. That meant challenging the formidable Marshal Stalin, who was nobody's fool: he would have known he needed Reilly's help.

Perhaps the most insightful description of the enigmatic Joseph Stalin's personality was given by American Ambassador Averell Harriman, after he worked with Stalin two decades later in World War 2. Harriman found it hard to reconcile Stalin's courtesy and consideration towards him with "the ghastly cruelty of the wholesale liquidations." Although many viewed Stalin as a tyrant, Harriman recognized his high level of intelligence, his "fantastic grasp of detail, his shrewdness and his surprising human sensitivity that he was capable of showing." He found Stalin "better informed than Roosevelt, more realistic than Churchill, in some ways the most effective of the war leaders."

As Robin Bruce Lockhart wrote, "More and more of the world's intelligence services and students of intelligence history—particularly those in the United States – have come to learn that today's Soviet intelligence activities have matured to their present peak of efficiency through refinements of older techniques which they had developed in the late 1920s and during the 1930s. This was primarily achieved through learning, adapting and improving British espionage methods, then considered to be the best in the world . . . And it was none other than Sidney Reilly who provided the Russians with the information, leads and many ideas which gave birth to a re-vamped organization which grew to become, in Philby's words, an "elite force—the KGB."

The photo released by the Soviets of part of a man's body lying on its back on a slab had looked convincing for those who felt happier with an illusion of closure concerning the Reilly Affair. But in the secret world of intelligence gathering and distortions of the truth, it meant nothing else except that somebody wanted the public to think that Reilly was dead.

Whether Reilly had been executed by the OGPU or had defected and was still alive was still only a matter for conjecture, just as Reilly himself had always been. In any case, the photo of Reilly's alleged corpse was taken by the OGPU on November 5, 1925, since when—according to Robin Lockhart—there had been numerous reports that he was still alive.

He and a few others believed the OGPU had used a fake Reilly in the deception staged at the frontier. Typical of Soviet subterfuge, the actor playing the role of Reilly had to be killed to prevent disclosure. It was his fake body that was photographed afterwards, while the real Sidney Reilly was being interrogated in the Lubianka prison under threat of torture.

13
The Fate of Prisoner Number 73

"IT IS ONLY AT THE END OF THINGS that we begin to understand them," wrote contemporary English philosopher Sir Roger Scruton in his book called *England*.

It is certainly the case with Sidney Reilly, who was admired as a courageous hero by the diplomat Robert Bruce Lockhart, who had worked alongside him, and his son Robin who praised his virtues in two books. More recently, he was vilified by a contemporary historian who evidently disliked him personally and made all kinds of sweeping accusations about him, in an effort to discredit him, with little or no evidence for his scathing claims.

In the same year as that book depicting Reilly as a villain was published in Britain, another biography of Reilly was published in the United States that endorsed the Lockharts' original account of Reilly as a decorated hero who deserved appreciation for his bravery in times of danger, and for what he achieved for Britain, Russia, and the United States in two World Wars.

The American biographer was almost excessively thorough in his research. He benefited from being able to sift through previously disclosed information which had already been scrutinized and analyzed by all previous authors, as well as possessing new information which had not been available to them then.

The approach used in these pages differs in being more like a detective story in which readers are brought into the historical background and can sift through the evidence for themselves.

The man whom the American version depicts as a hero is the same Sidney Reilly whom both Lockharts described because they knew from Sir Robert's own experiences with Reilly that he *was* a hero. Since Reilly and Bruce Lockhart were central to the "Lockhart Plot" in revolutionary Soviet Russia, the Lockharts knew Reilly better than anyone else.

Whereas the authors of previous books about Reilly were unaware or diffident about claiming that Reilly might have been a double or triple agent, and could provide no clear evidence for either possibility, the American author commenced his own probe with a belief that Reilly was not what he appeared to be and a theory that he most probably worked for any number of different governments, including Britain, Soviet Russia, Japan, and even Israel—despite the fact that the new State of Israel did not yet exist when Reilly was alleged to have been executed in 1925. It meant that Richard B. Spence, who wrote *Trust No One: The Secret World of Sidney Reilly* in 2002, was convinced that Reilly was still alive.

The main problem of revealing Reilly's activities as a secret agent is that anything is possible, but all evidence is likely to have been carefully destroyed. There was certainly not enough evidence to account for all of Robin Lockhart's new claims. What had complicated all the investigations had been the adroit way in which Reilly habitually concealed his presence by distorting the truth. He was like a stage magician using smoke and mirrors to create illusions. It required numerous names to be replaced by false ones, and most activities to be concealed by fabrications.

What is so remarkable is that Reilly managed to keep his secrets for three quarters of a century. One of the more important of them was whether he was still alive or dead after defecting to Soviet Russia. And if alive, what he was up to.

Robin Bruce Lockhart's last book held firmly to the opinion that Reilly was not executed by the GPU. He did so even without considering the political and military implications of the wild rise of the rebellious and mentally unhinged young Hitler, and the bizarre and psychotic Nazi Party composed of society's misfits in Germany by 1925. None of Reilly's biographers refer to the direct influence on Reilly's fate of Hitler's criminal intentions which he revealed in *Mein Kampf*. And yet, it influenced the outcome of Reilly's arrest and confinement in the Lubianka prison in Moscow.

Many of the readers of Hitler's turgid and rambling book failed to understand what its rebellious author was ranting on about among all his own personal envies and resentments, grievances and discontents. His revenge for being a mediocrity was nothing short of the Nazis' intention to destroy Russia and its entire population in order to annex the territory as part of a Greater Germany. The enormous size of Russia's population and the wealth of its resources that made it potentially the richest country in the world had been the object of envy and fear by its neighbours since before World War 1. It could even be claimed to have been the real cause of that war, and also of World War 2.

The contrarian biography by Cook, who played the Devil's Advocate, was published in Britain in 2002. Despite its author's personal distaste for his subject, he began to show admiration for Reilly's extraordinary courage as the prisoner who was about to be tortured and executed in cell Number 73 in the Lubianka prison. But, whereas Cook believed that Sidney Reilly was the prisoner in cell No.73, Spence was certain he was not.

14
A Hall of Distorting Mirrors

BEFORE DESCRIBING THE PRISONER in the cell numbered 73, there are still a few more loose ends to consider about how and why Sidney Reilly was arrested by the Soviet secret police and locked up in the Lubianka prison.

One such loose end is whether Commander Boyce was over-reaching or clumsy in his fatal efforts to persuade Reilly to penetrate "The Trust." Or whether Boyce was a double agent in the pay of the Soviet OGPU. The same suspicion might also apply to Hill or Alley, since governments have a habit of reducing their intelligence budgets as soon as possible after a war ends, and letting staff go; as Churchill frequently complained when in office.

Most were let go in this particular case when intelligence budgets were cut and Cumming reorganised the Secret Service around 1922.

The contrarian Cook asked rhetorically, "Would it therefore be fair to conclude that Hill was knowingly or unknowingly an OGPU source?"

What he meant was that, since Hill was no longer in the pay of the SIS, he might have collaborated with the OGPU instead. He needed employment when the SIS no longer wanted him.

That question was most likely posed as a result of an article which appeared in the *Sunday Times* as recently as 2001. The article was headlined "Double Agent may have sent Ace of Spies to his Death." It went on to state that "Boyce was a long-term double agent working for the Russians and was motivated solely by hard cash."

The claim was made by an author named Edward Gazur. FBI Special Agent Gazur contended that "Orlov told him that Cmdr Ernest Boyce, an MI6 officer and colleague of Reilly's, played the key role in entrapping the spy."

Despite Gazur's claim, we should be skeptical because of the lack of any "hard and fast evidence" against Boyce. Cook referred to it as only "educated guesswork."

Suspicion inevitably hovers over anything to do with the Secret Service and foreign secret police, because their activities *are* secret and we are curious and easily drawn to possible conspiracy theories. Suspicion is also aroused by every statement issued by the OGPU, which stated; "No. 73 was collected from the morgue of the OGPU medical unit by Com. Dukis at 8.30 p.m. on 9 November 1925 and driven to the prepared burial pit in the walking yard of the OGPU inner prison, where he was put in a sack so that the 3 Red Army men burying it could not see his face."

Since there is no evidence that the prisoner in cell number 73 at that time was Sidney Reilly, there must have been a very good reason why the Red Army men were purposely prevented from seeing the dead prisoner's face. It indicates that the dead man was not Sidney Reilly.

Reilly's was not the only name of a secret agent to surface in Russian spy trials after he had allegedly defected to Soviet Russia. In July 1925, Moscow announced that a group of conspirators led by ex-naval officer Albert Hoyer (or Goier) had been discovered and brought to justice. Hoyer had past connections to Reilly and Dukes, and had recently been controlled by Commander Boyce.

In the months that followed the announcement, Soviet prosecutors and the press media repeatedly accused Boyce of having initiated plots against the state, and of terrorism. It was a self-defeating strategy if Commander Boyce really was an important OGPU asset, since the publicity could result in the SIS being obliged to let him go now that he was no longer a credible agent. The question was whether Reilly's exposure as a possible Soviet double agent had also exposed Boyce to suspicion of disloyalty or treason. Or "had someone in Moscow figured out that he was not on their side after all?" Suspicion spreads like a virus in the shadowy world of espionage.

There are far more questions like that than answers, because suspicions are continually aroused by leaks about secret agents, and by communications from so-called "confidential sources." Whereas Boyce was once thought to be a hero and a patriot, then accused of acting for the Soviet secret police in destroying Reilly, now his real loyalties were being questioned by both sides. More than one source jumped to conclusions. For example, when Ernest Boyce had failed to meet Pepita in Paris as arranged, she had instinctively "considered the possibility that Boyce might be an OGPU double agent who had entrapped her husband."

"Nay, I thought, why should Commander E, himself not be in the pay of the *Tcheka*?"

Suspicion goes with the territory, whether founded on truth or not. One possibility was that the real culprit was not Boyce at all, but his assistant Harry Carr. The OGPU might easily have mistaken Carr for Boyce when Carr was acting for his boss. It was at the time when Boyce had disembarrassed himself from the "Trust" catastrophe and returned to England after Reilly vanished in 1925. Mistakes happened frequently, particularly in the case of identities, and especially in the contrived and make-believe secret world of espionage. The tricks of the trade had a habit of rebounding on the perpetrator. In his attempts to look like someone else, he could easily resemble the guilty man pointed out in an identity parade.

The secret services of both sides were playing guessing games in their attempts to outwit each other, and were probably as wrong in their suspicions and conclusions at least as much as they were right. In fact, it was more than likely that they were even more wrong than right. But, in a regime where human life was not recognized as possessing any value, right or wrong hardly mattered.

What was remarkable was the number of times that anyone who had been associated with Reilly in the past was disposed of by execution in Soviet Russia, or simply disappeared. Was it because they knew too much about Reilly's activities as a Soviet secret agent, and the only way to prevent leaks was to dispose of them?

No one was at greater risk in the cover-up process than the heads of the Soviet Secret Police, who had files on just about everyone, from Stalin to Reilly, and each other. But that does not make it any easier to pinpoint the reasons for the mysterious deaths of Dzerzhinsky (Dedicated revolutionary and Director of the Soviet OGPU in 1923 to July 1926). Or Yagoda (Director of the Soviet NKVD Secret Police in 1934-1936). Although some considered it was because they were covering up for Reilly, other thought it was because they knew too much about Stalin.

The choice, once again, depends on whether we believe that Reilly was a Soviet agent all along, or not. As Spence remarked somberly, "they took their secrets to the grave."

But one apparent clue of what had happened to Reilly came from Opperput, the agent who switched sides according to circumstances. He "claimed that the Kremlin had abandoned hope of spreading Communism in Europe and now placed its hopes on the East, above all China."

Despite what is now known about the spread of Communism across Europe over two decades later, during the Cold War period, with the "Iron Curtain" across Central and Eastern Europe, Opperput was right at the time. And Reilly had previously vanished into the uncharted parts of China for a period after working in Manchuria on the Russo-Japanese War for Melville.

Opperput, too, disappeared from Europe after a shootout with militia, and was thought dead, but turned up afterwards in China. According to the British news media, Opperput received an Order of the Red Banner "for his recent feats."

It is possible that Reilly was already in China by that time, also working under an assumed name. He had used Relinsky and Steinberg and Massino before, and had assumed several other code names, too. But what happened in China was another story. What we really want to know is what came of Reilly's interrogation in cell Number 73 in the Lubianka in 1925?

We know that, in 1925, Commander Ernest Boyce was a passport officer, running a network of agents out of Helsingfors in Finland. His assistant was Harry Carr, who had been born in Archangel. So many stories were being floated about Reilly being alive in 1926 and 1927 that Pepita Reilly wrote to Churchill to press for an official inquiry into his whereabouts. Churchill's private secretary Edward Marsh responded to Pepita by reminding her that her husband had chosen to go to Soviet Russia at a time when he was no longer working for the SIS, so they had no responsibility for him.

Margaret Reilly was convinced he was alive in 1926, and eager to get her hands on his money. She attempted to obtain information from the Foreign Office in 1928, and was told that they had no confirmation of his death; nor did they have any information about who was the executor of his will.

Both of Reilly's former wives were persistent in their attempts to get their hands on his assets. For, although Reilly had constantly moaned about his financial problems, it was thought that he had concealed get-out money in bank accounts in Switzerland and Germany.

By 1931, Margaret was described by the British Embassy as unstable and liable to commit some desperate act if not treated carefully. Pepita lived on "in impoverished alcoholic obscurity." It appeared that she owed her survival partly to "Jolly" George Hill, now known as a drunk who helped Robin Lockhart with his book about Reilly in 1966.

Hill's work with the NKVD when Russia was one of Britain's wartime allies, had left him in a fog of suspicion. No one was sure who he worked for now. He claimed that Russian officer friends of his had told him Reilly was still alive and had been working for the Soviets. Columnist Richard Deacon, who wrote for Britain's *Sunday Times*, was of the same belief.

15

Hunted Down

APPARENTLY ONLY ONE INDIVIDUAL made what appeared to be a thorough attempt to investigate what happened to Reilly. He was a Russian émigré journalist named Nikolai Alekseev, who had met Reilly in London in 1919. Alekseev had served in the army in South Russia and worked for the Soviet in Moscow, Germany and Yugoslavia, and also for Krassin in the foreign trade bureau. Although he now worked for a Russian newspaper in Paris, he was still suspected by some to be a Soviet agent.

Alekseev first faced the questions of whether Reilly was Russian or English or Jewish, and whether he was collaborating with the Bolsheviks or fighting against them. Among those he interviewed was Aleksandr Matzebovich, who revealed that he had worked in the Bolshevik underground with Reilly in Lenin's time. He insisted that Reilly's true fate was unknown.

It was from another source that Alekseev learned that Reilly had recently reappeared and had been travelling between London and Moscow on business. Some other former colleagues said they had seen Reilly in Paris towards the end of 1929. Another informant who had known Reilly, had accidentally run into him in Paris at more or less the same time, but Reilly gave him the slip—somewhat like the mysterious figure of "Harry Lime" disappearing into the shadows in the 1940 movie of *The Third Man*.

Being able to blend in instinctively with every possible background and society, is a prerequisite of spying. And Reilly was a natural multifaceted chameleon who could change his image with ease in any situation that required cover.

Alekseev became convinced that Reilly was still alive; that he was working as a secret agent for the Soviets, and probably always had been. "With signs pointing to his presence in Paris in the latter part of 1929, Alekseev suspected that Sidney had played a part in the January 1930 abduction of Gen. Kutepov, who had been snatched by OGPU agents right off a Paris avenue. Kutepov was smuggled back to Moscow, interrogated and later shot."

But which of those characters was Reilly? Alekseev might well have been suffering from the same type of wild imagination as those authors who reached far and wide for coincidences and vague possibilities whenever they arrived at another dead-end. They felt frustrated at finding nothing more tangible than flimsy circumstantial evidence which could not be pinned down as hard proof, but were just clever tricks using smoke and mirrors.

Alekseev even called on Pepita Reilly in Paris in 1930 and urged her to tell him the truth about where Reilly was. But if she had known his whereabouts, she would have already absconded with his money and vanished from sight, enjoying a secret life of luxury as a rich widow. So Alekseev apparently gave up searching.

On the other hand, the likelihood was that Alekseev was really a Soviet agent of disinformation, who repeated rumors and gossip, and created red herrings to cover up the truth that Reilly was, and always had been—what? Another Soviet agent? Perhaps Alekseev's alleged search for Sidney Reilly was simply a trial run to ensure that Reilly had left no trace behind him. Otherwise Alekseev would have been hastily bundled off in exile to Syktyvkor, like Pimenov who knew too much about Reilly.

Other stories that emerged included one that Reilly had come to an agreement with the OGPU in 1925 and worked for them in Europe for the next decade, passing information simultaneously to the SIS—as double-agents customarily did—before turning up in Manchuria and continuing working as an agent into the 1950s. But for whom?

Another source described Reilly's so-called execution in 1925 as having been a carefully orchestrated defection to Soviet Russia by Feliks Dzerzhinsky, and that Reilly's task now was to help recruit British agents for Soviet Russia.

When he lost Dzerzhinsky's protection and the NKVD liquidated Reilly's other collaborators, Reilly left Soviet Russia in 1938 for Manchuria. "Along with Yagoda, almost everyone connected to Reilly's 1925 arrest perished during 1937-39."

But apparently not Reilly: he was a survivor.

Reilly had begun writing a diary in his prison cell in the Lubianka, on October 9, 1925. The OGPU had not tortured him physically, yet. So he must have concluded that they preferred him alive rather than dead or disabled. That meant they intended to use him in some way. They had apparently outlined what they wanted from him: "to employ him as a secret collaborator and agent of influence abroad."

They increasingly threatened him if he failed to comply. Even so, he refused. Now his guards forced him to change into work clothes, removed all his possessions and let him wait to think about what might happen, before they woke him up again and took him to a downstairs room near a bath. There they told him that he was about to be executed immediately. When he still refused, they dumped him back in his cell to reconsider. They returned an hour later, leaving the heavily armed executioners outside but within clear sight. Then they handcuffed him.

Evidently Reilly had anticipated each stage of their charades, and refused them once again. He was, after all, a gambling addict, and cool as a British cucumber when it came to life-and-death conflicts. Apparently he was convinced that he could outwit them.

He had not yet been shown the instruments of torture, but they were carefully described to him. According to Styrne, who was one of his interrogators, when

Reilly still refused, "he was forced to watch a grisly execution in the Lubianka cellar." It was a tactic that usually worked, since it created a fierce desire to avoid having to experience a similar gruesome and pointless death.

"After about forty-five minutes, an exasperated Styrne called in the executioner named Dukis, and his men. They handcuffed Reilly [again] and left him in his cell while the distinct loading of arms took place beyond the door."

After another moment for reconsideration, they pushed Reilly into a waiting vehicle outside with its engine running, and took him for a drive, after which Reilly expected he would be shot. Instead, they returned to the prison complex through a different entrance into the Lubianka, so that anyone who had seen him leave never saw him return. Styrne casually told him that he had postponed Reilly's execution for the moment.

Back in his cell, Reilly wrote in his diary that he missed his sleep because of bad dreams. He was given a sedative the next day to calm him down. After a medical test by a doctor, he was told to put on an OGPU uniform, and was taken for another drive. This was followed by a walk in the countryside. Then they took him for a friendly tea and a meal in a comfortable apartment with Styrne and Ibragim.

He was given a document, which he signed, since it was an agreement. Styrne passed the signed agreement to Dzerzhinski. After which Styrne returned and told Reilly that his execution had been cancelled.

Further discussions took place along the lines that Reilly had previously suggested. And he was asked to write down and clarify the six main points of their agreement. He and Styrne worked together on the British Secret Service report, which emphasized who did what, how and where. Reilly must have been greatly relieved when he wrote in his diary, "I see great things ahead."

What followed was another drive for prisoner number 73 at 8 pm on November 5, with Feduleev, Dukis the executioner, Ibragim the sharpshooter, and another agent named Syroeezhkin. They drove to Sokolniki, where the engine of their motor car appeared to fail when they came close to deserted parkland. They all got out of the vehicle, evidently in accordance with a plan, and entered the empty park.

Ibragim slowed down to fall behind the others, before drawing his *Mauser* pistol and firing at the prisoner's back. The sharpshooter watched the prisoner fall. His victim was still stirring on the ground when Syroeezhkin fired a last shot into his chest. Then they lifted the lifeless body into the car and drove back to the Lubianka prison, where a photo was taken of the corpse.

But who was prisoner Number 73? Although he was generally assumed to be Sidney Reilly, the OGPU wanted Sidney alive, because no one else possessed his knowledge, his personal connections, his sharp intelligence, or his special skills.

Spence claimed that "Yagoda had a very strong reason to keep Reilly alive. Sidney would have made sure that only he, personally, could access the money stashed away in Swiss and German banks. Despite his interest in the case, Dzerzhinsky took no direct part in Reilly's interrogation, leaving the matter firmly in Yagoda's and Styrne's hands."

Mikhail Trilesser, who ran Soviet Russia's INO Foreign Intelligence bureau (*Inostrannyi Otdel*), was convinced that Reilly was alive. He noted that—right after Pepita inserted a press announcement of his death—Britain's Foreign Office "had sent a confidential circular to all British missions." It instructed them to screen émigré and foreign economic publications for anything describing "Russian ventures or concessions." The SIS also made enquiries in Paris and Prague, and showed particular interest in Manchuria and the Chinese Eastern Railway.

"Opperput noted that two very different stories seemed to originate in Moscow. One still insisted the Ace-of-Spies had died in a frontier shootout, while another argued he had joined Savinkov and 'taken service with the Soviet Government.'" It was one of the few hints from Soviet Russia that Savinkov might still be alive. But it could simply have been Soviet disinformation to muddy the issue. Another rumor held that Reilly was alive but in prison. Still another insisted that a British demand for his release had prompted his execution.

In 1932 Churchill gave a different account of Savinkov's end in *Great Contemporaries*:

"After two years of subterranean negotiations they lured him back to Russia. Krassin was at one time the intermediary, but there were others. The trap was carefully baited . . . In June, 1924, Kamenev and Trotsky definitely invited him to return. The past would be condoned, a mock trial would be staged, followed by an acquittal and high employment . . . Anyhow they got him."

Churchill believed that Savinkov was not tortured: "Whether he was quietly shot in prison or committed suicide in his despair is uncertain and unimportant . . . Yet, when all is said and done, and with all the stains and tarnishes there be, few men tried more, gave more, dared more and suffered more for the Russian people."

Churchill was not free to make any such claims for Sidney Reilly's top secret affairs. Nevertheless, according to the esteemed nineteenth century French diplomat, Talleyrand, "What is treason today may not have been treason yesterday and may not be considered treason tomorrow."

According to the literature that accumulated about Reilly after Dzerzhinsky had been poisoned and Yagoda followed him to his own grave, "Along with Yagoda, almost everyone connected to Reilly's 1925 arrest perished during 1937-39; Stryne, Artuzov, Puzitskii, Deribas, Messing, Trilesser, Yakushev and Syrozhekin, all vanished into the "whirlwind" of the purges. So did Berzin and

Genryk Yagoda, head of the NKVD
(1934 – 1936).

Karakhan." Communism was as dangerous to its followers as to its enemies.

In 1938, Reilly "appeared in Harbin but soon left for Shanghai . . . Accompanying him were a wife and daughter, whom he either brought from Russia or picked up in Manchuria."

He married his daughter to an English official in Hong Kong, and followed them to Australia after the Japanese attack on the US fleet at Pearl Harbor in 1941. Then they left for Palestine. Biographer Michael Kettle claimed that he worked there under an assumed name for Israel's secret service agency, *Mossad*. Kettle's account has Reilly continuing to live in Israel until he died there at the age of 94 in 1968, without his daughter or son-in-law knowing his Reilly identity.

According to Spence, "Michael Kettle was convinced that all evidence of Reilly's presence in Israel was concealed because of his subsequent work for Israeli intelligence, *Mossad*."

After his successes in Britain's Secret Intelligence Service and the KGB, it must have been more than coincidence that Israel's intelligence service should now become, arguably, the most professional and effective secret service in the world.

Reilly had evidently done everything he could to protect his wife and daughter from being traced. Even so, as usual, he had plenty of other things on his mind. There was the rise of the Nazis as the leading military power and the vulnerability of Stalin's Russia. It presented a series of events that turned Russia into a nuclear power.

Although unconfirmed by hard evidence, which was always almost impossible to come by in attempting to penetrate the secure cover stories of any secret service agent, none of that is impossible. Indeed, all of it was likely with Sidney Reilly's debonair nature, his forceful personality, his quick wits and audacity, his charismatic personality, and his ability to survive in all sorts of different places and situations. It was the result of the well-honed skills of a highly intelligent but romantic, adventurous, and successful spy, who was always driven by a sense of responsibility and patriotic purpose, while he deliberately and carefully planned everything in advance.

With all the evidence available, it could be argued that it was Reilly, and not

Savinkov, who "tried more, gave more, and dared more for the Russian people." At the same time, he procured invaluable information for Britain which helped to secure its independence and survival as a free and democratic nation. And his contributions to the United States helped it and the Allies to win both World Wars.

Acknowledgments and Bibliography

Sidney Reilly was the most audacious, courageous, and successful spy in history. His exploits, although secret, were first mentioned briefly by Sir Robert Bruce Lockhart in his *Memoirs of a British Agent* in 1932. Lockhart headed the first diplomatic mission to Soviet Russia after the Russian Revolution in 1917 and worked closely with Reilly to organize a counter-revolution against Lenin's Communist Government. Reilly was awarded the Military Cross in recognition of his heroism as a British Secret Service agent. His extraordinarily daring and imaginative exploits were elaborated on in a book by Lockhart's son Robin in *Reilly, Ace of Spies* in 1984. But already some sceptical writers who doubted the reputations of all successful historical figures were determined to tear Britain's heroes from their pedestals and even vilify them without understanding or evidence for their conjectures. That is what happened to Reilly.

To add to the confusion resulting from those limited accounts and their wild suppositions intended to fill in the gaps in information, the BBC produced a fictional TV series called *Reilly: Ace of Spies* in 1983. Although enjoyable entertainment, it was not intended to be history. Historian Michael Kettle wrote a short book to correct its errors and fabrications.

Crucial new information about Reilly and his exploits have since been discovered, and make most of those accounts out-of-date, false, or irrelevant. But perhaps the biggest omissions in all of them is that their authors failed to understand and include at least four significant factors about the times before they themselves were born. They are the historical background which produced Reilly, the economic transformation taking place from rural societies to industrial ones, the political chaos in Europe that produced Hitler and the Nazis, and even an account written by one of Reilly's first mistresses in his formative years. Although that best-seller called *The Gadfly* is a novel, it was written by the woman who knew him most intimately, and its account of the young Reilly was claimed by Sir Robert Lockhart to be true.

To add to all the confusion about Reilly, his secret Admiralty Intelligence file formed the basis for Ian Fleming's series of novels or thrillers about a fictional secret agent whom he named James Bond 007 in 1953. This story takes all of those aspects in to account. The veracity of this book owes much to 359 valid sources by specialists in their field. They include the following books.

Sources are listed more or less in chronological order with the text, as well as diary entries and correspondence of a number of politicians, generals in the field, and Field Marshals, which are not listed in this bibliography, since this is a Story for general readers.

- Christopher Andrew. *Her Majesty's Secret Service.* (Penguin, NY 1986).
- Barbara Tuchman. *The Zimmerman Telegram.* (Macmillan, NY 1958).
- Richard Deacon. *A History of British Secret Service.* (Muller, London 1969).
- Winston S. Churchill. *The World Crisis: 1911-1918.* (Thornton Butterworth, London 1923-30).
- George Dangerfield. *The Strange Death of Liberal England.* (Stanford, CA 1997).
- The *Manchester Guardian* archives. 14 January 1939. Captain Franz von Rintelen. *The Dark Invader.* (Penguin, London 1936).

- *The Oxford History of Britain* (2010): "The Twentieth Century" by Kenneth O. Morgan;
- Winston S. Churchill. *Great Contemporaries.* (Butterworth, London 1937).
- Barbara W. Tuchman. *The Proud Tower.* (Macmillan, NY 1962).
- L.H.C. Edmond. *Origins of MI5.* MSS VII/3, Unpublished Memoirs. Ch. 20, MSS, III/5.
- Ulrich Trumpener. *War Premeditated: German Intelligence Operations in July 1914.*
- Admiral Alfred Mahan. *The Influence of Sea Power on History.* (Little Brown, Boston 1890).
- Keith Jeffrey. *The Secret History of MI6.* (Penguin, NY 2010). Minutes of Meeting of the Secret Service Bureau. 23 May, 1911.
- Somerset Maugham. "Looking Back," *Sunday Express,* 7 Oct, 1962.
- Thomas, Ransom, Knight Hinsley. *British Intelligence in the Second World War.* (HMSO, London 1981).
- R. H. Bruce Lockhart. *Memoirs of a British Agent.* (Putnam, London & NY 1932).
- Diary entry, 21 Aug. 1911, CCAC Grant-Duff MSS 2.
- George Makari. *Revolution in Mind.* (Harper NY, 2008).
- Michael Stürmer. *The German Empire: 1870-1918.* (Random House, NY 2000).
- C. L. Sulzberger. *The Fall of Eagles.* (Crown, London 1977).
- Léon Trotsky. *A History of the Russian Revolution.* (1930). (University of Michigan Press)
- Kagan, Ozment & Turner. *The Western Heritage.* (Pearson, NJ 2006).
- H. C. G. Matthew. *The Liberal Age. The Oxford History of Britain.* Ed. Kenneth O.Morgan. (Oxford University Press, NY 2010).
- Michael Kettle. *Sidney Reilly.* (St. Martin's Press, NY 1984).
- Norman G. Thwaites. *Velvet and Vinegar.*
- Roger Scruton. *England.* (Chatto & Windus, London 2000).
- Christopher Hassall's *Edward Marsh, Patron of the Arts.* (Longmans London, 1959).
- Paul Johnson. *Intellectuals.* (Harper, London 2007).
- Philip Longworth. *Russia.* (St. Martin's Press, NY 2005).
- Arthur Koestler. *Arrow into the Blue.* (Collins, London 1952).
- *Hansard.*
- Commander Mansfield Smith-Cumming's entry in *Who's Who.*
- Lockhart to Foreign Office, 28 March 1918. PRO, FO 371/3326, 57062.
- Captain G. A. Hill. *Go Spy the Land: Being the Adventure of IK8 of the British Secret Service.* (Cassell, London 1932).
- Harrison Salisbury. *Black Night, White Snow, Russia's Revolutions: 1905-1917.* (London 1978),
- Paul Johnson. *Modern Times.* (Harper, London 1983).
- Andrew Roberts. *The Holy Fox.* (Weidenfeld, London 1991).
- Paul Dukes. *Red Dusk and the Morrow: Adventures and Investigations in Red Russia.* (Doubleday, NY 1922).
- Spears to Churchill, draft, n.d.; Savinkov to unnamed French minister, copy, 25 Feb. 1920, CCAC Spears MSS SPRS 1/301.
- Leon B. Murray. *Political Hysteria in America.* (Basic, NY 1971).
- U.S. Bureau of Investigation 1918 Memorandum. John F. Cordley worked for Flint

& Co.

- Simon Sebag Montefiore. *Young Stalin*. (Knopf, NY 2007).
- Stephen Kotkin. *Stalin*. (Penguin, NY 2017).
- Caryll Houselander. *A Rocking Horse Catholic*. (Sheed & Ward, London 1955).
- Condoleezza Rice. *Democracy*. (Grand Central, NY 2017).
- George F. Kennan. *Russia and the West under Lenin and Stalin*. (Little Brown, Boston 1961).
- Mark Mazower. *Dark Continent*. (Vintage, NY 1998).
- Churchill to Austin Chamberlain, 22 Nov, 1924. BUL Chamberlain MSS AC 51/61.
- Norman Rose. *Churchill: An Unruly Life*. (S&S NY, 1994).
- George Orwell. *1984*. (Secker, London 1949).
- *The Maisky Diaries*. (Yale University Press, 2015). Ed. Gabriel Gorodetsky.
- E. L. Voynich. *The Gadfly*. (Henry Holt, NY June 1897).
- Robin Lockhart. *Reilly: The First Man*. (Penguin London 1987).
- Simon Sebag Montefiore. "Before the Terror." *The Guardian*, May 19, 2007.
- William Beaver. *Under Every Leaf: How England Played the Greater Game from Afghanistan to India*. (Zarak, UK 2012).
- Captain H. M. Hozier. *The Seven Weeks War*. (London, 1867).
- Alan Sked. *The Decline and Fall of the Habsburg Empire 1815-1918*. (Longmans, London 1989).
- Martin Gilbert. *The First World War*. (Weidenfeld London, 1994).
- Anthony Cave Brown. *"C:" The Secret Life of Sir Stewart Menzies, Spymaster to Winston Churchill*. (Macmillan, NY 1987).
- Phillip Knightly. *The Master Spy*. (Knopf, NY 1989)

Index

Cune Press

Cune Press was founded in 1994 to publish thoughtful writing of public importance. Our name is derived from "cuneiform." (In Latin *cuni* means "wedge.")

In the ancient Near East the development of cuneiform script—simpler and more adaptable than hieroglyphics—enabled a large class of merchants and landowners to become literate. Clay tablets inscribed with wedge-shaped stylus marks made possible a broad intermeshing of individual efforts in trade and commerce.

Cuneiform enabled scholarship to exist and art to flower, and created what historians define as the world's first civilization. When the Phoenicians developed their sound-based alphabet, they expressed it in cuneiform.

The idea of Cune Press is the democratization of learning, the faith that rarefied ideas, pulled from dusty pedestals and displayed in the streets, can transform the lives of ordinary people. And it is the conviction that ordinary people, trusted with the most precious gifts of civilization, will give our culture elasticity and depth—a necessity if we are to survive in a time of rapid change.

Bridge Between the Cultures (a series from Cune Press)

The Passionate Spies	John Harte
Music Has No Boundaries	Rafiq Gangat
Arab Boy Delivered	Paul Aziz Zarou
Kivu	Frederic Hunter
Empower a Refugee	Patricia Martin Holt
Afghanistan and Beyond	Linda Sartor
The Greatest Spy	John Harte
Stories My Father Told Me	Helen Zughaib, Elia Zughaib
Apartheid Is a Crime	Mats Svensson
Definitely Maybe	Stephen Fife
Girl Fighters	Carolyn Han
White Carnations	Musa Rahum Abbas

Cune   Cune Press: www.cunepress.com | www.cunepress.net

About the Author

John Harte was born in London, England, between the two World Wars. He witnessed at first hand the bombing of London and the Battle of Britain; the launching of the D-Day landings from England's south coast, and the enemy's rocket attacks intended to destroy London and its population.

He began his writing career as a playwright in London then became an investigative journalist writing for three leading publications in the UK.

After moving to South Africa to work in the advertising industry he continued to freelance, writing feature articles for two leading newspapers, which were syndicated worldwide by Reuters. He also broadcast his own stories on the SABC.

He now lives in Ottawa, Canada.

For more: http://johnhartebooks.com

CPSIA information can be obtained
at www.ICGtesting.com
Printed in the USA
JSHW030745240922
30798JS00001B/1